HALDANE
1915–1928

HALDANE IN HIS ROBES AS LORD CHANCELLOR

HALDANE

1915–1928

The Life of
Viscount Haldane of Cloan
K.T., O.M.

by

Major-General
SIR FREDERICK MAURICE
K.C.M.G., C.B., D.Litt.

IN TWO VOLUMES

VOLUME II

GREENWOOD PRESS, PUBLISHERS
WESTPORT, CONNECTICUT

Originally published in 1939
by Faber and Faber, Ltd., London

First Greenwood Reprinting 1970

Library of Congress Catalogue Card Number 72-110857

SBN 8371-4524-4 (Set)
SBN 8371-4526-0 (Vol. II)

Printed in the United States of America

PREFACE

My first volume of the Life of Lord Haldane ended virtually with his ejection from office in the spring of 1915 on the formation of the Asquith Coalition Government. But to round off that story I had to entrench somewhat on the war period in order to conclude the volume with Haig's dramatic visit to him after the Victory March through London, a generous answer to the campaign which had driven the architect of victory from office.

In this volume I go back to April 1915; and tell the story of Haldane's gradual return to public life. He began this return with a resumption of his campaign for the reform of our educational system as a prelude to reconstruction after the war. This brought him more and more into touch with the leaders of the Labour Party and his political sympathies with the aims of that party increased, until on the eve of the General Election of 1922, when there was at least a possibility that Labour would come into power, he was expected by the political gossips to become the first Labour Minister of Education.

In fact it was his interest in problems of national defence which brought him into the first Labour Government and caused him to make a curious bargain with Ramsay Mac-Donald.

His contribution to educational reform, to the reconstruction of Government after the war, to the reorganization of the Committee of Imperial Defence, and his relations with Asquith, Lloyd George, and Ramsay MacDonald, were the chief political interests of his later years; while his philosophic interests were absorbed by his contacts with Einstein and the philosophical aspects of the theory of relativity.

I conclude this volume with an appreciation of what Haldane's army reform and his speeding up of the process of mobilization meant to this country in 1914.

Alas, since my first volume appeared I have lost the invaluable help of Miss Haldane, who, as her brother's literary executor, knew where every paper was, and whose advice and judgement were unfailing guides to portraying with due balance a man whose interests were unusually wide and whose activities were very diverse.

F. MAURICE

December 1938

CONTENTS

xi

CONTENTS

CONTENTS

CONTENTS

ILLUSTRATIONS

Chapter I

THE WAR

1915 to 1916

Haldane, on exchanging the turmoil of the Woolsack for the peace of Cloan, had spent some of his leisure in preparing an account of his visit to Berlin in February 1912, which he circulated privately to some of his friends. Most of them urged him to publish the memorandum. Sir George Prothero put it to him that it was his duty to do so. 'No one', he wrote, 'can regret more than I do the baseless attacks that have been made upon you, but I regret that not only on your account, but because the suspicions and doubts from which they arise lower the tone of public life, and because, if not cleared up, they encourage similar attacks upon others and spread a general want of confidence which is very damaging to the state, especially in such times as these. Your resignation will not clear the air. It will not undo the mischief that has been done by no fault of yours. It will rather tend to confirm the unfounded rumours and appear to those who have circulated them rather in the light of an acknowledgement that they were correct and at least that—as people say—"there was something in them." And this will be a great misfortune, for such suspicions ought not to be allowed to exist, whether the Minister, whom they touch, is in or out of power, if they can be exposed, as in this case they can be.'

To this Haldane replied: 'I am very grateful to you for your letter and I have given most careful thought to all you urge, but my mind is made up. Anything that I publish now must be taken as a personal defence against the attacks which have been made upon me. This is no time for airing private grievances. "Inter arma silent leges" and it is inevitable in a time like this, that there should be hasty judgements and injustices. If I set the example others will follow and there will be division and controversy when there should be unity. It is for the Government to decide when publication is in the public interest, the decision cannot rest with me.'

There now began to reach him, interspersed in the stream of abusive and mostly anonymous letters, and those from indignant friends, resolutions of appreciation and regret from Liberal Associations in many parts of the country. Encouraged by these and urged by his friends, he made his first public appearance at a formal banquet given in his honour at the National Liberal Club on July 1, Lord Lincolnshire in the chair. In his speech he made no reference to the attacks upon him and attempted no defence. Characteristically he devoted a good part of his speech to the defence of a friend who was being unjustly criticized.

One of the factors which had brought about the formation of the First Coalition had been the outcry provoked by the shortage of munitions at the front. We had made no attempt in time of peace to organize industry for the production of munitions in a great war, and no one had foreseen that munitions would be needed on the scale which the event proved necessary. The improvisation of munition factories and the attempts to speed up production had inevitably created difficulties and caused friction. Asquith had in April 1915 gone to Newcastle to appeal to industry in general, both capital and labour, to pull together so that production might reach the scale required. In making this appeal he had said, on information supplied to him by Sir John French through Lord Kitchener, 'I saw a statement the other day that operations, not only of our own army, but of the Allies, were being crippled

2

or at any rate hampered, by our failure to provide the necessary ammunition. There is no truth in that statement.'[1] As at
that time our guns in sectors where we were on the defensive
were limited to two rounds per gun per day and the savings
thus made had proved quite inadequate to prepare the way
for successful attack at Festubert, this statement by the Prime
Minister had produced consternation at the front, which in
its turn led to agitation at home. Kitchener was attacked by
the Northcliffe press, but the public would have none of that
and the *Daily Mail* was solemnly burned on the Stock Exchange. So another victim was chosen, and the dismissal of
General von Donop, who was the Master General of the
Ordnance, was demanded. Manufacturers new to the task of
producing high-explosive shell complained that they were
unduly hampered by War Office requirements and regulations. These grumbles reached Fleet Street and were the basis
for the demand for von Donop's head.

After the usual compliments to his hosts Haldane said: 'I
have not come here to talk of myself. There is to-day no
question of individuals, there is the question of the nation. I
am not here to weep over what we have not done. I am here
to exhort you to do all that we can do. We can win, we and
our allies with the resources which we have, if we can only
organize them effectively. We must distribute the task of
winning victory justly with our Allies. It is three years since
I was at the War Office, but the General Staff used to teach
me in those days the necessity of clear conceptions on military
method. There was a good deal of loose and irreflective talk
at the beginning of this war about a rapid invasion of Germany. That invasion could only come after the German Army
had suffered from a process of attrition; her strategic railways
are too well organized, her military strength is too well developed. If we chose attrition we must prepare methods
which are different from those of invasion by manœuvre,

[1]*Life of Lord Oxford and Asquith,* vol. ii, p. 149.

as Germany has herself found out. We must develop heavy artillery, we must prepare munitions on a vast scale. . . . There is a national tendency in time of stress and excitement, which bring with them disillusionment and disappointment, to look for scapegoats. It is in the national interest a dangerous practice. We have not so many first-class men that we can afford to throw them away. We must use our best men and above all we must be careful not to blame the right man because we expect from him the impossible. I have been reading the attacks which have been made on General von Donop. When I was at the War Office I picked General von Donop as the man who of all our generals stood unrivalled in his technical knowledge, in the directness and firmness of his mind and in the sanity of his advice. I would like to know on what grounds it is alleged that he ought to go.

'In the month of October last, when I was still a member of the Cabinet, there was a committee assembled by the Government which included Lord Kitchener, Mr. Lloyd George, Mr. Churchill, Mr. McKenna and myself. Our attention was drawn to the urgent necessity of a vast increase in the supply of munitions. The condition of trench warfare had made this necessary. We consulted General von Donop and afterwards summoned the great manufacturers and placed orders with them which they undertook to carry out. The manufacturers did their best, but there arose difficulties between capital and labour which confounded all the calculations of the manufacturers, and that is the cause of the trouble to-day. It is not General von Donop.'

Haldane's audience with ears cocked to hear his answer to his detractors was impressed and moved by the dignity and generosity with which he passed by any personal defence in favour of the defence of another, and when Lord Lincolnshire read from the chair the following letter from Asquith it burst into prolonged applause:

'It is with sincere and keen regret that I find myself disabled by a call of public duty from being present with you this evening. I had looked forward to the opportunity of hearing what Lord Haldane had to say on the subject of our national duty in these critical times and of paying such tribute as I could to the signal service he has rendered and the splendid example he has set to the Empire. As I cannot be with you I should be glad if you would convey my message to your meeting. Lord Haldane is the oldest personal and political friend I have in the world. For the best part of 35 years we have been associated in close and unbroken intimacy. We have worked together and fought side by side through many vicissitudes of fortune in the pursuit of what we have believed to be great and worthy causes, without as far as I can recall more than a passing shadow of difference in opinion and always with the same ideals in view.

'I can never adequately express the debt which I owe to the width of his outlook, to the large range of his varied knowledge, to his acute perception of political perspective, and above all to his selfless loyalty and devotion. It has been given to few men to find and keep such a friend.

'But quite apart from and beyond these personal ties, I wish to put on record my sense of the inestimable value of the work which in very different spheres he has done for the State. As a profound and accomplished lawyer he has worthily sustained the best tradition of the Woolsack. *Inter arma silent leges* and now we are engaged in the greatest war in our history or in that of the world, I should wish my countrymen to realize that it is more due to him than to any other man that our army was ready to undertake the mission to which it has been called. The Territorial Force, which is winning its laurels, and covering itself with fame in every theatre of the war, is his creation.

'The magnificent work which is being done by the Staff is largely the result of his initiative and inspiration. Long years of patient and intensive effort conducted under his guidance and stimulus are bearing their fruit in the addition every day of fresh chapters to the glorious annals of the British Army.

'I may take the opportunity of contradicting the statement which I am told is still believed in some quarters that at the outbreak of war Lord Haldane claimed or desired to return to the War Office. There is not a word of truth in this silly story. I was myself at the time Secretary of State and Lord Haldane was good enough to assist me for a few days at the Office to cope with the overwhelming pressure. He was from the first moment a strong advocate of Lord Kitchener's appointment.

'Let me add that no man in our time has made more fertile and lasting contribution to the reconstruction and better organization of national education in its best and broadest sense, a reform which has already done much and when developed and completed is destined to do more to enable this country to hold better its own in the growing rivalry of the peoples of this world. You do well to honour him to-night, and I predict with undoubting confidence that your recognition of his character and services will be ratified by history and posterity.'

Lord Oxford's biographers say that the fact that the Prime Minister neglected to write to Haldane on his retirement rankled. They do not mention this letter, to which Lord Haldane answered on July 6:

'MY DEAR A.

'My reception at the National Liberal Club and most of all your very generous tribute warmed my heart. I am more than grateful. Passing clouds do not dim the memory of years of friendship.'

I can find no trace in Haldane's papers that he ever bore Asquith any grudge, while, as will be seen, there is abundant evidence that his affection for his old friend and ally was not affected by the demand of the Conservatives that he should be excluded from office.

Shortly after the meeting Haldane received an invitation from Sir John French to come and stay with him at his general headquarters in France. He went out at the end of July. Of this visit he wrote to his mother from Saint-Omer: 'Nothing could be warmer than the welcome which I have received from my old friends. Sir John made many enquiries about you and sends you his warmest greetings. On my arrival I was greeted by a German air raid, but I gather that it did not do much damage and no bombs fell anywhere near me. I have just been to see Haig at his Headquarters. He is just as calm, quiet and determined as he used to be in the old days at the War Office. He introduced me to his staff as the man who had saved the British Empire and France. I fancied I could trace awed incredulity on their faces. Everyone I met is equally confident that we shall win but they see a long and heavy task ahead of us and wonder if that is sufficiently realized at home.'

The situation at the time of Haldane's arrival was that the campaign in Artois in which Foch had tried and failed to capture the Vimy Ridge had come to an end. Our contribution to this campaign had been costly and very moderately successful attacks in the battles of Aubers Ridge and Festubert. The first divisions of the Kitchener Armies were arriving and we had formed a new Third Army, which took over from the French a portion of the front south of Arras. The French Army had been considerably increased and Joffre believed that the supply of guns and munitions would be fully adequate to his needs in the action. The Germans were winning a succession of victories over the Russians on the Eastern Front and the French Commander-in-Chief was eager to resume the offensive in the greatest possible strength before the Germans called a halt in the east and brought back troops to the Western Front. He proposed that Foch should again attack the Vimy Ridge, while we co-operated with an attack on Foch's left across the plain of Loos. At the same time as these attacks were made in the north four French armies were to make a great attack in Champagne.

Of his visit Haldane wrote to Kitchener on his way back: 'I have just been spending a few days with French. I gather that Asquith has been over lately so I do not suppose that I can tell you anything new, but as my old friends may have spoken their minds more freely to me than they did to the Prime Minister, I pass on my impressions for what they are worth. I have had several long talks with French and I think that I have done something to clear the air. He is rather jealous of your new divisions going to the Dardanelles but his chief demand is heavy guns and shells. I reminded him that when he was Chief of the Staff the General Staff deliberately refused to equip the Expeditionary Force with heavy guns, because this would hamper their mobility and that the artillery men as deliberately chose shrapnel in place of high explosives. I pointed out that we poor civilians could not be blamed for not having foreseen what none of the soldiers foresaw and that manufacture on a large scale could not be developed by waving a wand. My words had the more weight owing to something which has happened to the French next door. It appears that the French Ministry of Munitions has been pressing on production without due regard to quality, and as a consequence Foch's army has in the recent battles lost large numbers of guns, the figure of hundreds was given me, owing to the premature bursting of shells. I went to the French lines and climbed up to Notre Dame de Lorette, whence I watched a bombardment going on and while I was there a French gun burst in a battery near by. I find this to be one of the chief topics of conversation amongst those I have met. The French with their large stocks of reserve material have been able to replace these losses quickly, but Haig told me that if the like had happened to him in his recent battles it would have meant disaster. I hope that you will not allow our volatile Minister of Munitions[1] to get rid of von Donop. I have had some considerable experience of the problems of explosives and I know no one who can shield us better from the results of impetuosity. I think French now realizes what you are doing and what the difficulties are, and he will be more patient in the future. As to the next campaign I find that neither French nor Haig are enthusiastic about Joffre's plans. Both are against his proposal that we should attack over the open plain north of Loos. French is as usual willing to co-operate loyally with Joffre to the best of his resources, but has his own ideas as to where we could best help. Haig's views are much more decided. He says that we should not attack again until we can do so on a front of at least twenty miles so as to be protected against gun fire from the flanks. For this he wants about a thousand heavy guns and a vast quantity of shells. He told me he has about 60 heavy guns now. He is very definite that it is mere waste of life to attack until we can mask the enemy's machine guns with an overwhelming bombardment. I met Foch during my visit. He takes a contrary view and says that the French Army is never likely to be stronger than it is now, that to wait means that the German defences will grow stronger and stronger and that there is every prospect that the Germans will be able to shorten their front in the East and bring over many divisions to the West. You will have a difficult task in reconciling these conflicting views.

'Everyone is full of admiration of your new divisions. I saw a part of one of them, the 9th. Truly a splendid body of men.'

There were, as Haldane anticipated, many anxious discussions on the plans for the autumn campaign. The overriding factor was that Joffre had complete faith in the success of his plan and in the importance of striking a heavy blow at

[1]The Ministry of Munitions had recently been started under Mr. Lloyd George.

the earliest possible time. The French had 98 divisions on the Western Front and we had 28. Kitchener therefore decided that French views must prevail and in the middle of August he told our Commander-in-Chief that 'we must act with all energy and do our utmost to help France in their offensive even though by so doing we may suffer very heavy losses'. So in the fourth week of September we began the battle of Loos, which was but little more successful than our previous efforts, while the losses were much heavier. This battle, in which Haig decided to use gas to make up for his deficiencies in heavy artillery, was the baptism of fire of Kitchener's new divisions and the losses incurred touched many more homes in Great Britain than any previous battle. There was bitter disappointment at the repeated failures of 1915 and there were angry comments on the conduct of operations. The prime cause of our lack of success was the complete failure of Foch's attack on the Vimy Ridge, to which our attack over the plain of Loos was intended to be subsidiary. This our public could not be told. A second cause was a vital difference between Sir John French and Haig as to the methods of attack.

At the beginning of the spring campaign in Artois a portion of the centre of Foch's Moroccan division had broken through the German lines and for a brief period had crossed over the centre of Vimy Ridge. Being unsupported these troops had been driven back. A study of this experience led the French to the conclusion that it was vital that any success won by the first waves of attack should be promptly supported by the reserves. Therefore it was decided that in the autumn campaign all reserves should be close up to the front and be thrown in at once to confirm and extend any success gained. Haig accepted this principle and had disposed his troops accordingly. Sir John French had formed an XIth corps for the battle composed of the newly created Guards division and the 21st and 24th divisions of the new armies which had but recently arrived in France. This reserve Sir John decided to keep in his own hands till he saw how the battle was going. In the event it was placed at Haig's disposal too late to enable it to follow up the success won in the first attacks. The 21st and 24th divisions were flung into the battle, without adequate preparation for their advance. They had had no previous training in France and had to make their attack through the confusion of a battlefield. They were heavily counterattacked and suffered a heavy reverse. Stories of mishandling drifted home and there was an outcry against the incompetence of our staffs. One of the consequences of this was that the Prime Minister asked Haldane to go to France and report upon the battle of Loos and more particularly upon the charges of bad Staff work. Haldane put his conclusions in a more intimate form than is possible for an official document in a letter which he wrote to Lord Esher, who was then in Paris.

'This popular outcry against the Staff is unfortunate as it tends to undermine confidence within and without the army, and, as is usual in such cases, it is taking a wrong direction. The public is seeking some relief for its disappointment at the meagre results obtained by the battle of Loos and, hearing that there has been failure in staff work, is clamouring for the heads of those responsible for preparing the plans for the battle. I have been very carefully into these both with Robertson's and Haig's staffs, who were the responsible people, and am fully satisfied that both the General Staff at headquarters and with Haig's Army are as hard-working and intelligent a body of men as one could expect to have. The main causes of failure were not bad staff work but this is not the time to go into these. There have been mistakes and failures in the application of the plans by the subordinate staffs and the reason for this is obvious. We have not enough trained staff officers to equip the staffs of the new divisions, and obviously new troops want more and better help from staffs than do well trained troops. I still think that if Kitchener had used the

Territorial Army for his expansion, as you and I intended that it should be used, the difficulties would not have been so great. We had a nucleus staff of trained staff officers, who knew their officers and men, in each division, and it would have been easier to expand from these than to build up from nothing. However, we have to take things as they are and make the best of them and I am conscious that I am far from blameless. It was, I think, in 1907 that I pointed out that the age of our officers who were studying at the staff college was much higher than those in the staff colleges of France and Germany, and I suggested that our upper age limit should be reduced by five years. I was told that this would be difficult to implement, would be unpopular, and that the greater experience of our officer students, gained in all parts of the world, made them better material. I had so much on hand that I let the matter drop, but if I had insisted we should now have an additional five years output of the Staff College available, that is about 150 more trained staff officers.[1]

'Bronsant von Schellendorf in his *Duties of the General Staff* points out that staff officers, being *ex-officio* in a privileged position, are naturally the subject of jealousy and that they must make it their business to overcome this. Before the war we had, as the General Staff became established, done a good deal towards this, but this business has done mischief and will take some living down. It is our habit and inclination to improvise and we must pay the price.

'I saw Foch yesterday for a few moments. He is clearly much distressed by his failure and looked years older than when I saw him last only a month ago.'

When Haldane got back to London he found that the agitation against the Staff had gathered momentum during his absence. The wildest stories were flying about. Ladies were said to be frequent visitors to General Headquarters, which was full of incompetent young men, foisted into the Staff by

[1]This reform was introduced by Mr. Hore-Belisha in 1938.

family influence, while the hard-working regimental officer who knew his job was left in the mud of the trenches. On November 16 Lord St. Davids arranged a full-dress debate on the subject in the House of Lords, and in this he repeated most of the charges which were flying about. Haldane's reply ran:

'If you go to that quiet little French town which is the head-quarters of the British Army, as I have done more than once, you will find a certain number of officers, who have had very little to do with military affairs in the early part of their life, and who are there to carry out the business and everyday administrative arrangements of the General Commanding-in-Chief. But if you walk a quarter of a mile away you will come to a plain building where the real staff of the Field-Marshal commanding is at work. You will find there just about as competent a General Staff as anyone could wish to see, presided over by General Robertson, one of the most competent heads in any army that is engaged in this great war, who has some 24 experts under him, many of whom I know personally to be about the best trained officers we have turned out in the last ten years.

'It is quite true that we have suffered in this war from the want of an organized staff and by that I mean a General Staff, not what is commonly known as the Staff. When we are comparing our Army with Armies that have had a general staff for a hundred years or more, as is the case with the German Army, no doubt we have been at a disadvantage, and no doubt our disadvantage has been the greater because we have had to expand our army in France to something like five times the size at which it started. . . . It is quite true that in a war like this a great deal depends upon staff work. In the old days we used to win by bravery and determination and sometimes by numbers. In these days you cannot win by mere bravery and determination and you may not be able to win even by numbers. The military problems are of a difficulty and intricacy which require mind to be brought to bear. For years I thought that where we were asleep in connection with the Army was in our want of recognition of the absolute fact that the next great war would be a war of mind against mind. If you are going to play chess against a body like the Great General Staff of the German Army you must train your chess players for a long time beforehand. I have felt for long that the really great problem of the British Army was the problem of its General Staff, and I rejoice to think that among our generals to-day there are some men, who, sharing that conviction, have made it the business of their lives to train as General Staff officers ought to be trained. We cannot give too much attention to that. We cannot overlook the necessity of so fashioning our organization that brain and organization may be the chief things, with the confidence that the national spirit will add everything else. But brain and organization cannot be improvised. You have to prepare beforehand, and if we have too small a staff to-day, and if it is not perfect, it is because, as I said, we did not wake up to this great military problem early enough.'

Haldane walked away from the House after this debate with his successor on the Woolsack, Lord Buckmaster, and as they strolled up Whitehall he said: 'We are living in a forcing house now and can produce many things much quicker than we could in peace. We can force strawberries but I wonder how long it will take us to learn that we cannot force gardeners.'[1]

The incident of his journey to France to investigate the circumstances of the battle of Loos and its sequelae left a deep impression on Haldane, and from it may be dated a new mission to be added to those of which he was already missioner. He desired passionately so to fashion the organization, not only of our fighting services, but of government in general and of industry, so that 'organization and brain may be the chief things'.

[1]Letter from Lord Buckmaster to the author.

On April 8, 1915, a few weeks before he left office, Haldane sent to the Cabinet a note on 'The Future Relations of the Great Powers'. The concluding paragraphs of this paper were prophetic:

'The conclusion of the present war when it comes is likely to be attended with a new set of problems. These problems will arise from the inevitable fact that this war, unlike some others, cannot be allowed to terminate as a drawn battle, or even as a victory evidenced by mere cession of territory or payment of indemnities. It is conflict with a power which threatens, should it win, to dominate ruthlessly a large part of the civilized world. It is therefore essential that it shall not in the future be likely to succeed in a second attempt at armed supremacy. To insure this it is, from the point of view of other nations, desirable that military hierarchy in Germany should be dethroned. Against this dethronement the leaders who are at present supreme in Germany will fight to the last, and no hopes can be built on a refusal of the German nation to follow these leaders, unless a crushing defeat threatens and cannot in any way be averted. In that event the German people may insist on the establishment of a different kind of Government. The task of making such a defeat inevitable must rest with the forces of the Allies. It is only when the Allies have succeeded in this task that a new situation can arise. But even success may be followed with complications. By the agreement of the 5th September the Allies agreed not to make any peace the terms of which had not been agreed on in common. It is hardly likely that any terms will be acceptable to the Allies generally unless they provide for cessions of much territory and the payment of some indemnities. Here is a fruitful source of difficulty in bringing the war to a satisfactory end. For the more these things are demanded, as demanded they are likely to be, the more certainly will Germany and Austria struggle to the last against impending disaster, and endeavour to enlist the sympathy of the neutral Powers.

'Still the prospect of still worse disaster if the war is prolonged after it has become clear that the Allies are about to succeed may lead Germany and Austria to submit to hard terms, if only those terms leave them another chance in the future. It was hope of the kind which Stein and Scharnhorst, and the bolder spirits in the Government of King Frederick William of Prussia, entertained after the campaign of 1806-7, and entertained not in vain. If Germany be left free to begin once more to build up her military system she may well, such is her energy and organizing capacity, be able to build it up so that she will be more formidable than before. On the present occasion it is in diplomatic skill rather than in military ability that she has shown deficiency. She will profit by her lesson.'

He went on to adumbrate, as the remedy, an Association of Powers on the general lines which eventually developed into the League of Nations. He concluded:

'There is a postscript which I wish to add about a point which is germane to what I have written above. The organization sketched is suggested only tentatively and in outline. The important matter is the underlying principle. But in whatever shape such an organization is born, vigilance on the part of nations individually will be required to keep it from slumbering. Such vigilance seems to imply careful and continuous study, by trained minds, working undisturbed, of situations likely to arise in the future. Although armaments ought, if the principle were successfully established, to be much less extensive than at present, the necessity of most careful staff work of certain definite kinds will thus remain. In this country we have not excelled in developing the general staff mind, and the result has at times been surprise from want of prevision. To-day we are somewhat better off than we used to be. But the war and general staffs of the Navy and Army have not acquired the habit of close co-operation in study in advance. The Committee of Imperial Defence is too miscellaneous and unwieldy a body, and too much separated from both of them, to be able to guide their work into a definite co-operation. The result is that the real general staff system has not yet been produced in this country. The true general staff mind evolves and studies its problems systematically, continuously and in seclusion. The best type of this mind brings expert and special knowledge of different sorts to bear on problems with several aspects, and it seeks to study these problems in advance, and so in time. Not the least valuable service which a general staff of the best order can render is that of looking ahead for developments which may be escaping public observation.'

That his experience in France in the autumn of 1915 and the reaction of events there upon opinion at home had caused him to widen his views on the application of general staff principles is shown by a letter which he wrote to Lord Knutsford on November 19:

'This agitation about the Staff has opened my eyes. For more than five years I was immersed in the War Office in the endeavour to apply general staff principles to military reorganization, later I tried to get the same principles applied to the Navy. But occupied with all this I did not fully realize how ignorant we are as a nation of what a staff is or should be. To the general public it has a purely military connotation and any officer who is not employed with his regiment is looked on as a staff officer. Besides the mass of functionaries who are required in any great organization there must be a staff of two kinds, an administrative staff, to organize and provide material needs, and a general staff which is primarily concerned with plans and the creation of plans. We as a people have the gift to a greater extent than other peoples of dealing practically with problems as they arise, but we fail lamentably in thinking ahead, in being ready for the problems before they arise. Indeed we have a natural distrust of plans prepared for hypothetical cases. We say "that is all very well in theory but it won't work in practice". Yet any scientist will tell you that nothing is well in theory which will not work in practice. Plans which won't work in practice are due to slovenly thinking. Germany has been able to do what she has done against what, on paper, are overwhelming odds, because she has applied general staff principles not only to her military but to her national organization. If we are to get the best out of ourselves both in war and in peace we must do the same. The political parties should have their general staffs to work out policies, so should our great industries, iron, coal, shipping, cotton, etc. It is evident from what has happened and is happening that our public will need a good deal of persuading that organized thinking pays, but I mean to do my best in persuasion.'

In December 1915 Sir John French was recalled from France to be Commander-in-Chief of the forces at home and was succeeded by Sir Douglas Haig. Haldane wrote to his mother:

'You will I expect be sorry to see that your old friend Sir John French, who is to become Viscount French, has been removed from the command in France and is to be succeeded by Haig. I know them both intimately. We owe a great debt to French for his courage and leadership during the critical first months of the war. He is a leader in a way in which Haig can never be, for Haig is too reserved and too inarticulate to be able to make a personal appeal to men. But on the whole I think the change is justified. Haig's character is yet more solid than French's and he is technically far better equipped. I owe a great deal to his sound judgment and wide knowledge both of principles and detail, which were invaluable to me in getting my reforms through. He is, I think, best fitted to deal with the new type of warfare which has come upon us. Also I hope that he will get on better with the French than did his predecessor. Sir John has never forgiven the French for leaving him in the lurch at Mons and always looks on their proposals with a suspicious eye.'

MRS. HALDANE, IN HER 81ST YEAR
FROM A PICTURE BY THOMAS GRAHAM, R.S.A.

By the end of 1915 attacks on Haldane had ceased, and he came to the conclusion that he could again take part in public affairs without embarrassment to the Government. He began to take part in the legal work of the House of Lords, but this did not occupy more than a moiety of his time, so he arranged with Lord Crewe to take a seat on the front Opposition bench in the Upper House, and again became a regular attendant at its debates. He wanted a platform of his own and formed it on his old love, education, which now was closely linked in his mind with his new love, organization. Early in 1916 he wrote to his mother:

'I dined with the Asquiths last night. They were as affectionate as ever. Asquith seems to be tired, and is feeling the strain. He is worried about Kitchener's position. There is apparently a strong anti-Kitchener clique in the Cabinet and A. is wondering how Kitchener will get on with Robertson. I told him that I knew Robertson[1] well, that he was a first class general staff officer and knew what a general staff should do and that he need have no fear that Robertson had political ambitions. He is not of the Wilson[2] type. There is a growing agitation for conscription, in which K. apparently can't make up his mind and A., though he did not say so definitely, seems to fear a split in the Cabinet on the question. I told him of my plans and he was full of encouragement and said he had more than one job which he would like me to undertake.'

The Workers' Educational Association had been established in 1903 and ten years later its tutorial classes had been recognized by the Board of Education as eligible for grant from public funds. This had given a great fillip to the movement, but the war had inevitably put a check on progress. Haldane consulted Albert Mansbridge, R. H. Tawney, and other leaders in the cause of adult education and determined to

[1]On the change in command in France Sir William Robertson had become Chief of the Imperial General Staff at home.
[2]General, later Field-Marshal, Sir Henry Wilson.

start a campaign which would prepare the way for a great revival and extension when peace came. The new universities were now firmly established, but they, like Oxford and Cambridge, were mainly concerned with their own students. Haldane made a series of visits to all university centres in the country with the object of pressing upon them the claims of possible extra-mural students. He found a very general interest in the subject, and was convinced that when the younger lecturers came back from the war there would be plenty of them with the time, ability, and inclination to take up adult education work, provided they could receive a reasonable reward for their labours. As usual money was needed, and this meant getting the Board of Education and the Government interested. In the course of his consultations with educationalists up and down the country Haldane came to the conclusion that as the war had put a check on all the normal activities of peace there must be a general reconstruction after the war, and that now was the time to prepare for this in the field of education. He therefore undertook a general survey of our educational system and decided to widen his plans, beyond increased provisions for adult education, into a programme designed to fill what he conceived to be the gaps in that system.

Haldane was in Leeds on this work on June 6, when the news arrived of the sinking of the *Hampshire* and the death of Lord Kitchener. He wrote to his mother:

'I do not recall that the death of anyone since that of Queen Victoria has aroused so much genuine feeling as that of Kitchener. He had won by his achievements and character a truly remarkable influence, without resorting to any of the ordinary methods by which popularity is won. There is a feeling amongst hard-headed Yorkshiremen here that his death is a national calamity, worse than the loss of a great battle. I do not think so. His work is done, the great expansion of our Army which he initiated is complete, and his death in harness is for him a happy one. His position in the Cabinet was becoming daily more difficult. His mind was that of an autocrat and he was not equipped for work in counsel with colleagues. To the public he was a great organizer. I do not think he was ever that. He never attached much importance to plans and principles, and without those a sound organization cannot be built. He was a sincere and devoted patriot, a great improvisor, and he had an extraordinary flair for divining the course of events. In 1914 statesmen, financiers, economists, and soldiers, or at least the overwhelming majority of them, were of opinion that the complicated fabric of Europe could not stand the strain of a long war. There was a very general opinion after the battle of the Marne which I know was held by such diverse authorities as Joffre in France, and Bonar Law in England, that the war would be over by Christmas. Kitchener held to it that we were engaged in a long and bitter struggle and prepared for it. That is his monument.'

Meanwhile the jobs of which Asquith had spoken took shape. In April Haldane accepted the chairmanship of a commission on the organization of university education in Wales. In May a demand for the creation of an air ministry had gained much support and, in a debate on the subject in the Lords, Haldane had said that he agreed with those who believed that the time had come to give the organization of air power a precise form, but that the problem would not be solved by appointing an air minister and telling him to get on with the job. We must first decide the principles on which air power was to be organized and then decide the functions of an air ministry. The result of this was that he was called in by the Government to advise on the creation of the new ministry, and at once he became conscious of a serious conflict of opinion between the airmen, the admirals, and the generals. He wrote of an early meeting of the Air Committee: 'I heckled my old friends the generals and pointed out to them that when we were making a start with an air service and establishing the air factory at Farnborough the prophecies they made then had now proved to be in nearly every case wrong. No one could to-day foresee what the developments of air power will be, except that it is quite certain that we are only at the beginning and that the development will be great. I said that in my opinion the new service must be allowed to develop freely in its own way, and that it could not do that if it was controlled by men whose minds were on the ground. All their arguments that aircraft are and must be an integral part of the army merely mean that there must be intimate and effective co-operation, which can be arranged without giving the generals control of policy, training and organization.' The struggle for the independence of the air-service was long and at times bitter, but Haldane was consistently on the side of the airmen.

A third job came to him in June, when Asquith asked him to be chairman of a Home Office Committee on coal conservation. This committee consisted of a number of experts in mining, geology, the chemistry of fuel, iron production, and electrical engineering with Mr. R. Smillie, the President of the Miners' Federation of Great Britain. On it Sir Richard Redmayne acted as Haldane's right-hand man. Its terms of reference were to consider:

(i) what improvement could be effected in the methods of mining;

(ii) what improvement could be effected in the use of coal;

(iii) whether it was desirable to secure the development of new coalfields.

Haldane, who was always happy when conducting a scientific inquiry with experts, threw himself into this work with enthusiasm, and in the intervals which this and other work left him he was putting the finishing touches to his plans for launching his educational campaign. He wrote to his sister from Queen Annes Gate:

'I had L. G. here to-night to meet McCormick,[1] Blair,[2] and Heath.[3] I sketched my educational programme to L. G. who was deeply interested and has promised to try and put it through. In the Ministry of Munitions he has been employing a large number of boys to save men for the forces, and he has organized classes and a general supervision of their welfare. This is a valuable experiment in the value and practicability of continuation classes. L. G. and I are once more forming an educational alliance. I am arranging for a day early next month for my motion in the Lords.'

So by the mid-summer of 1916 Haldane was once more fully occupied as he liked to be. The upper smoking-room at Queen Annes Gate was the resort not only of his intimates but of experts in education, and coal, and of officers home on leave, and the atmosphere after dinner was heavily charged with discussion on very varied topics and the smoke of his long cigars. He wrote to his mother on the last day of June:

'I am very full of work and of work which seems likely to lead to results worth achieving. There is a great deal of satisfaction at working at things in which one is interested, with men who are equally interested, free from the minor worries and friction, which office inevitably brings. I do not think that I have ever been more contented with my work. *Laetus sorte mea.*'

[1]Sir William McCormick, chairman, University Grants Committee.
[2]Sir Robert Blair, Chief Education Officer, L.C.C.
[3]Sir Frank Heath, Secretary, Department of Scientific and Industrial Research.

Chapter II

THE ORGANIZATION OF EDUCATION

1916 to 1917

On July 12, 1916, Haldane rose from his place on the front Opposition bench in the House of Lords to move a motion calling attention to the training of the nation and to the necessity of preparing for the future. As soon as he had done so the Duke of Buccleuch, white with emotion, sprang to his feet and said:

'Before the noble Lord directs your Lordships' attention to foreign policy I suggest he should explain his past conduct in misleading Great Britain upon the German danger, and in misleading Germany upon British policy.'

A scene in the Lords is a very rare event and the whole chamber and the galleries were stunned by this dramatic intervention. Lord Haldane quietly replied:

'We are not here to discuss foreign policy and I have only to say in answer to the question of the noble duke that nobody more than myself desires that the whole facts should be brought out as to what was done before the war and the preparations that were made. There has been an extraordinary stream of misrepresentation, untruths, inaccuracies, and the sooner these things are brought to the test the better. Nobody desires the moment to come for the most complete judgment of the nation on the full facts more than I do. That is all that I have to say to the noble duke.'

He then went on with his speech:

'For twenty years I have taken the deepest interest in edu-

24

cation, and I have done all that I could, in and out of office, to advance the cause, often with very indifferent success; but at least I have been privileged to watch and observe progress, and it is to me a source of gladness that so much progress has been made in these matters since the beginning of the present century. But, my lords, if we have been making progress, other countries have been making progress too, and making it more rapidly than we have. I am not talking of enemy nations at the moment. It is sufficient for me to take the case of two neutral nations, one a small one, the other a very large one—Switzerland and America. Switzerland puts us to shame in respect of her national system of education and in the training which she gives to the mind of the young, particularly of those who are engaged in the great industries; and there is a keenness and activity everywhere present in the United States which shows the sort of rivalry we shall have to meet if we are to preserve our great industrial and commercial position. Our problem, therefore, is to make education, which is a tiresome word to most people in this country, interesting, by showing its concrete nature and by showing what it means, not only theoretically but practically. It means not mere examinations, not the mere putting of science into the test to which people who are aspiring as candidates for office are subjected. It means far more than that. It means the training of the mind in the widest and most comprehensive sense, so that the youth of the country may be able when the time comes to turn, it may be to science, it may be to the other humanities, it may be to any of the thousand and one subjects which are covered by the field of knowledge in this twentieth century. . . .

'These are reforms which will cost money, a good deal of money. I have said before in this House, and I repeat, that it is an expenditure on which you dare not economize. You must spend more, not less. As readily save the money that is necessary for preparing the field to yield the crop as save the money necessary to train the future generation of industrial experts to retain the position of this country in the markets and factories of the world. There is no worse economy possible than on education, and I am glad to think that people seem to be realizing this more at the present time than they did some months ago. Speaking for myself, if I had a limited amount of money to spend I would spend it first, not on special subjects, not on this or that branch of science, not on this branch of training engineers or the other; I would spend it on improving the profession of teachers throughout the country, and particularly on improving the quantity and quality of the teachers in the secondary schools.

'So far I have merely endeavoured to convey the general principle which seems to me to lie at the root of the whole problem of reform in this direction, and I must now come for a little to the hard and painful facts which are so much ignored and yet are so important. It is an appalling reflection yet true —and I will give your lordships the proof of it a little later on —that in this country 90 per cent. of our young persons, nine out of ten, get no further education after the age of fourteen. What chance have they of rising? Very exceptional talent may rise, but even that is probably lost. I have often wondered how many Watts, Kelvins, and Darwins have perished in the vast mass of untrained talent which the children of the working classes afford. Our greatest mistake in this country has been in concentrating almost exclusively upon the education and training of the well-to-do. We do not recognize that a bifurcation takes place about the age of thirteen. At that time compulsory elementary education ceases, and for the child of the workman what provision is there unless he has a very exceptional and keen father? Why, none whatever. Whereas it is the custom and nearly invariable practice among the middle and upper classes to send their sons and daughters to schools where they will get further training, in the case of the working classes there is no such provision, with the result that, as I say, 90 per cent. of our population have not that education which is required if we are to make the best use of our available talent. . . .

'I pass now from that great class which is to me the class that is most important, and which we literally throw away for want of a proper system, though it contains a reservoir of potential benefit and profit to the nation. I go to the other class that passes up the educational ladder, the 10 per cent., some of whom have the keenness and the opportunity to go to the secondary school and then on to the University. Now between the German system and ours, there again, there is a great difference. In Germany the secondary school is the strongest point in the whole educational movement; it is thoroughly organized, and though it is not compulsory it is virtually compulsory, because unless you go through it and get a military certificate you will have to serve two or three years instead of only serving one year. Moreover, unless you go through it and get the leaving certificate you cannot go to the University and get a degree. And the courses are much longer than ours. What are called preliminary studies are not taught at the Universities in Germany; they are taught in the secondary schools there, but they have to be taught here in the Universities. It is a great feature in the German secondary schools that they teach these preliminary studies, and so set the Universities free for their proper work. . . .

'In Scotland, there have been great reforms. In 1908 there was an Act passed with which, in the planning, I had something to do. It was the work of the best educational experts in Scotland, and the Prime Minister took it up and passed it rapidly through. Under it great changes have been made in Scotland. Not only has something in the way of trade continuation schools, of which I spoke in connection with Germany, been introduced, but great opportunities have been given for developing secondary education; and that had been preceded by a reform of educational endowments.

'But when one comes to England the position is enough to make one weep. Not only are there not enough secondary schools, but such as there are are indifferently organized and staffed compared with what is necessary if they are to do the work which the country requires to be done. An Education Act was passed in 1902 by Mr. Balfour's Government. It was in many ways an admirable Act—I can speak of it although I think I was the only member of my party who supported it in the House of Commons—and I do not think I was wrong in the anticipation which I then formed that out of the Act would come immense good. It broke down a great many of the barriers which hindered the development of secondary education, and it gave to the new education authorities the power to do a great deal. Much has been done under that Act for secondary education, but not nearly enough. In regard to the number of the teachers and the quality, and the number of the schools and the standards, reform is urgently required. Practically there is very little provision, in the secondary schools which are available for the middle class and the lower middle class boys of over sixteen. The result is that when they go on to the University—such of them as do go on to the University—they have to do over again the work that ought to have been done in the secondary schools. Therefore I say that the problem of the secondary school is one of the most pressing that we have in this country.

'Look at the defects of our general system. We have no last elementary year, as in the foreign system. We do not go to the boy and girl in the last year of the elementary school and ask them what they wish to be in life, and tell them that they shall not only be taught by their master and in the trade school but be made fit persons in the occupation they choose. We have nothing of that kind that counts. And then when you come to the secondary school, again we are deficient. It is quite true that those deficiencies arise a good deal from a certain want of outlook. We suffer from them even in the great public schools, which are in some respects very remarkable institutions. Our great public schools have the quality, which is much admired on the Continent, where they have striven so far vainly to imitate them, of training boys to be rulers of men; they have that in a fashion which no Continental school possesses in any degree approaching it. On the other hand increasing science and the application of science are becoming a necessity for the training of a very large portion of our well-to-do class. But they discourage that, and they discourage it by not making some adequate provision, because nearly all the scholarships and bursaries are allocated to the classics. The dead hand, which did that many years ago when people did not see what would be the necessities of to-day, ought to have its grip relaxed by legislation, so that some better encouragement towards getting a university education in science should be given to boys at Eton, Winchester, Harrow, and other great public schools, on the same footing as when they go in for a classical career.

'I am surveying one or two defects in order to bring out the difficulties that attend the situation. The result of these things has been that people have come to think that reform of education is impracticable in this country. An education debate is not a very popular debate in the other House of Parliament, and I am afraid it is not always a very popular debate in this House. The reason is that we make education so uninteresting; we have taken it out of contact with life and have not made it take its place in the whole of a great system of national training which should prepare, not only for theoretical activities, but for practical activities, which should aim at giving the very highest excellence and refinement, cultural, moral, spiritual, and physical, which it is possible for an education system to attain. Therefore it is not enough to do anything short of reforms which will improve our training system itself, which will improve the quality and quantity of the teachers, and make education more interesting, so that when boys wish to go forward to a career of industry or science, they may at least go with their minds so trained, so apt, that they are able to take up and absorb the scientific ideas which they are to put in practice in the industries which they undertake. Let me illustrate what I have said by one or two concrete instances. We suffer in this country from want of experts. Instead of experts being diffused, as they are in Switzerland, which has a most admirable system of training them, and as they are becoming diffused in the United States, where that very practical people are waking to it, we have taken too few steps to produce experts. It is no use saying to the manufacturers, "Employ more chemists". There are no properly trained chemists to employ. Our training machine is not adequate to produce the supply we require. At the beginning of the war I was chairman of a technical committee which had to go into one of the great chemical industries, and I found, rather to my horror, that we had become dependent upon Germany to an alarming degree; in fact to such an alarming degree that in regard even to great discoveries that we had made in this country it had been left to the Germans to produce what we wanted. I asked why it was, and I was told "We cannot get chemists. The Germans organize so well and make the product in such a way that it is our best course to buy from them." When the war came, one result of this was that we were almost without aniline colours, and your lordships will remember the acute distress that was caused in the dye trade owing to that want. It was entirely due to our not training men who were required for an industry which was originally a British industry, but which we had allowed to languish.

'The other day I had occasion to inquire how many trained chemists there were available for the hundreds of chemical industries that there are in this country, because I had been struck by the fact that many of the chemical works were without chemists. On inquiry at a source on which reliance could be placed I found that there were only 1500 trained chemists in this country altogether, and the reason was that we had not the means of encouragement to produce the business kind that was wanted. Our public schools do not aim at preparing an aptitude in the boys' minds for the study of chemistry; nor do our secondary schools; nor have we any trade continuation schools which stimulate the working man's son of exceptional talent to go on with this. Nor are our Universities equipped to produce these men in large numbers. But we have made progress in that direction, as I shall point out later. We have only 1500 trained chemists in this country. On the other hand four large German chemical firms, which have played havoc with certain departments of our trade, employ 1000 highly trained chemists between them. Those men were trained and produced by the great schools which exist there for that purpose. I will take another illustration of what we suffer because of the want of experts. I had the honour of knowing the late Lord Kelvin, who used to talk to me about energy, and I used to ask him about the possibility of using the energy of the sun and the tides in case of the giving out of our supplies of coal. Lord Kelvin would smile and say, "A pound of coal is worth far more than anything that you can hope to get from the sun or the tides or anything else; there is plenty of it for a long time to come, if you will only use it economically." And I got to know this the other day from a well-known expert, that whereas the ideal capacity of a pound of coal—what you could get if you had the proper scientific appliance—would be one-horsepower per hour, as a matter of fact and in practice it requires five pounds of coal to produce one horse-power per hour, which one pound would produce if properly used. Another great chemical expert has calculated that we could, by the use of expert knowledge, which exists, produce the whole of the motive power which we use in this country from one-third of the coal which we actually consume in doing so. My noble friend who sits near me (Lord Joicey) knows what I mean when I speak of the wonderful transformation of coal into electrical energy in the north, and the splendid scientific way in which it has been done by certain engineers.

'Then take another case. It has been calculated by high experts that every year in the various stages of consumption and of the making of bye-products, and so on, we waste as much coal as would pay the interest on £500,000,000 of War Debt after the war. That is a compassible practical figure, and it is only a question of applying the requisite expert knowledge and the requisite methods. But we have not got the experts although the expert knowledge exists. It is a great mistake to suppose that in this country we have not got the very highest science. We have the very highest science and knowledge, but we have not enough individuals possessing that high science and knowledge to go round. The result is that we suffer. . . .

'I will sum up what I have to say by giving your Lordships a few figures; they are new figures but they have been calculated by very high authorities. In England out of 2,750,000 boys and girls between twelve and sixteen, nearly 1,100,000 get no further education after the age of thirteen. Of the remaining 1,650,000, the great bulk are educated only for a very short time, mostly in the elementary schools until fourteen. Only 250,000 go to proper secondary schools, and they are there only for a short time in most cases. Thus quality as well as quantity is deficient. I now pass to the period after sixteen. Between sixteen and twenty-five there are in England and Wales 5,850,000 young persons roughly. Of these, 5,350,000 get no education at all; 93,000 only have a full time course for some period, which is generally a very short period; 390,000 have a part time course, which may also be a very short period, at the evening schools. Are not these appalling figures—390,000 only out of somewhere near 6,000,000! What chance have we against other nations which are administering their affairs on a diametrically different plan and setting stress on the power of knowledge to stimulate industrial activity and industrial capacity? ...

'I wish to say something about the physical side, about the training of the future generation. It is impossible to speculate as to what form the organization of the future armies of this country will take. It is too soon to know; it depends on the result of the war and the state of the world. But this I think is certain, that whatever system we adopt, whether it be a purely voluntary system, one which throws much into reserve, or whether it be some compulsory form of Army organization, we shall be very much the better if we attend to the physical side of the question, and attend to it early. I begin very early, because I begin before birth. The birth-rate is a very important thing, particularly with the diminution of the birth-rate from other causes, which is a striking feature of the situation not only in this but in other countries. It has been estimated—and here I am touching on ground which Lord Sydenham knows more familiarly than I do—that 15 per cent. of the children who might be born into the world are not born owing to causes which are preventable. There are two scourges mainly responsible, both of which in a large measure are capable of being dealt with in such a way that this 15 per cent. could be very much diminished. Then, again, after birth 10 per cent. of the children die in the first twelve months whose lives might with care be preserved and made healthy. Needless to say, if these two economies in the wastage of life were effected we would not have to trouble about the reduction in the birth-rate. I am not sure that the reduction is altogether a bad thing, because it shows that people are more careful about the *status* they can give to their children. However, it is a wide and controversial question, and there is not only one side to it. But it is important that the wastage in birth and in child life should be attended to.

'Then between the end of the first twelve months and the

school age, there is the care of the child. Splendid work has been done by Dr. Newsholme of the Local Government Board, and by Sir George Newman of the Board of Education; and I am glad to see that Mr. Walter Long, who is energetic in these matters, is taking the subject up and directing practical attention to these questions. But when you have got the child through that period into the elementary school, what then? To my mind it is essential, if you are to have a complete system of elementary education, that the physical training should be looked to. I should like to see the Boy Scout system made an integral part of elementary school education up to thirteen or fourteen. I think the country owes more than it knows to Sir Robert Baden-Powell for his great discovery of the Boy Scout system. Then you pass to the secondary school, and, I hope, in the future to the continuation schools. I should like to see cadet training from thirteen or fourteen on to eighteen; I should like to see it a part of the whole system of education—as large a part of the schooling as the teaching of Latin or the teaching of science. I think it is most important that in connection with the schools you should organize cadet training, and it is certainly a thing that can be done. Attention was given to it a little time ago, and it was only the outbreak of the war which precluded further attention being given. When you reach the later stage, the University, then come the Officers' Training Corps, which give an opportunity to every young man of talent to qualify himself for an officer; and I need not remind your Lordships of the value of the Officers' Training Corps in this war. . . .

'We have the advantage of possessing in this country the most admirable educational experts. I have seen a good deal of educational experts, and have lived with them, but I do not know finer expert minds than we have in Great Britain at the present time. All you have to do is to put this thing into the hands of the experts and make a beginning. I will indicate the beginning in a moment. But what are you doing at the present time? The Minister of Education[1] is a right hon. friend of mine, a man who has rendered and is rendering great service to the nation. He has great gifts. But the Government have taken him away from education and set him to solve labour disputes. Nobody is better than he at that. But he is absorbed by his work at the Ministry of Munitions, with the result that the Board of Education is practically without a Minister at the present time. It is impossible for Mr. Henderson to do the work. You ought to set him free to devote himself with his whole energy to working these things out and carrying them into immediate effect. The experts are there; the machinery is ready; all you have to do is to set it going; and the only thing required to set it going is the resolution and decision of the Government to act at once. I am not reproaching the Government for these committees. As I say, they are very valuable. But for Heaven's sake do not let us have any committees on a thing which your experts understand thoroughly and which can be put into operation without a day's delay. The plans are sufficiently worked out. All that is wanted is the Government's decision to give effect to them.

'If this debate has any effect in interesting the public in the present position and in bringing home what our situation is, it will have been a valuable debate. I hope something may come of it. I feel that too few people take an interest in this tremendous problem that is confronting the nation. I am not reproaching the Coalition Government. They have had their hands full of the war, and it is their chief problem. But it would not interfere with their attention to the war if they took action and set this thing going. I have never known a Government that was not really indifferent to education. Cabinets are all more or less indifferent, and education is squeezed into the last moments of the sittings of the Cabinet. The Cabinet reflects Parliament, and Parliament reflects the

[1]Mr. Arthur Henderson.

opinion of the nation. Matthew Arnold was fond of speaking of our inaptitude for ideas, and the nation has been very unhappy with regard to ideas about education. This is reflected in the Cabinet, in Parliament, and in the country. Therefore the only way is for the leaders to take a definite decision without waiting for any particular mandate, and carry out what is absolutely essential if the national life is to be preserved at its ratio of strength.

'I think that this indifference is partly the result of the training of the old Universities. I know I tread on difficult ground. That training is magnificent for the Senate and for the forum, but no good for administration. You make splendid debaters and splendid rulers, but that precise habit of mind necessary for administration you do not train and never have been interested in training. The new Universities may produce men of a different stamp. But while I hope for the larger outlook, I do not forget the splendid things the two old Universities have done. I remember having a remarkable conversation with the late Mr. Chamberlain. I was, with him, looking at the University of Birmingham, and we were talking of this very question and of the indifference displayed. Mr. Joseph Chamberlain was a man who had a very real interest in education. He saw with his practical instinct what was necessary, and he had shown his great driving power in what he had done in connection with Birmingham University. He cared for education because he saw that it was a national deficiency. I remember him saying: "Now let us in the work we are trying to do, agree about one thing. Do not let us do anything which will in the slightest degree injure that atmosphere and tradition of Oxford and Cambridge. They are splendid and irreplaceable."

'I entirely agree with what he said. But we want not merely this training for the senate and the forum, but training for administration; and when we have got that there will arise in the Government a keen interest in education such as we see in other countries. We lack the reflective habit of mind, the reflective habit of mind that likes thought before action; and our lack of it is reflected in every stage of social life. It was all very fine in the days when we had no competition, when our energy had made us what we were. What is necessary now is energy directed by high science; and I am appealing to-night for the high science which is essential if that energy is to be directed to the result which will maintain our place.

'If I were to suggest what could be done practically I would suggest this to the Government. Let the Minister of Education devote his whole time to the question of education; he might be relieved from his Cabinet duties for this purpose. Let him devote his attention, first of all to improving the last year at the elementary school, so as to give that choice of direction of occupation to the pupil of which I have already spoken. Then develop the continuation schools and the boy supervision policy of the Ministry of Munitions. I am not suggesting that you can do everything at once, but you can make a beginning, and if the beginning is made the progress will be rapid. Then improve the teaching and number of the secondary schools. Also carry out the Report of the Consultative Committee—my noble friend knows what I refer to— of five years ago, which was directed to instituting the leaving certificate of the secondary school and freeing the University from preliminary studies which ought to be conducted in the secondary school. And, lastly, there is the physical training in the schools of which I have spoken, and which I think might be introduced without friction and without delay. If money is spent on these things it will come back, not ten times or a hundred times, but a thousand times. It is all vital to us. The old order is passing away, and we are face to face with a new order. Our old methods will not avail us any longer. That is why one hopes that the Government will take the lead in preparing the nation for the struggle that lies before us as soon as this war is over—a struggle not less deadly, and not less terrible, because, as I have said, it will not be obvious and it will be slow. The sands are sinking in the glass. When the war is over this struggle will be on us almost immediately. At present we have taken no adequate steps to prepare ourselves. Let us see to it that we do prepare ourselves. Shakespeare put into the mouth of Brutus words which apply to this position:

> *There is a tide in the affairs of men,*
> *Which, taken at the flood, leads on to fortune;*
> *Omitted, all the voyage of their life*
> *Is bound in shallows and in miseries.*

'My Lords, let us see to it that the nation, with a great emergency looming in front of it, does not lose the Tide.'

Now twenty-two years after this speech was delivered almost everything there advocated is in full process of development, the extension of the elementary school age, the extension and improved equipment of secondary schools, inducements to pass from the elementary to the secondary schools, and from them to the universities, the development of technical schools, pre-natal and infant welfare, and physical training. It cannot often have happened that so much that was desirable and attainable has been advocated in a single speech. Haldane had wondered 'how many Watts, Kelvins, and Darwins have perished in the vast mass of national talent which the children of the working classes afford'. While he was speaking Professor Gowland Hopkins was beginning to make his name as professor of bio-chemistry in the University of Cambridge. He had gone from school to a seat on an office stool in an insurance office. There his urge for a scientific career and the help of an uncle had got him into a junior post in the laboratory of Allen & Hanbury. After three years with that firm he took a short course at the Royal School of Mines and at University College (London) and sat for the examination for the Associateship of the Institute of Chemistry. His work at that examination attracted the attention of Dr., later Sir Thomas, Stevenson of Guy's Hospital, who made him his laboratory assistant, and gave him the opportunities and kindly encouragement which opened the door to a career of the highest distinction. To-day he has made for himself as bio-chemist a name which ranks with those mentioned by Haldane and is a living example of the result of the educational opportunities which Haldane was advocating.

At the end of Haldane's speech the Lords paid him the unusual compliment in that House of clapping loudly, a demonstration which was probably, in part at least, an expression of sympathy with him in the Duke of Buccleuch's attack upon him. That attack was the signal for another campaign in the Press, led this time, strangely enough, by the *Morning Post,* generally regarded as the organ of the Army. That paper thundered: 'We think it monstrous that, while Lord Haldane is conscious—for he must be conscious—of the way the nation regards him, he should go about lecturing on education or on any other subject. If he knows the feelings of his suffering countrymen, if his front were not brass, he would not desire to speak nor to see nor to be seen. He would relapse into silence and seclusion until such time as it was thought safe for the world to hear his defence. When that time comes his place will not be to lecture but to plead. In the meantime his appearance in public is an outrage.'

Now, however, the reaction was immediate, too many people had read Haldane's memorandum and knew the facts, and the letters of indignation and sympathy were now more numerous than those of abuse. He wrote to his sister on July 22: 'Grey came to see me last night, full of indignation and sympathy. He talks of initiating a debate in the Lords in my defence. I spoke to him pretty plainly about the delay of the Foreign Office in publishing at least a summary of the events which had led up to the 1912 visit and some account of the

39

visit itself and its results, making it clear that the full facts are not withheld in my interests. He is still averse to publishing the papers, but says there is now no reason why the facts should not be stated unofficially, so I am going to let my friends go ahead. Gosse is particularly insistent that continued silence is mischievous.' Questions were asked in the House hinting broadly that publication was delayed in Haldane's interest, and of one of these Asquith wrote to him on August 8:

'DEAR HALDANE

'I have recently been asked in the House of Commons, whether the papers relating to your visit to Berlin can now be published or whether I will consult you on the subject. A question by Rupert Gwynne is on the paper for to-morrow again making this request. I have here the opportunity of reconsidering the question of publication and of hearing the views of the Foreign Office.

'I feel strongly that our previous decision against publication is still right. Publication will involve disclosure of the negotiations with regard to the Portuguese Colonies and to the Baghdad railway, and to my mind, during the war at least, this cannot be contemplated.

'In view of this consideration do you agree?

Yours affectionately,

H. H. A.'

To this Haldane answered:

'MY DEAR A.

'The public interest must govern the answer to the request for the publication of the records of my Berlin conversations. But the responsibility for their non-publication ought not to be put on me; nor should the answer be framed in such fashion as to suggest that it is my interest that these conversations should not be published. As regards the subsequent Portuguese and Baghdad negotiations in which I had no part, the Foreign Office apparently does not realize that they have been made known in Berlin. Count Reventlow's recent third edition of his book on German foreign policy between 1888 and 1914, evidently with material from official sources, gives a pretty full account not only of my visit but of the subsequent negotiations about the Portuguese Colonies. There is in consequence little that is left secret about them, though I doubt whether the Foreign Office had ever seen this book. Anyhow other people have. The recent Foreign Office communiqués, i.e. the one that suggested that Bethmann-Hollweg's original formula was not at once rejected by me, but only by Grey subsequently, has been used mercilessly against me, yet the suggestion has no foundation as you can see if you look at the records.

'If it is now suggested that I am unwilling to have the conversations published, the few remaining rags of character which I have left, will be torn away. The suggestion I refer to would, of course, not have arisen, nor would have several others, if these conversations had been made the subject of a short statement, far short of full publication.

'Why should not this be done?

'I was recently driven by stress of misrepresentation to ask Grey's permission to show the documents confidentially to a few important people. He said he did not mind so long as they did not get into the papers and had no objection to a discreet and unofficial account of the events, without reference to the territorial topics, if these are still to be a mystery.

'What do you think? In any case you should I think make it clear that it is neither by my request nor in my interest that the publication is withheld.

Yours affectionately,

H. of C.'

Asquith agreed that Haldane's memorandum could be used by discreet friends in his defence. So Mr. Harold Begbie published a book entitled *The Vindication of Great Britain*, which was in effect a vindication of Haldane. Lord French paid a warm tribute to his work for the Army in the House of Lords. Mr. Winston Churchill and Mr. Gosse wrote articles defending him, and a series based on the privately circulated memorandum appeared in the *Manchester Guardian*. Action produced reaction, and on October 30 Gosse wrote:

'I have some information to give you which is very unpleasant. The hounds of Hell are again being laid on to your track. A friend of mine who is of importance in the journalistic world tells me that a few days ago Northcliffe gave a luncheon at the Aldwych Club to prominent journalists. He made a speech entirely directed against you. After the bitterest diatribes he adjured all those newspaper men to see to it that you never regained political power in this country. He told them that there was a campaign afoot to reinstate you, but that they all must combine by all means known to them to defeat it. He assured them that you were the greatest enemy to the English state.

'One of these journalists, moved by all this, asked him, since he was in possession of all this evidence against you, why he did not rise and expose you from his place in the House of Lords. This took him aback for a moment, but he answered that this would lead to controversy, which would be dangerous and unsatisfactory. "What you have to do", he went on, "is perpetually to insinuate into the public mind suspicion and hatred of Lord Haldane, so that the moment there is a question of his reappearance in public life, public opinion may automatically howl him down."

'I think you should make this odious conspiracy known amongst your friends.'

In the event the odious conspiracy did not have much effect. Haldane went on with his educational campaign, and was very warmly received. In November he was speaking on edu-

HALDANE AND WINSTON CHURCHILL
AT THE DOOR OF 16 QUEEN ANNE'S GATE

cation at Huddersfield, when a man shouted 'traitor', but he
was promptly silenced by the audience, who gave Haldane an
ovation. In that speech he gave a clear indication of the direction in which his political sympathies were moving:

'If it were not that the working classes are more and more
feeling a strong desire to give their children better opportunities than they themselves had,' Lord Haldane continued,
'I should feel rather hopeless about stirring up sluggish people;
but I do see that the working classes are desiring better chances
for their children than they had themselves, and I do see an
awakening in the national sense that we must have such a
measure of education as will put our nation on a level with
other nations that have rather got ahead of us. There is an
awakening sense, and I think this war may, with all its
miseries, have brought one advantage—it has wakened us up
out of our dogmatic slumber, and made us see what as a
nation we are called on to do for our own. It may be that this
war will have rendered us such service as nothing short of a
calamity could have done.' 'I could wish', he went on, 'that
the Trade Unions would think a little more about education
and a little less about some other things. I look, in vain, in the
speeches of their leaders for any real first class appeal for education. If the Labour Party would make education a plank in
its programme we should carry it to any extent, but they have
not yet wakened up.'

On November 28 he wrote to his mother:

'The Viceroy has telegraphed to me from India urging me
to come out there to preside over the enquiry into educational
reform as a cure for Indian unrest, and the India Office are
strongly supporting the request. But I can't leave my work
here, I have put my hand to the educational campaign at
home and have many more commitments which I cannot
with honour dismiss, so I have refused definitely. I dined last
night with Asquith and Margot. Very friendly as usual. Raymond's death has been a heavy blow to him. He looks weary

and I hear he is losing his grip in the Cabinet and that intrigues are afoot. I am glad to be out of it.'

In the first week of December it was clear that Asquith's Government was tottering, and on the evening of December 3 the Prime Minister informed the King that a reconstruction of the Government was inevitable. During the next two days it became clear that reconstruction would not be easy, and on the afternoon of December 5 Asquith tendered his resignation to the King. There was doubt whether Mr. Lloyd George would be able to form a government and the King feared that he might be asked to dissolve Parliament. He therefore sought advice privately and that night Lord Stamfordham wrote to Haldane:

'Will you be very kind and tell me if the King were asked to dissolve Parliament as a condition of anyone undertaking to form a Government could His Majesty constitutionally refuse to do so? Or if refusal be legally impossible could the King decline on the grounds of expediency owing to the War, a faulty register, the absence of so large a number of voters at the front and the immediate necessity of a Government to carry on the war and the general business of the country.'

To this Haldane replied the same night:

'1. The Sovereign ought at no time to act without the advice of a responsible Minister, except when contemplating the exercise of the prerogative right to dismiss his Minister. The only Minister who can possibly give advice as to a dissolution of Parliament is the Prime Minister.

'2. The Sovereign before acting on advice to dissolve ought to weigh that advice. His Majesty may, instead of accepting it, dismiss the Minister who gives it, or receive his resignation. This is the only alternative to taking his advice.

'3. It follows that the Sovereign cannot entertain any bargain for a dissolution with a possible Prime Minister, before the latter is fully installed. The Sovereign cannot, before that event, properly weigh the situation or the Parliamentary position of the Ministry as formed.'

In the event Mr. Lloyd George formed his Government and on the day the change was announced Lord Buckmaster met Haldane in St. James's Park and expressed his apprehension. Haldane answered: 'Asquith is a first class head of a deliberative council. He is versed in precedents, acts on principles, and knows how and when to compromise. Lloyd George cares nothing for precedents and knows no principles, but he has fire in his belly and that is what we want.'[1]

On January 2, 1917, Haldane wrote to Asquith:

'The old machine, by means of which I used to try to work, is now destroyed, and I do not see any prospect of another coming into existence, which would either take me on or which I could take on. So I am just going on with the cause of national training. I may do a little good, and I cannot do harm.

'I think with you that Lloyd George's trouble will come with Carson.[2] He has not got a constructive mind and is a wrecker. But Jellicoe is sensible and full of driving power. I only wish Fisher were twenty years younger.'

A few months later he was more cheerful. In April 1917 he wrote to his sister:

'It is curious to find the change in the Government so plainly visible. The Liberals are wholly out of it now and one gets little information. But as far as I can judge the public likes the new régime. It is showing energy and does not waste time. The changed position in Mesopotamia[3] is a feather in their cap and a tribute to Robertson's reorganization of the General Staff at the War Office, of which I hear well. I have had many talks with Fisher, the new President of the Board of Education. He is very sympathetic to my programme and quite agrees with me that the fact that we are at war is no

[1] Letter from Lord Buckmaster.
[2] First Lord of the Admiralty in the new Government.
[3] Baghdad was captured on March 1.

45

reason why we should not prepare for better things in peace. There seems to be a real prospect of getting something done. He is putting nursery schools, continuation schools, improved secondary education and physical training in his programme. I am deeply engaged in planning reconstruction after the war. People are beginning to see its vast extent of meaning. It includes not only education but much besides. Last night I had the Prime Minister to dine to meet some of those busy in thinking out reconstruction. We had that day passed a great scheme for the supply of power to industry and I had the most important members of my committee and the President of the Board of Trade[1] to meet the Prime Minister, who was keenly interested.

'As he left the P.M. took me aside and said: "You must come in. All difficulties must be put aside, for the nation wants your brains badly." However I simply smiled and said I would help as I was doing from outside.'

On April 19 Mr. Fisher introduced his first education estimates, and speaking on these on May 9 in the Lords Haldane referred to two problems which are still with us. The first of these had been considered by his Coal Conservation Committee:

'After the war we shall have to face the payment of interest on an enormous debt. For my part I see no prospect of taxes going down. I think we shall require all the revenue we have now for the three-fold purpose of paying the interest and sinking fund on the National Debt, for providing pensions for a long period, and last but not least for so improving our institutions that the generation, on whose shoulders the burden of these things will mainly rest, shall be capable of dealing with them by a great increase in the productivity of the Nation.

'It must be a better generation in every respect if we are not to break down under our burden. Take only one of the topics which are fructifying at the moment—I mean the supply of energy from coal. I am not speaking at large. I am repeating

[1] Sir Albert Stanley.

46

the results which have been worked out by some of the first expert authorities in this country, when I say that the situation is broadly as follows. We use, in order to obtain the energy which we require for our industrial purposes, some 80,000,000 tons of coal. It is estimated, not on the basis of calculation but on experience gained in parts of the country, where the thing has been done, that the same results, the same kind of energy could be got with 25,000,000 tons instead of 80,000,000. The reason is that we waste our coal prodigiously. Instead of taking it at the pit head, we transport it, thereby losing a great deal that is not fit for transport, we take it away to small generating stations which are run very expensively, in place of having got the energy which the coal at even moderate computation would furnish us with, we have rather less than a third of what we ought to have obtained. Besides that we lose the benefits of the bye-products which the conversion of the potential energy of the coal at the pit head might enable us to recover. And at the present time it is estimated that if our system were what it should be every workman would have at his disposal twice the amount of energy in the shape of proper machinery and tools, and a much larger output, even double, would be the result, with the consequence to the workman that he would be able to obtain in shorter hours a much larger wage by reason of a greatly enhanced output. The working classes are thereby directly interested in a reform of this kind, which rests, not upon speculative considerations, but upon knowledge and on the interest of the public.'

The second problem on which he touched in this speech was the part of physical training in national efficiency:

'Mr. Fisher has proposed to deal with the subject of physical training. There, of course, I am entirely with him. But this is a very large subject and I do not think it is a Board of Education question.

'Nobody can tell until peace is made what sort of army we shall require after the war is over. It may be an army of one

47

sort, or an army of another sort. I think it is not improbable, at any rate it is a case which has to be considered, that we may require to keep the great garrisons in India and overseas, and an Expeditionary Force to reinforce them. It may be greater or smaller. It may be much like what we had before the war. But at least we shall require an Expeditionary Force capable of extremely rapid mobilization. And then I think the lesson of the war is this, that the nation must be more willing to lend itself to arrangements for a Second Line Army, capable not only of comparatively rapid mobilization, but of great expansion. . . . You will probably find that we shall have to raise a First Line Territorial Army—I gather from Lord Derby's speech in the House of Lords that he meant to preserve the Territorial organization based on territorial principles and raised through the County Associations. But you would want expansion. Expansion may take the form of Army behind Army—a First Line Territorial Army, a Second Line, a Third Line, and so on through the population. You can only train the First Line adequately; for the others you will have to go back to the population. I think you will find it difficult to get people over eighteen to submit themselves to compulsory training after the war, and if you do, you may get into difficulties in raising your overseas garrisons, which have to be raised on a voluntary basis and for long service. But I do not want to mention controversial subjects. Whatever line you take about that, you could make use of the schools as a means of preparing your future potential soldiers. In Mr. Fisher's scheme compulsory vocational training is required. Why should not one of the periods of education after the elementary school be a period in which this compulsory training should be required to fit men to be called upon in after life, if necessary, to become rapidly capable and trained soldiers? Of course one does not wish to touch the elementary schools. The Boy Scout organization will be very valuable there, and from the earliest point I should like to see the nature of that organization, the *esprit de corps* and the standard it raises, brought into our educational life; and when you get to the post-elementary stage, the period between 14 and 18, and I do not propose myself to carry it further—then I should like to see the compulsory education which is to belong to the continuation school include training in a cadet corps and the annual camp, which is necessary for this purpose.'

So he went on quietly thinking and planning for the future and sooner than he expected he was given far greater opportunities than he could possibly have had as a private member.

He wrote to his mother in mid July: 'Ll. G. is out to liberalize his Government. Curzon I am told, is kicking, but I back the little man to win. Addison is to be moved to the Ministry of Reconstruction and Winston comes in as Minister of Munitions, and Montague as Minister without portfolio with a special eye on reconstruction. I am now Chairman of a Committee on the Machinery of Government. It is about the best committee over which I have ever presided and we see our way to producing a real plan for the Government of the nation in the days ahead. Whether any Government will have the courage to put our plans into operation remains to be seen.'

Haldane's Coal Conservation Committee was now placed with a number of others under the direction of the Ministry of Reconstruction. Twenty-four committees were set to work—the number of these was later increased—to examine almost every aspect of national life, and of these committees, in addition to that on the Machinery of Government and on Coal Conservation, of which he was chairman, he became a member of the committee on our system of education. As he continued to take his full share of legal work in the House of Lords and in the Privy Council, he was now fully occupied, as he liked to be, with constructive work, and his educational campaign in the country had to cease. In October and November a double blow fell on his dear friends the Horners

—Mells, the Horners' beautiful home in Somerset, which he had always called his English home, was burned down and a few weeks later Edward Horner died of wounds received in the battle of Cambrai. 'What a convulsion this is,' he wrote to his mother. 'The terrible thing for the future of the country is that when peace comes we shall be found with problems, more difficult, more pregnant of good or evil than any with which this horrible war confronts us, and the men who could succeed us and bring back with them from their trial by fire, new inspiration and fresh ideals are being swept away by the hurricane. Raymond Asquith, Bron Lucas, and Edward Horner have gone from our own circle, and the gaps in the number of these to whom we could hand on our task grow wider daily. After moments of despair I return with new zeal to my thesis, better education, greater opportunities for those who are left to us.'

A few weeks later he wrote: 'My hints to the Labour Party have not fallen on deaf ears. More and more labour leaders and prominent trade unionists are coming to consult me. They are really interested in my education programme, though some of them are rather disposed to regard me as an emissary of the War Office and to be suspicious of my ideas of cadet training. However, when I explain that you can't have physical training without drill or run camps successfully without discipline, they begin to see that there may be something in what I have to say. The real interest of most of them, more particularly the trade unionists, is in improved secondary and technical training. Indeed I am finding more real interest in these subjects amongst labour men than amongst my fellow Liberals.'

At the end of the year 1917 he brought his Royal Commission on University Education in Wales to a conclusion with a report which was adopted unanimously, and formed the basis on which Statutes giving the university new form and life were framed and adopted in 1922.

Chapter III

THE ORGANIZATION OF GOVERNMENT
1918 to 1919

Full of work which interested him, Haldane watched the stirring events of the year 1918, in which political and military crises followed each other in swift succession, from the wings with an observant and critical eye. In February Mr. Lloyd George proposed that the British Military Representative on the Supreme War Council at Versailles, which had been created in the previous autumn, should be entirely independent of the Chief of the Imperial General Staff. Field-Marshal Sir William Robertson, who held the latter post, insisted that military advice to the Government should be presented through him, and pointed out that the French Military Representative at Versailles was General Weygand, who was a subordinate of Foch. Robertson refused to give way and was dismissed, and the Prime Minister made General Sir Henry Wilson, who had been our military representative at Versailles, Chief of the Imperial General Staff in his place, and he soon after appointed a subordinate of his as our Military Representative at Versailles. The object of this manœuvre was to get rid of Robertson, who was, Mr. Lloyd George believed, opposed to unity of command. This affair gave rise to much controversy and to attacks upon the Government. Of these Haldane wrote on February 20:

'Ll. G. has tackled his opponents with his usual courage and has made a pretty conclusive case for himself on the main issue. He is impulsive and rushes in without thinking out his way and so makes unnecessary trouble for himself, and he doesn't know how to handle the soldiers. I prophesy that he will be before long regretting the exchange of Wilson for Robertson. The Liberals have been full of excitement. There is an intrigue on foot to form an Asquith-Lansdowne coalition to replace Ll. G. It would never work and hasn't the remotest chance of success. I will have nothing to do with it.'

A few weeks later he again wrote to his sister: 'Last night Ll. G. and the Sidney Webbs dined here alone. It was a great success. We are to dine with him before long to meet Milner, who is going to the War Office in place of Derby. The object of our talks is to think out the lines of the channels in which the democratic flood can safely flow. Ll. G. was very tactful with the Webbs and told them that the future would lie between two new parties, with the old Liberal party split between them. He said that he would always be with the democratic side. We had much talk about the reorganization of Government. He sees that at the end of the war everything will be in the melting pot and that we have an unique chance of repairing old omissions and errors. After the Webbs left he stayed on and we went for a midnight walk guarded by a vigilant detective. He told me that the newspaper proprietors of to-day were like the Whig Dukes of the old days and could burst up any Government and had in time of crisis to be secured. He was quite frank and knew the case against himself, but his plea was the impossibility of keeping the national government together otherwise in times of crisis. I don't like his methods but he has intelligence and real driving power, and he is full of courage over the prospects of the war.'

The great German attack began in the third week of March, and as soon as the military crisis had been tided over a political crisis followed. The Government was hotly criticized for not maintaining the strength of our Army in France, and on May 6 I wrote a letter to the Press challenging certain statements which had been made on that subject by ministers.

Haldane wrote to his sister on May 9, the day on which my letter was the subject of a debate in the House of Commons, when Mr. Asquith moved that a select committee of the House be appointed to inquire into my allegations:

'The Government does one foolish thing after another and they have handled this business of General Maurice badly, but the Liberals have handled it worse. There is no real alternative to the present Government and I said so plainly in the House of Lords yesterday. I hear that 20 Cavendish Square[1] has been much upset by my declaration, but the feeble way in which Asquith's motion was handled was not a good advertisement for a change. I do not think that there is any doubt but that Lloyd George backed his military judgement against that of the soldiers and was wrong, but he has managed to wriggle out of his trouble with his usual dexterity.'

The sequel to this incident may follow here. On November 15 he wrote to his sister: 'Sir Frederick Maurice came to lunch with me to-day and we had a very interesting talk. He showed me the papers relating to the events which led to his writing his letter challenging the statements of Ministers in May, and told me that the reason why he acted as he did was that he had definite information that Ll. G. and General Wilson were agreed that the time had come to get rid of Haig, that statements which were not correct and tended to throw the responsibility on Haig for our failure in March, which brought us so near disaster, were made to prepare the mind of the Cabinet and of the public for Haig's removal. He determined to prevent this by challenging the statements publicly, being sure that the real facts would then be known to the Cabinet. He assured me that he had no political motive and had gone into hiding immediately after sending his letter to the papers to avoid being drawn into any political controversy. If he is right in his facts events have proved that he did his country good service. He is going to be Principal of the Working

[1]Mr. Asquith's London house.

Men's College, where I first began to work at Adult Education.'

Almost simultaneously with the crisis on the Western Front the situation in Ireland became critical. On April 9 Mr. Lloyd George in introducing the Military Service Bill, designed to provide more men for the Army, had announced that Home Rule would be conferred on Ireland and that a measure of conscription would be applied to that country. The Easter Rebellion had occurred and had been suppressed and on May 6 it was announced that Haldane's friend Lord French was to be Viceroy. On hearing this he wrote to French:

'With your usual courage you have accepted a very difficult task. We are old friends and you will not mind my saying that I am doubtful if you were wise in doing so. I do not believe that the Government seriously intends to apply conscription to Ireland or that it would be possible to do so, if it does. I think that Ll. G. made his announcement of conscription for Ireland as a sop to public opinion here, without reckoning what the effect on Ireland would be. The mere fact that you are a soldier and a soldier of great distinction will make your task the more difficult. You will need all the patience and judgement you can exercise. You should make a point of seeing Morley before you leave. Remember that coercion never has succeeded and never will succeed in Ireland.'

Haldane was confirmed in his view that the application of conscription in Ireland was impossible by a letter which he received from Mr. W. B. Yeats from Dublin:

'DEAR LORD HALDANE

'I have just returned to Dublin from the West of Ireland, where I have been living for months. I am alarmed at the state of feeling here and there. I write to you because you are a man of letters, and we, therefore, may speak the same language. I have no part in politics and no liking for politics, but there are moments when one cannot keep out of them. I have met nobody in close contact with the people who believes that conscription can be imposed without the killing of men, and perhaps of women. Lady Gregory, who knows the country as few know it, and has taken down, for instance, hundreds of thousands of words in collecting folk-lore from cottage to cottage and has still many ways of learning what is thought about it—is convinced that the women and children will stand in front of their men and receive the bullets. I do not say that this will happen, but I do say that there is in this country an extravagance of emotion which few Englishmen, accustomed to more objective habits of thought, can understand. There is something oriental in the people, and it is impossible to say how great a tragedy may lie before us. The British Government, it seems to me, is rushing into this business in a strangely trivial frame of mind. I hear of all manner of opinions being taken except the opinion of those who have some knowledge of the popular psychology. I hear even of weight being given to the opinions of clergymen of the Church of Ireland, who, as a class, are more isolated from their neighbours than any class anywhere known to me. I find in people here in Dublin a sense of strain and expectancy which makes even strangers speak something of their mind. I was ordering some coal yesterday, and I said: "I shall be in such and such a house for the next four months." The man at the counter, a stranger to me, muttered: "Who, in Ireland, can say where he will be in four months?" Another man, almost a stranger, used nearly those very words speaking to me some two weeks ago. There is a danger of a popular hysteria that may go to any height or any whither. There is a return to that sense of crisis which followed the Rising. Some two months after the Rising I called on a well-known Dublin doctor, and as I entered his room, an old cabinetmaker went out. The doctor said to me: "That man has just said a very strange thing. He says there will be more trouble yet, for 'the young men are mad jealous of their leaders for being shot'." That jealousy is still in the country. It is not a question as to whether it is justified or not justified, for these men believe—an incredible thought, perhaps, to Englishmen—that the Childers Committee reported truthfully as to the overtaxation of Ireland, that the population of Ireland has gone down one-half through English misgovernment, that the union of Ireland, in our time, was made impossible because England armed the minority of the people with rifles and machine-guns. When they think to themselves: "Now England expects us to die for her", is it wonderful that they say to themselves afterwards: "We shall bring our deaths to a different market." I read in the newspaper yesterday that over three hundred thousand Americans have landed in France in a month, and it seems to me a strangely wanton thing that England, for the sake of fifty thousand Irish soldiers, is prepared to hollow another trench between the countries and fill it with blood. If that is done England will only suffer in reputation, but Ireland will suffer in her character, and all the work of my lifetime and that of my fellow-workers: all our effort to clarify and sweeten the popular mind will be destroyed and Ireland, for another hundred years, will live in the sterility of her bitterness.

Yours sincerely,

W. B. YEATS.'

While the state of Ireland was going from bad to worse a dramatic change in the fortune of war began in July with the defeat of the Germans in the Château Thierry salient, and this was followed by the series of victories which ended in the Armistice of November 11. When the news of this reached Cloan Mrs. Haldane composed a little hymn which Haldane showed to Gosse, who sent it to *The Times* with the following letter:

'Sir,—When the news that the armistice was signed reached Scotland, my venerable friend, Mrs. Haldane of Cloan, who is advanced in her 94th year, improvised the following verses, which I have her permission to send to you:

A HYMN OF PRAISE

The victory is won!
To Him be all the praise
Whose arm this work has done,
Praise Him always.

'Twas not by power or might
Were moved the hearts of stone,
But of imperial right—
His word alone.

Then let us with our hearts
And tongues his praises sing
Who peace and joy imparts,—
Of kings, our King.

So may our voice intone,
Our praises loudly ring,
Till all the world shall own
Our God and King.

Am I wrong in thinking that many hearts will respond to the patriotic enthusiasm of these simple lines, written on the 17th of the month by one who was alive when Byron died?

I am Sir, your obedient servant,

EDMUND GOSSE.'

Just at the time when this appeared Haldane received the letter from Haig[1] in which, writing of Haldane's work as

[1]Vol. i, p. 373.

Secretary of State for War, he said: 'You then sowed the seeds which have developed into the tremendous instrument which has vanquished the famous German Army and brought about a victorious peace.' It is characteristic of Haldane that he was more pleased at the reception accorded to his mother's little hymn than he was at getting that letter. He wrote to his sister: 'Everyone is talking of mother's hymn, and what a wonderful achievement it is for one of her age. Two such diverse personalities as the Archbishop of York[1] and General Sir Herbert Miles stopped me and asked me to send their congratulations on it and both said that she was one of the most remarkable women alive to-day. James Barrie whom I met casually said to me, "you know she has more personality than you have or had when you were sitting in your robes on the woolsack. You ought to tell the world that your spiritual home is your mother's room."

'I have had a remarkable letter from Haig, who writes of what the Army owes to me. I will bring it with me when I come up. Of course it cannot be published but it is an interesting possession.'

With that strange sensitiveness which annoyed his friends Haldane refused to ask Haig whether he might publish the letter, and it did not appear until his autobiography was completed by his sister after his death.

On November 23, two days after the arrival of Haig's letter, Lord Stamfordham wrote to Haldane: 'I was with the King this morning and he directed me to write and tell you how deeply he appreciated all you had done to make our victory possible and how silly he thought the outcry against you which he thought was most unjustifiable.' On this Haldane wrote to his sister: 'I have had a very pleasant message from the King through Stamfordham expressing appreciation of what I did for the Army. It is odd how quickly public opinion veers round. I am now getting letters from all sorts

[1]Now Archbishop of Canterbury.

of people I do not know expressing gratitude and appreciation.'

In December the Report of the Machinery of Government Committee was completed. The drafting of this report was mainly done by Haldane, and he took the opportunity to expound what was now his favourite thesis:

'We have come to the conclusion after surveying what came before us, that in the sphere of civil government the duty of investigation and thought, as preliminary to action, might with great advantage be more definitely recognized. It appears to us that adequate provision has not been made in the past for the organized acquisition of facts and information and for the systematic application of thought as preliminary to the settlement of policy and its subsequent administration. This is no new notion. There are well-known spheres of action in which the principle has been adopted of placing the business of enquiry and thinking in the hands of persons definitely charged with it, whose duty is to study the future, and work out plans and advise those responsible for policy or engaged in actual administration. The reason of the separation of work has been the proved impracticability of devoting the necessary time to thinking out organization and preparation for action in the mere interstices of the time required for the transaction of business.

'But the principle ought by no means to be limited in its application to military and naval affairs. We have come to the conclusion that the business of executive government generally has been seriously embarrassed from the incomplete application to it of similar methods.'

In other words, the report advocated that every department of state should be provided with its general staff. When Haldane first entered the War Office he had asked three questions: 'What is the function of the Army? How should it be organized to fulfil that function? How does each existing part of the Army fit into that organization?' He adopted exactly the same procedure in his inquiry into the machinery of government and began by asking: 'What are the functions of the Cabinet? How should it be organized? Upon what principles are the functions of the departments of State to be determined and allocated?'

To these questions the Report answered:

'The main functions of the Cabinet may, we think, be described as:

'(*a*) the final determination of the policy to be submitted to Parliament;

'(*b*) the supreme control of the national executive in accordance with the policy prescribed by Parliament; and

'(*c*) the continuous co-ordination and delimitation of the activities of the several Departments of State.

'For the due performance of these functions the following conditions seem to be essential, or, at least, desirable:

'(i) the Cabinet should be small in number—preferably ten or, at most, twelve;

'(ii) it should meet frequently;

'(iii) it should be supplied in the most convenient form with all the information and material necessary to enable it to arrive at expeditious decisions;

'(iv) it should make a point of consulting personally all the Ministers whose work is likely to be affected by its decisions; and

'(v) it should have a systematic method of securing that its decisions are effectually carried out by the several Departments concerned.'

This last recommendation meant that the Cabinet secretariat and the system of keeping Cabinet minutes inaugurated by Sir Maurice Hankey under the direction of Lloyd George should be maintained.

In answer to the third question, upon what principle are the functions of Departments to be determined and allocated, the Report said:

'There appear to be only two alternatives, which may be

briefly described as distribution according to the persons or classes to be dealt with, and distribution according to the services to be performed. Under the former method each Minister who presides over a Department would be responsible to Parliament for those activities of the Government which affect the sectional interests of particular classes of persons, and there might be, for example, a Ministry for Paupers, a Ministry for Children, a Ministry for Insured Persons, or a Ministry for the Unemployed. Now the inevitable outcome of this method of organization is a tendency to Lilliputian administration. It is impossible that the specialized service which each Department has to render to the community can be of as high a standard when its work is at the same time limited to a particular class of persons and extended to every variety of provision for them, as when the Department concentrates itself on the provision of one particular service only, by whomsoever required, and looks beyond the interests of comparatively small classes.'

In order that the Cabinet should be small in number the Report recommended that Departments rendering like services should be grouped each under its own Minister and that each group should be under the general direction of a Cabinet Minister.

At first sight one of the most obvious of such groupings would appear to be that of the Admiralty, the War Office, and the Air Ministry under the general direction of a Minister of Defence, but the Report made no such recommendation. Instead it proposed that the three Departments of Defence should continue to be under the general supervision of the Prime Minister, exercised through the Committee of Imperial Defence, which should be to some extent reorganized and re-equipped to enable it to work more efficiently. This was to give rise to a controversy which is not yet ended.

The other main recommendations of the Report were that a Ministry of Information and Research should be created to be at the disposal of other departments of state, of the public services in general, and of industry, and that the work of the Lord Chancellor's office should be redistributed and reorganized. In both of these recommendations Haldane's influence is obvious. The first is the natural conclusion of his thesis that organization should be based on general principles formulated from ascertained and co-ordinated facts; the second was the result of his own experience of the Lord Chancellor's office. Of this he wrote a few months after the appearance of the report and after a conference of magistrates:

'I think there is nothing from which the public service has suffered more than the want of precise definition of function and of apportionment of responsibility. Without organization that makes provision for these the local Bench will look in vain for the light and for the refashioning of instruments which it requires for the adequate performance of great and essential duties.

'Law, with our local Bench, is inseparable from full understanding of the functions of the magistrate, and of the services which he is expected by the community to render to it. This, judging from the tone of the meeting last week, the magistrate seems himself to recognize. It is natural that it should be so. He has to consider administrative matters, even when dispensing justice, and administration is founded on science as well as on art. Practice can only be good if based on adequate knowledge. In the Civil Service itself this is becoming more and more clearly understood, and after a few years more it seems as though it would be insisted on. The Law Society not long since said something of the same kind with reference to Courts of Justice generally.

'It was the recognition that our standards of excellence are insufficient that led to insistence, as the first step needful, on definition of function with attendantly defined responsibility. Why this subject involves careful and scientific treatment was sought to be made plain in the Machinery of Government

Report of 1918. I had the honour of presiding over that Committee, but, what is much more important, I had as colleagues besides Mr. Montagu, such experts as the late Sir Robert Morant, Sir George Murray and Mr. Sidney Webb. We sought to set out the reasons why more than mere patchwork reform had become necessary. In Chapter X of the Report we set out in detail grounds on which we thought the necessity for this reform extended to the administration of justice.

'We did not seek to alter the status of the Lord Chancellor's office. He is required as the supreme constitutional and legal adviser of the Government; for the appointment of the Judges; as their head; and for other duties. But, as the late Lord Herschell said, in giving evidence on an earlier occasion, the work thrown on the Lord Chancellor under present arrangements requires, not one man, but three to do it. We showed in Chapter X of the Report what this work is. We set out a list of formidable duties of such a nature as necessarily to overtax the strength even of the energy and brilliant quickness of the present occupant of this great office.[1] What we recommended was that these duties should be re-defined and re-arranged, and that those which required, as some of them obviously did, the assistance of a trained staff should pass, not to a new Government Department, but to the Home Office, which, relieved of certain other duties by the analogous operation of principle of the Report, should become what it is, inherently, even now, the administrative Department of Justice.

'It is, I think, our neglect of the immensely important requirements of the administrative consequences of justice, and the failure to recognize that legal and administrative duties are of different characters, involving different training, that has laid our system open to some criticism, both at home and abroad.'

The Report appeared at an unfortunate time. A General

[1] Lord Birkenhead.

Election was in progress when it was published, and the General Election was followed by the complicated business of demobilization, by unrest and strikes at home, by disturbances in Ireland, and by the preoccupation of the Prime Minister and those in his immediate circle with the Treaties of Peace. So it failed to command the attention it deserved; the opportunity for a general reconstruction was there, but the time for it was lacking. Haldane wrote: 'I hate this election. Ll. G. always lives for the moment and never thinks of the lessons of the past. But one would have imagined even he would have remembered the khaki election of 1900. He is repeating Chamberlain's mistake, and will surely pay for it. The wild expectations which are being flourished before the public cannot be realized and the country is being whipped up into the worst possible mood for a wise settlement at home and abroad. The news I get from my Irish friends makes me anxious.'

Early in 1919 Lord French, the Viceroy, asked Haldane to come over to Dublin for an informal consultation on the state of Ireland and possible remedies. Of this visit he wrote to his sister during his journey back:

'I found the Irish Government in deep depression. Sinn Fein is something entirely new to them. It is non-material—idealistic, and as Lord Chancellor Campbell, who is a close friend of Carson, told me it is penetrating every class of society outside Ulster. French is, as usual, full of courage, but I reminded him that spiritual bayonets were much more difficult to break or down than the material bayonets which had confronted him in France. The Castle folk expect that very soon Sinn Fein will get control or supersede the local authorities all over the country and will find its way into the Central Government. I broke gently to French the idea which I had been meditating on at Cloan of making as soon as possible a great and generous offer, which would disarm American and Australian opinion, and that is a consideration of weight with him and his advisers. I proposed that an offer be made, publicly if possible, to the people of Ireland as a whole, not to the Sinn Feiners and their leaders, of self-government on the status of a Dominion under the Crown; that the financial conditions should be as generous as possible to Ireland, and that, pending agreement on these, customs and excise should remain under the control of the Imperial Government; that we should offer every assistance in the reconstruction of the Government so as to make its principles, administration and legislation conform as closely as possible with the best Irish ideas. I told him that Ulster would probably reject such proposals and that Sinn Fein would disbelieve in their sincerity. But publicly to make such an offer would disarm the U.S. and Australia and I said that they must follow it up and prove it to be genuine by reforms, which would pave the way for acceptance, reforms complete in spirit as well as in letter of the administrative and executive machinery of Government of such a kind as it might be conjectured a Home Rule Parliament would establish.

'I gave them a plan in outline to be worked out by a very small but powerful committee of three—an Ulsterman, a Sinn Feiner, and a neutral.

'French took time to consider this but after twenty-four hours he made up his mind in favour, strongly backed by the Principal Private Secretary, a son of Colonel Saunderson of Ulster fame. He asked me if I would be chairman of a committee like my Machinery of Government Committee, to work out the details. I said that must depend on what I found out after meeting his adversaries. I then shook off the splendours of Viceregal Lodge and disappeared into Dublin, and, through my own channels, got into negotiation on the general plan with Jesuit Sinn Fein priests, members of Parliament and other Sinn Fein leaders, including the two Mac-Neills, and I came to the conclusion that there was a chance of success. I told French that I would be prepared to make the attempt, if the Cabinet desired it; but that my terms would be immediate release of all political prisoners (there are about one hundred of them) and that my nationalist colleague should be de Valera himself.[1] I told French that de Valera would certainly be Prime Minister in an Irish Parliament and was indispensable if the plan were to go through. All those consulted by French have concurred and nearly two-thirds of them are Ulstermen or landlords. The Sinn Fein rebels whom I met were friendly and intelligent, and I only saw the best of them, but I thought highly of their quality and their sanity. The Cabinet may turn the whole thing down. I think they probably will, but the Lord Lieutenant thinks otherwise. I saw the letter he sent them last night and he is going over to London to urge Ll. G. and Carson to agree.'

Three days after writing this he heard from Lord French: 'I am very sorry to have arrived at the conclusion that it is useless for us to think of going any further, at present at any rate, in the matter of your proposed scheme. A terrible outrage occurred yesterday in Tipperary in which two policemen were brutally murdered and a quantity of gelignite was seized. It has been necessary to declare the whole county a military area. I must remind you that this horrible outrage occurred on the very day when we had reason to hope that secret influences were being brought to bear to prevent anything of the kind, which shows that the Sinn Fein leaders cannot control their own people.

'I have told Long that it is needless for you to see him now, at least as far as I am concerned, and that circumstances have prevented any further progress being made in the direction we wished.

'I am sorry to say that the reply which he sent me to the letter which I showed you was very uncompromising in tone, and I do not think any good would have resulted from the interview.

[1] Mr. de Valera was at the time in prison in England.

'I am more than sorry that for the present I can't avail myself of your valuable help, but I hope to be able to do so later.'

Haldane's comment on this was:

'This is folly. The Sinn Fein leaders are not murderers. They are idealists with a fanatical belief in what they believe to be principles, tempered by a shrewd recognition of realities and of what is practically possible. To class them with wild and irresponsible extremists and to refuse negotiation because these commit murders is I suppose what one must expect from Parliament in its present temper, but it is madness and the Government will soon be wringing its hands over lost opportunities.'

During the series of strikes which occurred during the first months of 1919 the Prime Minister used Haldane as a bridge between himself and the Labour Party, and there were a number of consultations between Mr. Lloyd George and the Sidney Webbs at 28 Queen Annes Gate. The coal-mining industry was amongst the most disturbed and at the Prime Minister's request Haldane negotiated with the Labour leaders on the appointment of a Coal Commission and on its personnel. He insisted that the chairman should be outside politics, and got both parties to agree to the appointment of Mr. Justice Sankey as chairman, with Sir Richard Redmayne as assessor. The Commission presented its interim report in March, recommending important changes in hours of work and in wages. On this Haldane wrote to his sister: 'The interim report of Sankey's Commission is good as far as it goes and I have had a good deal to do with it. The proposed changes in conditions should help towards peace but it will I fear be some time before the miners understand that the good times they had during the war cannot last for ever, and we have the grave problems of a surplus mining population brought in during the war to dispose of. Also during the war systematic development had to be sacrificed to the need for getting coal as easily and quickly as possible, so that many of the mines are now in a bad condition. I do not believe that there is any permanent cure short of nationalization. My Coal Utilization Committee proved that the waste is at present tremendous and I am sure that we could get such results from a complete and scientific reorganization of the industry as would enable us to pay handsomely for nationalization.'

With no commission on his hands and no work to be done beyond his legal work in the House of Lords and the Privy Council Haldane now had some leisure to give to other things and at long last gave way to the pressure of his friends that he should state his case publicly. Gosse wrote to him:

'It is not fair either to yourself or your friends that you should refrain any longer from answering the slanders, which you have borne with too much patience. The occasional words of commendation of your work for the country, which fall from those who know the facts, are quickly forgotten and continued silence only means that there are mutterings amongst those who won't admit that they were wrong, of "there must be something in it". Jack Squire has been urging me to stir you into action and has sent me a rhymed epistle all on one rhyme. I must copy for your amusement a fragment of it:

> *The noble Viscount I repeat,*
> *Is really annoyingly discreet,*
> *If he weren't so damnably discreet*
> *He'd find himself in another street,*
> *With all the public at his feet,*
> *And even the scribes who with horrid heat*
> *For five long years have steadily beat*
> *His pate for plotting our defeat*
> *And the victory final and complete*
> *Of the Hunnish Tirp and his beastly fleet*
> *Would be bound perforce their words to eat*
> *(I admit a most rancid and nauseous meat)*
> *And stand in a row in a pure white sheet,*

and so on and so on, monstrously clever Squire is. I hope his appeal will move you.'

It did and Haldane wrote a series of articles giving an account of what he had done for the Army and of his negotiations with Germany, which appeared in the *Westminster Gazette*, and an article for the *Atlantic Monthly* on the latter subject. The *Atlantic Monthly* offered him 500 dollars for the article, but he refused payment on the ground that he had used public documents to complete it. He then put the two together and with some additions published them as a book under the title *Before the War*, early in 1920. The book was well reviewed but it was not a really adequate presentation of his case. As Squire said, the noble Viscount was 'too damnably discreet'. He never seemed able to take the same interest and trouble about the preparation of his own defence as he had been wont to do when defending the interests of a client.

As soon as this was out of the way he turned back to education and busied himself, with the assistance of Mr. Fisher and the Master of Balliol, in the reorganization of the educational trust which he had persuaded his friend Sir E. Cassel to found.

On Haldane's advice Sir E. Cassel had given the sum of five hundred thousand pounds for the advancement of adult education. Haldane at Cassel's request became chairman of the trust, and his co-trustees were Lord Balfour, Lord Oxford, Mr. Herbert Fisher, Mr. Sidney Webb, Sir George Murray, and Miss Phillipa Fawcett. One of the first acts of the trustees was to make a substantial grant for the establishment of the British Institute of Adult Education, of which Haldane was the first President. He also became President of Birkbeck College. That college had been founded by Dr. Birkbeck in 1823 as a Mechanics Institute and had developed into an institution for providing facilities for higher education for those who were at work in the day time. The Royal Commission of the University of London over which Haldane had presided said of Birkbeck College: 'We think that the original purpose of the founder of Birkbeck College and the excellent work that institution has done for the education of working students, who desire a university training, marks it out as the natural seat of the constituent college for evening or other part-time students.' Haldane as president now set himself to implement this recommendation. He approached the London County Council and secured financial backing from that body. With this he went to the University of London and secured the admission of the college as a school of the university in 1920.

Einstein had propounded his theory of general relativity in 1915. The war had naturally diverted attention from this important event, but as soon as peace was restored scientific and philosophical societies in this country began an eager discussion of Einstein's theories. Haldane, with his deep interest in any new scientific development, followed these discussions closely, more particularly those concerned with the philosophical aspects of the problem. He began a correspondence with Einstein, but as he was neither a mathematician nor a physicist and Einstein was not a philosopher the correspondence languished, and the two men did not really begin to understand each other until Einstein visited England. Despite the difficulty of getting useful contact with the author of the theory, Haldane set himself to work out its application to his philosophy, and he wrote to Asquith in May:

'I want to thank you for Barbellion's *Journal*. I have read it through with pleasure *and profit*. I think it is probably a genuine book. Wells could not, I think, write like that. Someone who was influenced by Maurice de Guérin and by Marie Bashkirtseff must have set these things down. The morbid strain in it is not the important feature. It is the truthful self-rendering. This suggests genuineness to me strongly. I had heard of the book, and was thinking of sending for it, when it came from you, and it is more than up to my hopes about it.

'I have been working pretty closely and have finished the

Address to the British Academy on "Degrees in Knowledge and Reality" to be delivered on June 25. I find that I have semi-unconsciously moved on, and the idea is developed in a form that it has not taken before. But I am a beastly bad writer, alas, else I could make some stir with this, which will probably fall flat!'

He followed this address to the British Academy with another, which was his inaugural address as President of Birkbeck College on 'The Relativity of Knowledge', and these were his first contributions to a subject which was to absorb more and more of his mind during his last years.

Like a good many other people he was far from satisfied with the Treaty of Versailles. He wrote to his mother: 'The peace terms make me anxious for the tranquillity of the world in the next generation. They are not high-minded terms. From Paris I hear privately bad accounts. The French are backing the Poles. They want to cripple Germany permanently. There might be something to be said for it, as a policy, were it not that forty-five million people cannot cripple seventy million. But they can lay the seeds of war for the future. There is a liberal Germany which could be built up and a German culture which has its message for humanity, but this treaty submerges both in a state of misery and despair, which will in due course have their reactions.'

In the celebrations of peace Haldane had one small but sigcificant part. On July 5 the London Territorials marched past the King at Buckingham Palace and His Majesty paid their founder the well deserved compliment of inviting him to stand on the dais beside him during the march past. Then came the Victory March and from his study window at Queen Annes Gate he saw the troops marching up Birdcage Walk to salute the King. Then followed the wholly unexpected visit from Lord Haig. Of this he wrote to his mother: 'I had an affectionate visit from Lord Haig yesterday. He presented me with his dispatches in two volumes with a remarkable inscription.[1] I will bring the book down next week. He tells me that they are planning to reconstruct the Army after the war, almost exactly on the lines which we worked out together; that the Territorial Army will in the future be the official instrument to expand the Regular Army in case of need and that all the experience of the greatest war in which we have ever been engaged shows that very little amendment in the Field Service Regulations, which we drafted, is required. I hardly know which is the bigger compliment, Haig's inscription, or the vindication of my system of administration.'

[1]'To Viscount Haldane of Cloan—the greatest Secretary of State for War England has ever had.' Vide vol. i, p. 376.

Chapter IV

THE HIGHER DIRECTION OF WAR

1920

Strikes and labour unrest, particularly in the coal and transport industries, continued during the first months of 1920, and Lloyd George continued to use Haldane as a link between himself and the Labour leaders. The negotiations which resulted caused alarm in Conservative circles and Lord Selborne in February put down a motion in the Lords calling attention to these negotiations and, in moving it, made an attack on the policy of the Labour Party and suggested that the Prime Minister was giving it undue encouragement. Haldane rose to reply and said: 'I am not a member of the Labour Party, I have not joined it, but I am in great sympathy with certain purposes with which it has associated itself, and on these I shall have a word to say presently.'

The two points on which he expressed general sympathy with the policy of the Labour Party were the nationalization of the coal industry and education. Of the former he said: 'Nationalization is a very difficult question. I believe myself that to the end of time four-fifths of the industries of the country will be run by private enterprise, for the simple reason that nothing but private enterprise can run them. But just as in a score of cases, tramways, light, water, and other things have been taken over by the local authorities, so I believe it is at least conceivable that other things may be taken over by the State. If anybody asked me whether I would support a proposal to run the mines by the existing Civil Service I should say "Certainly not". And if anybody asked me if I thought that one of the plans put forward, at any rate the other day, by the miners for running the mines was a good one, I should answer "Certainly not". But if anybody asked me whether it is inconceivable that we should reach a stage in which the mines could be taken over, controlled and worked by a new body of State servants, with the initiative, the enterprise, and the skill which private ability has hitherto produced, then I say I cannot tell until I see what methods are possible for the training of the people who would be required to manage the industry in such a fashion. It is a matter on which it is well to keep an open mind and to confine criticism to detailed proposals rather than to great principles which you may not hereafter be able to sustain.'

The other point was the 'paramount importance of education as the greatest thing in the State. The Labour Party is insisting on that, I think, more vehemently than any other party. It welcomes what has been done by the Government in the great measures of education which it has passed for England and Scotland, but it says that it seeks more—that education should go on in the life of each man, not only till he attains the age of 16 but till the grave. It insists upon the necessity of the education of the adult, and points out that the educated adult is a very different and a far more reliable man than the adult who is uneducated and unable to use his hours of leisure in such a fashion as will rouse his mind, not only in the accomplishment of his daily task in life, but for that communion with literature and the traditions of the past, which will make him a better citizen and more fit to exercise the franchise.'

Haldane's political sympathies were moving to the left. He made this clear in a declaration of his new political creed: 'This country to-day needs not a new party, but something which shall inform and transform the existing parties. Our political system belongs to conditions which have passed away. The workers have emerged. So far as they are concerned we have passed from status to contract. Yet the Labour Party, great though its possibilities are, lacks a background. You may put it another way, and say that it has made its roof high enough to give space to great ideals, but not broad enough to cover all men of good will.

'And what in these circumstances are we to do? It is most certainly not a matter of starting another party. There is already an enormous amount of sectionalism, and we have to go deeper than that. It has seemed to me and to a few friends of mine that the thing to deal with is the mind of the people. We have made for ourselves the machinery of democratic government, but we have failed in the past to give the people a chance to fit themselves to use the machinery. Fifty years ago Matthew Arnold warned the Liberal Party of the certainty of the coming of the trouble which has actually wrecked it to-day. He pointed out that for the ordinary man material prosperity could not be enough. There must be opportunities for broad, human intercourse, for the cultivation of and delight in beauty. He asked, in so many words, whether material prosperity would permanently reconcile men to living in places like St. Helens.

'That which he foresaw has come to pass. The workers are in revolt against a scheme of things which, as they see it, reserves all the best things in life for a small and not too obviously useful class. Their minds are filled with suspicion and jealousy, neither of which is unnatural in the circumstances. It is with their minds that we must deal rather than with the actions to which their minds lead and drive them to-day. We have to get rid of that suspicion, that jealousy. And that means that we must so order our world that the worker—by which I mean, of course, the manual worker—shall have no reasonable ground for envying anyone else. To that end we have to confer on the worker two freedoms—freedom from the domination of capital, and freedom from his own ignorance.

That is the aim we must set before ourselves; that is the object to which I and some others propose to devote the years of life which may remain to us.'

The year 1920 was a busy one for him. A number of important appeals to the House of Lords and the Privy Council had been held up by the war, and the work in both of the Supreme Courts of Appeal became heavy. He was active in the development of the British Institute of Adult Education and of Birkbeck College, was engaged in negotiations with Mr. Fisher for the acquisition of the Bloomsbury site for the central buildings of the University of London, and was engaged on a book on the philosophical aspects of Einstein's theory. The publication of *Before the War* gave an impetus to the swing of public opinion in his favour, and he became the object of a number of demonstrations of sympathy. A luncheon was given in his honour at the Reform Club of which Gosse wrote an account to Miss Haldane:

'I have just come from the luncheon of honour given to Richard at the Reform Club. It was a tremendous success. Asquith proposed Richard's health in his usual easy felicitous terms and with a good deal more warmth than usual: "My oldest friend, to whom the Empire owed its victory as much as to any other one man." Lord Haig followed with still more warmth and less felicity of phrase and with very sincere and even indiscreet praise. The American Ambassador[1] tuned in happily. Then came Richard's turn to reply. I felt extremely nervous and anxious, but he was as cool as a ripe cucumber. I never heard him so happy, not too long, not in the least egotistical, full of gracious praise of Asquith and Haig, and with some happy touches of humour. I left with Asquith and Richard, and in Pall Mall we met Carson, whom I made to stop and listen to my account of what my two companions had been doing and how they had acquitted themselves. Richard says I skate on very thin ice but I always get safe to shore.'

[1]Mr. J. Davis.

In March Haldane went down to Bristol for an official visit to the university as its Chancellor, and of this he wrote to his mother: 'I have had an extraordinary time here. A vast crowd of students and others met the train. I was carried to my car, which they overwhelmed and broke its springs, and I was transferred to a cab, which they hauled through the streets, the crowd chanting "Who saved England?" the response being "Haldane". I arrived very dishevelled at the University and addressed the Council, a fine meeting. Then a big dinner at the house of Mr. Wills, who has been the chief, and a princely benefactor to the University. He told me that it was his motor car which was broken down, but that anticipating what would happen he had provided an old one. Bristol is very proud of its University, which looks on me as its father, hence the enthusiasm. I had an equally tumultuous send off on my departure next day and was rather weary when I sank into my seat in the railway carriage. It is curious to see the reaction, but you must not imagine that Bristol is a fair specimen of the feeling of the country; there are still plenty of people who won't admit they were wrong.'

From these many and varied activities Haldane was called back to a subject in which he had never ceased to take the liveliest interest, the organization of Imperial Defence. The problem of the reconstruction of our defence forces after the war was exercising the minds of many people, and there arose an insistent demand that the Army, Navy, and Air Force should be placed under the general direction of a Minister of Defence, provided with an Imperial General Staff chosen from all three services. Haldane was resolutely opposed to any such measures and in order to have an opportunity of stating his case against them he tabled a motion in the House of Lords to call attention to the Committee of Imperial Defence and its relations with the staffs of the Navy, Army, and Air Force:

'To talk of a joint Naval and Military Staff is to indulge in confusion of thought, because two-thirds of the problems with which the Navy have to deal have nothing whatever to do with military operations on land, and are best kept apart from them. It is quite true that the Navy has to transport troops. It transported the Expeditionary Force splendidly, and other troops also with most conspicuous success, during the war. But two-thirds of the work of the War Staff of the Navy is, or ought to be, done in peace time. We are an island, and with a great scattered Empire it is necessary that we should have command of the sea, with, of course, the possible control of other and weaker countries, which has been the source of a great deal of grumbling in the past, but is a necessity of our safety. But the essence of success in that command depends upon the study and understanding of commerce and trade routes. The bulk of the Staff work of the Navy is, as I understand it, devoted to the question of how we are to be protected in the food and raw materials that are being brought across the ocean to us, and how our supplies can be maintained in time of war. That was a tremendous problem during the late war, and it involves every sort of question connected with submarines, convoys, and a multitude of other matters. It is essentially a problem to be thought out by seamen, and by seamen in close connection with the Mercantile Marine, who have devoted themselves to these problems for a long period during peace. If that be so, what profit would there be in putting them under a semi-Military Higher General Staff? It would be simply to invite the diversion of these activities from their proper purposes—purposes which can only be realized in the proper surroundings in which the Navy ought to exist.

'The Staffs, whether they be Naval, or Military, or Air, have all the same divisions of work. They have to train their officers, they have to collect and study intelligence, and they have to devise operations, and divine as far as possible what are the operations they will have to meet. Those are divisions which occur both in the Army and Navy to-day, and of course it is extremely desirable that these Staffs should not exist separately altogether. Their members should meet and consult, but they will consult all the better if they come as grown intelligences, not dependent upon someone else, and put their minds together in a common pot and think out the objectives they have in common with the special knowledge which belongs to each. No doubt if it were true that the only or main work of the Navy was the landing of troops for military operations on land, there would be a good deal to be said for a combined Staff, but I hope that I have shown that that is a very small part of the Navy's work to-day, and it is a much smaller part than it was in former days.

'It is one of the misfortunes connected with the recent history of the Navy that not having had a proper War Staff it lived on traditions. In its war schools there was a good deal of study of what were called "dumping operations", the landing of small forces in different places, as I have known from my own observations. The traditions have survived from the days of the Seven Years' War, when landing operations on a small scale really were of some use, because by sending five thousand men to Britanny you could make the King of France bring back his Army from the frontiers of France; but, to-day, with strategical railways and the study of these things made on the Continent and elsewhere, these landing operations have become of no account and are even matters of foolishness in many cases. The modern naval Staff sets itself to include in its own knowledge an amount of military information which enables it to set aside as useless many of the things on which time was wasted in days gone by, and there is no reason at all why officers of the two Staffs, Naval and Military, should not have a good deal of intercourse, take courses at each other's colleges and work together, provided that in the end the conclusions you get are the conclusions of seamen in the one case and of soldiers in the other, working together for a common purpose, each with expert knowledge and each bringing to bear the fully developed personality, which can only arise from the sympathy and inspiration of their own Service, as the home in which they have been bred and as the place where they rise to pre-eminence.

'I have said all that I wish to say at present. We have in the position of the Prime Minister at the head of the Defence Committee what seems to me an ideal organization for the development of the strength of the individual Staffs. It is true that the Prime Minister does not administer it. That is the strength of the situation. As head of the Government he is in such a position that his word is law. We ought to have, as he has had, the best Staff for study and for consultation that he can obtain. His position is rather that of a Judge than of one who initiates, and it is therefore always possible for him to delegate that position on occasions. It was extensively done during my experience, and there is no reason why it should not be done to-day. But the importance of the Prime Minister being at the head is that he alone can command the necessary position with the rest of the Dominions of the Crown, and he alone is in the position to speak with that gentle authority which is sufficient to bring people together. With that and with constant intercourse—because I hope your Lordships understand that I am insisting on the desirability of constant intercourse—between the Staffs it should be possible, and I think always is possible, for common objectives to be worked out and general purposes to be visualized, and the means of their attainment investigated. It is because an organization of that kind, loose, as it may seem, is more in accordance with our own Constitution in these Islands and still more in accordance with the Constitution of the Empire and its necessities, that I respectfully ask the Government not to come to any conclusion in favour of some alternative system, the nature of which I hardly believe to have been thought out, and to take time to consider the matter in the light of the peculiar necessities and standard up to which we have to work if we are to maintain and develop the interest of Imperial Defence.'

Early in 1921 the rise in taxation had created an insistent demand for a reduction of expenditure, and the Prime Minister appointed a committee under the chairmanship of Sir E. Geddes to examine national expenditure and propose economies. The recommendations of this committee, which became known as 'the Geddes axe', were drastic. The axe fell heavily on education and to Haldane's deep regret Fisher's continuation schools were lopped off, and the programme of the raising of school age, the development of adult education, and the improvement of secondary schools was postponed indefinitely. One of the measures of economy which the committee recommended was the amalgamation of the Admiralty, War Office, and Air Ministry into a Ministry of Defence. This recommendation was an important reinforcement to those who, led by Mr. Winston Churchill, were advocating such a measure as the best means of ensuring efficiency in the three defence services. There was at the same time considerable agitation in the Navy and Army against a separate Air Ministry, the two senior services concluding that as aircraft was an essential element in their work they should have direct control of weapons which they considered to be as much part of themselves as, say, guns. The Prime Minister therefore appointed in 1923 a strong sub-committee of the Committee of Imperial Defence, with Lord Salisbury as its chairman, to examine and report on these two questions, the relation of the Air Force to the Navy and Army, and the desirability of setting up a Ministry of Defence.

Haldane gave evidence on this second question and said: 'The Committee of Imperial Defence is an organization that has nothing quite resembling it in any other country. The reason is that no other nation resembles the British Empire, with its island centre for a number of countries, some of which are self-governing, and all of which are united by un-written and elastic obligations. We have evolved this Com-mittee to meet Dominion as well as home necessities, and to meet the former it is far better adapted than any special Ministry of Defence could be. . . . But a still more instructive feature of the existing organization is that it has been evolved to meet the situation where sea power comes first and where the other two Services are, in some measure, merely its ad-juncts, however great and important. That is why the scope of the Committee must be sufficiently catholic to admit of the co-operation within it of distinguished experts at the head of very different services.'

The sub-committee in its report said that this statement was specifically endorsed by the Chief of the Imperial General Staff.[1]

Haldane in his evidence made no specific recommendations for the organization of the Committee of Imperial Defence, but in an address to the Staff College he made his ideas on this clear. The following are the salient parts of this address:

'I know of few questions military or constitutional in which such obscurity prevails as in those concerned with the higher direction of war. The obscurity arises almost entirely from the necessity of bringing into harmony two different conceptions that are unavoidable. One is the directing power of the military leader, the other is the supreme authority of the State. As the conduct of war almost invariably raises political questions, for instance the right of blockade, a con-flict of ideals becomes almost impossible to avoid. The con-flict may even manifest itself in the conduct of a single per-sonality. One of the best books that has been written about Napoleon is Count Yorck von Wartenburg's *Napoleon as General* (translated into English in the Wolseley series). The author, who was a distinguished member of the Prussian General Staff, has written the story of Napoleon's career

[1]Cmd. 2029—1924.

from an unusual point of view. His doctrine is that the more his hero became prominent as an Emperor the more he deteriorated as a leader of troops. The surroundings of court life gradually deadened the old energy and disposition to devote his immense abilities to the supervision of the details of both battles and campaigns.

'The duties of a commander-in-chief in the field may be of a purely military character, but in modern war his duties will rarely be so simple. Political complications with other nations such as was the case with the Americans and with other neutral powers early in the Great War, which has recently finished, are apt at almost every time to ensue, and provision must be carefully made for those complications if victory is to be secured. It is not only complications with foreign nations that require to be dealt with, but possible difficulties in the relations with our own Dominions. Neither in our preparations for the Great War, nor during the war, was there always that perfect co-operation between our naval and military forces which should exist. We have now a third force to consider and the problem of co-ordinating the efforts of the three, so that they may be combined effectively in carrying out the policy decided on by the Government, is a grave one. It follows from this that, if war is to be directed successfully, the commander-in-chief in the field must receive guidance in which the technical naval, military, and air considerations are duly weighed with the political considerations.

'It has been loudly said that these things would be best provided for if a Ministry of Defence was appointed in advance to take charge of the preparatory work of the three services and of the war if it came. I cannot agree. In the first place I do not think that the Dominions would be likely to be willing to put their vital interests under the control of a British Minister sitting in Whitehall and not responsible individually to their Parliament. In the second place I do not think that the British public would accept such an arrangement. We are trained here to look to a Cabinet which will act in consultation with the Dominion Ministries in what it does. No doubt the problem would be different if we had an absolute Monarch. But then it would be far from certain that he would act wisely, or could be trusted to surround himself with the best advice. Even Napoleon in the end broke down under this system. A one-man business is not what we must look for in these modern times.

'What then is our best course if we are to try to perfect our organization for war? My first observation is that we must be sure that we understand what we mean by its higher direction, and by the necessity of bringing together the military and political roles which are both essential in that direction. To understand this adequately we require principles to guide us. To me the first of these principles is that we should realize the great doctrine that it is for the Government to define the objectives, just as it is the duty of the Government to answer the preliminary question between peace and war. When this is done the carrying out of what is aimed at is for the leaders of the naval, military and air forces. Even if we have got so far we are a long way from having eliminated the civilian element wholly. For the broad reasons already given the service leaders will have to be constantly on the outlook for civilian complications, and in so looking out they will be dependent in part at least on civilian advice. But a first step will have been taken towards a definition and apportionment of functions. This requires the general supervision of the Government, and it is pretty plain that such supervision can be carried out effectively only if the naval, military, and air leaders, who will have to make the war plans, and the politicians are brought to work in harmony. Now consultation, which such harmony requires, cannot be left to accident or take place haphazard. It must be carried out in advance by a scientifically organized body. In the late war this was only imperfectly done. Civilians were apt to interfere in military affairs, and soldiers in those that were political. But this arose largely at least from want of knowledge on the part of our rulers in what the higher direction of war really consists. More systematic thinking than was then considered to be necessary was required. Rejecting the plan of a Ministry of Imperial Defence as being just as impracticable as of an Absolute head of the State and both on the ground that neither plan would give us security that the direction of affairs was in the hands of the most suitable leader, I turn to what seems to me to be practicable.

'We have not yet had time to realize either what the Committee of Imperial Defence is, or what it can be made. The Committee is under the Prime Minister and under no other Minister. The supreme authority of the Prime Minister must be maintained, but he is a very busy man and can rarely have the time to give his whole mind to the many and varied problems of Imperial Defence which arise. He should therefore have a deputy, a cabinet minister, who can give his whole time to the business of what is in reality one of the most vital pieces of our machinery of Government. The Committee must have a first-rate staff, the very best men we can find, and I should like to see it established that service on the staff of the Committee of Imperial Defence brought promotion automatically. The Secretary must be a very able and a very industrious man. Fortunately these qualifications are possessed in a very high degree by the present Secretary,[1] but they might not be in the same degree in another occupant of the office. It is necessary that the person holding the position of deputy should belong to none of the three Services, and should be a civilian member of the Cabinet. A suitable occupant thus qualified is not always easy to find, and the selection made by the Prime Minister might well give rise to friction. But this is a difficulty of detail and not of principle, and it must be overcome.

[1]Sir Maurice Hankey.

'What is the proper position of the Committee of Imperial Defence? It clearly is to devote itself, not to administrative business at all, but to investigation of strategical questions and to thinking about them. It consults, but is not bound by the opinions and material laid before it by the three official heads of the Navy, Army and Air Force. It consults the Cabinet Ministers who are at the head of these departments of the State. The result is that the Prime Minister is furnished by it with definite opinions which he can lay before his Cabinet for discussion. He and the other Ministers there are the supreme authority. And they act, or ought to act, with full materials before them. Instead of disjointed views representing what is thought in each department separately, in all sufficiently great questions the process of joint consultation has been gone through in the Defence Committee. The result ought to be the reduction of the points of supreme importance to questions of principle and not of detail. How we are to be defended, how we are to act if we have to strike, become matters which are not decided, but on which the Prime Minister and his Colleagues in the Cabinet are supplied with the fullest and most complete knowledge attainable.

'How does such an organization bear on the supreme direction of war? Obviously very closely! The head of the Government is able, with a well-informed mind, to give advice which his Cabinet colleagues may follow or not. And if it is well thought out advice they are likely to follow it. The Cabinet is relieved from having to go into detail over problems which are purely technical, further than to decide questions of principle. The strategy can be left to work itself out, and experience shows that if this is done there is no desire on the part of civilians to determine what are in the main military questions. It is true that during the Great War this was not always the case. But that seems to me to have arisen from the extent to which the distinction was not generally maintained between the proper work of the Committee of Imperial Defence and that of the Cabinet, for which its work ought to have been purely preparatory and distinct. It may be said that this principle is nothing new. But my own experience of the Committee of Defence was that when it sat in full session the civilian element had *de facto* an undue preponderance over the technical advisers. Sailors and soldiers are rarely as well adapted for oral debate as are trained civilian Ministers of the Crown. When they meet in council the latter are therefore apt to be preponderant. If the Defence Committee is to form a true General Staff for the Prime Minister it seems better therefore that the work should be done, not without the presence of a picked civilian element, but in such a fashion that the sailors, soldiers, and airmen should have fuller scope. After all they are not there to determine policy but simply to assemble materials jointly, and to advise upon them. But the matter is one on which only the Prime Minister himself can give the final decision. No doubt the burden will lie heavily on the Prime Minister of determining when such decisions are required. But his burden in time of war must always be a very heavy one. If he has a competent Chairman of the Committee of Imperial Defence to whom he can delegate the problems of advising him on questions of this kind, he can be relieved of much. And then he has a thoroughly trained and able secretary of the Committee, with a staff under him equal to almost any emergency. If the situation is thoroughly understood by the Services, and if their permanent Chiefs feel that they can be sure of opportunities of getting their views expressed and adequately considered, experience shows that they are neither likely to differ among themselves on the real points they have to consider, nor are in danger of introducing confusion or delay in the preparation of technical advice.

'The conclusion therefore seems to emerge that the higher direction of war in a country with a constitution such as is characteristic of our Empire must centre in the Prime Minister at Whitehall. He alone can take counsel with his fellow authorities in the Dominions, in India and throughout the Empire. Whatever idealists may say about special Ministers of Defence and of the desirability of leaving things to Napoleonic personalities, it does not appear that there is any such alternative way, and for this reason amongst others I think it important that a deputy to the Prime Minister should always be provided and the staff of the Committee enlarged.'

Lord Salisbury's Committee reported in November 1923, and Haldane found himself in complete accord with its recommendations, which were that the Air Ministry, with a separate air service, was to remain, that a Cabinet Minister to act as deputy to the Prime Minister should be Chairman of the Committee of Imperial Defence, and that one of the chairman's chief functions should be to preside over a permanent sub-committee composed of the Chiefs of Staff of the three Services, which should keep the defence situation constantly under review.

It happened that this report appeared just at the time of the political crisis which resulted in the formation of the first Labour Government, and it fell to Haldane to be the first to give effect to its recommendations. Indeed it may be said truly that his keen sense of the vital importance of this question was the factor which made him decide to join Ramsay MacDonald's administration.

To pick up my threads I must return to 1920. In that year conditions in Ireland grew steadily worse. Intrigues by the Republicans became more numerous, especially in the west and south. The Government had at last produced the Home Rule Bill, promised when conscription, which was never in fact enforced, was made applicable to Ireland in April 1918. The Bill provided for a parliament for Ulster, and another parliament for southern Ireland with its seat in Dublin. The constitution offered to southern Ireland was never in the least likely to be accepted, and the immediate result of the measure was a revival of Sinn Fein, which had been losing ground, and an encouragement to the extreme Republicans to proceed to what was in effect civil war. To meet this situation the Government imported into Ireland a specially raised police force, popularly known from their uniforms as the Black and Tans. This force engaged in reprisals for outrages, and the effect of this policy was to embitter the struggle. Haldane, who had many correspondents in Dublin and elsewhere in the south, wrote to one of the most regular of these, his friend Mrs. Green, in October:

'Ll. G. used to storm at us constantly during the war for being too late, but if ever any Government has been too late it is the Coalition over Ireland. As you know, I am firmly convinced that an offer of Dominion status early in 1919 and generously applied, would have gone a very long way to-wards peace. A pinchbeck Home Rule late in 1920 is not an olive branch, but a tocsin. Ll. G. talks of an Ireland with Dominion status, with a fleet of submarines of its own, and harbours ready to receive hostile fleets. Southern Ireland will now get something much more than Dominion status, and this will not come as a generous gift but will have been wrung from us. Even so there won't be submarines and harbours for a German fleet, which incidentally does not exist, but there will be an aftermath of bitterness which will, I fear, last for a generation. The root of the trouble is that Ll. G. has never taken the trouble to get to know the men who could form a Government for Southern Ireland. If he had done so he would have found out, as we know, that they are not murderers, but that they have a very clear idea of the minimum which they can accept. The policy of the Coalition has driven away their followers into the ranks of the wild men, and things must, I fear, become worse before they can become better. Did you see Asquith's letter in *The Times* of October 4? Full of good sense and sound reasoning.'[1]

[1]*Life of Lord Oxford and Asquith,* vol. II, p. 333.

Before the year ended Haldane found himself immersed in yet another controversy over the University of London, in which he had for long years taken a paternal interest. The Royal Commission on the University, over which he had presided, had recommended that the university should have a permanent centre of dignity and importance, and had proposed for this a site in Bloomsbury behind the British Museum. The war had postponed any further consideration of the question, but in 1919 Haldane had reopened negotiations with the Minister of Education, and in April 1920 Mr. Fisher had offered the Bloomsbury site to the university. This offer became linked with another, that King's College, which occupied the east wing of Somerset House, should vacate this in return for a payment of £375,000 and move to Bloomsbury. But King's College did not want to move, and this put the whole scheme in the melting-pot, while about the same time many advocates of Holland Park, a part of which was in the market, as a preferable site became vocal. The battle of the sites was continued for several years, and in the interval the Government's offer lapsed, and it was not until 1927 that, thanks to the efforts of Sir William Beveridge, then Vice-Chancellor, who obtained a generous benefaction from the Rockefeller foundation, and secured the co-operation of the Government and the London County Council, the Bloomsbury site was recovered. In this prolonged controversy Haldane was, naturally enough from his early association with the problems of the university, much concerned and the controversy was not confined to the sites. On November 9, 1920, he gave an address on 'The Nationalization of Universities' to the Old Students' Association of the Royal College of Science, then a part of the Imperial College, which he had been instrumental in creating. He concluded the address with a review of his ideas of the future of the university:

'The University of London can be no mere teaching body. It can be no mere local institution in a great city. It ought to be what it is not to-day—it ought to be the chief centre of learning in the entire Empire, perhaps the chief centre of learning for the entire world. Here ought to be concentrated the highest talent, the highest level in that passion for excellence of which I have spoken, the highest atmosphere, such as only can come in a great capital at the heart of a great country. The University ought to be an institution spread over the great city, to the various parts of which people will go and find that, according to circumstances, that which is most appropriate is assembled in an atmosphere, inspiring not merely by its magnitude, but by the variety of what is there. You ought to find a University the very name of which will attach weight to its degrees and carry in itself a guarantee of a standard of excellence which can be attained by no isolated bodies acting, however vigorously, without co-operation. It must be an intimate union in which, at the same time, freedom and self-government are combined. Such a conception, I believe to be, in the days we have reached, a possible one. The difficulties which stand in the way may seem formidable, but they are difficulties, believe me, of detail rather than of principle, and if the great purpose is grasped firmly, and if the means for its attainment are insisted upon, and if the nation is in earnest about it, then I, for my part, look forward to the pride of seeing possible in my own time, my own country as the possessor of such a teaching and inspiring institution as the world's history has never yet seen.'

From this it will be seen that he conceived of the university as constituting a union of its colleges and of its future as depending in the main on the development of those colleges. This conception was to provoke yet more controversy when the time came to translate the recommendations of his Royal Commission into a new constitution and new statutes. Haldane had never really understood or had much sympathy with the external side of the university, under which candidates could sit for degrees without attending a prescribed course at a university college. But the external side was firmly established, had done much valuable work, and had powerful advocates, and in the event the Constitution recommended by the Haldane Commission was drastically revised to provide for equal representation of the two sides in the government of the university.

Chapter V

THE AGE OF RELATIVITY

1921 to 1922

The political field in 1921 was still chiefly occupied by the dispute with the coal-miners and with Ireland. On the coal question Haldane still straitly maintained his thesis that the only permanent solution was nationalization. At the request of some of the younger Labour leaders he allowed the evidence which he had given before the Sankey Commission to be printed as a pamphlet with introductory notes by Professor Laski and Mr. R. H. Tawney. Haldane sent them to Sankey, who replied:

'Many thanks for sending me the reprint of your evidence before the Coal Commission with the introduction by Laski and Tawney. I almost knew it by heart before I wrote my report and I adopted it because I believed then, as I still do, that it gives us the true solution of the question. There are none so blind as those who won't see, and the coal owners have been very adroit about your suggestions. They keep on saying they do not want Whitehall bureaucrats in the coal trade. They are setting up a bogey only to knock it down again. They ignore it because it is unanswerable. I should like it used as propaganda. How you find time for all you do I can never understand, because I realize that your pronouncements are not the momentary efforts of a politician, but the result of deep and prolonged thought. And, I know from what I hear, that they are having an influence more perhaps than you imagine.'

In the summer the Government opened negotiations with the leaders of Sinn Fein, which led to a settlement in December. When the negotiations began Haldane wrote to his mother:

'The whirligig of politics brings about the strangest changes. I am assured that Lloyd George has been resolute to fight Sinn Fein to the death and in his refusal "to shake hands with murder". He has never understood that the wild men of the west are not the men who will govern the Southern Ireland of the future, and that these, when they get the chance, will suppress murder a great deal more effectively than he can. It is indeed a curious development for him with his background. The majority of the Cabinet has defeated him and I am also assured that the leader in insisting that the time has come to negotiate is Birkenhead, who as "Galloper Smith" was at Carson's right hand in organizing the Ulster Army in 1914. The decision was due to the fact that soldiers told the Government that it would take 100,000 men to conquer Southern Ireland. We have not got anything like that number available and there is not the least prospect of the country consenting to raise such a force for such a purpose. All now depends on whether Sinn Fein has thrown up the right men.'

While these major questions were in debate two of Haldane's old friends came up for final settlement. As Lord Chancellor in Asquith's administration Haldane had planned a Law of Property Bill, which, like a good many other plans, had to be put back in a pigeon hole. Now Lord Birkenhead took it out, and introduced it with some improvements, with a very generous acknowledgement of Haldane's work. Of this Haldane wrote to his mother:

'Another tree which I planted is now about to bear fruit. For more than two years as Lord Chancellor I was at work on a Law of Property Bill, to codify and simplify the whole law of the transference and tenure of landed property. Now Birkenhead has taken it up and made some valuable improvements, and it is certain to go through. It is a revolution of the law of real property and will keep the solicitors pretty busy. It is a curious thing but it always takes two Lord Chancellors, one a Liberal and one a Conservative, to carry through a big legal reform. It took Cairns and Selborne between them to get through the Settled Land Act, the Conveyancing Act, and the Judicature Act, and I think that what Birkenhead and I have done will be classed by the lawyers of the future with the achievements of our predecessors.'

The other friend appeared as a sequel to the famous case of the Scottish Churches in which Haldane had made his first appearance as a Chancery barrister.[1]

In supporting Lord Birkenhead's Scottish Churches Bill, which passed successfully through all its stages, Haldane told the story of the case:

'Seventeen years ago I stood at that Bar, convinced as an advocate of the justice of my cause. I fought for what I believed to be its just title of spiritual liberty of Conscience on the part of the United Free Church of Scotland. We turned out to be wrong in our contentions. By a majority this House decided that the United Free Church of Scotland had turned itself, in virtue of its trust deed and declaration of doctrine, into a body which could hold its property only on a trust to promulgate and pursue particular doctrines of an older type than seemed to the majority suited to the time, and that to deviate from those doctrines meant the forfeiture of over £2,000,000 of property, the peculiarity of which was that

[1] I wish to correct an error in my account of this famous case in vol. I, p. 142. I there said: 'Principal Rainy, the leader of the United Free Church, an old man of eighty, as he listened to the judgement solemnly and slowly read out by Lord James of Hereford, felt that the bottom had dropped out of his world, and broke down!' This statement was due to a misinterpretation of mine of a letter of Lord Haldane's. I have now had clear evidence from others who were present at the reading of the judgement that Principal Rainy heard the judgement with complete calm, and, far from showing emotion, endured this heavy blow to his hopes with the greatest courage.—F. M.

nearly the whole of it had been subscribed and collected by the very people from whom it was taken. It was taken from them, and they had to pay the costs of the litigation.

'Parliament said, "That may be the law, but it is a law that we are not content with. These funds have a greater public application. We propose to appoint a Commission and apportion them between the people who are entitled to them." That Commission was appointed by an Act which was passed in 1908, and the greater part of the property was given back to the United Free Church with freedom to apply it to purposes which meant that the Church was a real Church; not a mere trust for the promulgation of certain doctrines, but a Church with spiritual powers of self-government which enabled it to mould and determine its own needs, and to enjoy the knowledge of spiritual liberty.

'I want to refer to that for a single purpose, which is to draw your Lordships' attention to the fact that the success of the appeal which the United Free Church made to Parliament to pass the Bill was largely due to the generous support given by the Established Church of Scotland to her sister Church in its dire necessity. The Established Church came forward and fought for the Bill as if it had concerned itself. The late Lord Balfour of Burleigh took a very active part in the struggle, and the result was that at that time, with the co-operation of the Church of Scotland, the United Church won her liberty of Constitution, and she won it because she was enabled to make and maintain what she had already put forward, the very declarations in substance which are contained in the schedule of this Bill—and declare them to be her own constitution, and to embody the purposes to which she wished to consecrate her fortunes and her means.

'When that was done, when the United Free Church of Scotland was emancipated from the shackles of the old Trust deeds, naturally she began to look to union, to the healing of old strifes, and the Established Church on its part also began to look to the healing of old strifes and to union. The Established Church was in a position not altogether dissimilar from that in which the United Free Church had found itself to its cost. It was hampered, not by old trust deeds, but by statutes of the fifteenth, sixteenth and seventeenth centuries, old Scottish statutes passed before the Union which put great obstacles in the way of the Established Church of Scotland having freedom for the moulding of her own needs; and being able to make an effective fight for spiritual liberty. That is what stood in the way of union with the United Free Church, which had come out, in the disruption, for the purpose of vindicating its liberty and failed to do so because of the very old trust deeds. The Established Church said:—"Let us be free from the Statutes." That was the basis of the negotiations which, begun in 1917, have been continued up to the present time, and were not interrupted, I believe, by the war, although there was a cessation of activities during the war.

'The noble and learned Viscount on the Woolsack has with perfect accuracy described the nature of this Bill. It is not a Bill to set up a constitution. The Church would not ask that constitution from Parliament. What the Church says is:—"We ask Parliament to say that if we wish to pass that constitution we shall be free to do so, notwithstanding the existence of these old statutes which have hitherto blocked the way." '

The United Free Church obtained what it sought, and Haldane had lived to see the results of what he had begun seventeen years ago.

But in 1921 Haldane's chief preoccupation was not political. In May his *Reign of Relativity* was published. Besides the activities which I have mentioned, legal work had been heavy, the Lord Chancellor was abroad at the beginning of the year, and Haldane had frequently to take his place on the Woolsack, he was occupied with a number of important judgements, and he was still constantly travelling up and down the country addressing meetings on education. We may well wonder, with Lord Sankey, how he found the time to complete and see through the press an important philosophical work of 427 pages, dealing with most abstruse problems. It was the most successful book he had ever published. It went through three editions in six weeks, a large edition was required in America, and the book was translated into German, French, and Russian. Much of his success was, of course, due to the wide interest which Einstein's statement of his theories had aroused, but the book had its origin not in Einstein, but in the development of Haldane's philosophical thought. It was a natural progression from the second volume of *The Pathway to Reality*. He had begun to meditate on this progression as soon as he left office in 1915 and *The Reign of Relativity* was the result of years of thought and of much reading and research. Einstein had acted as a spur to what was already moving in his mind. In the earlier work he had maintained the principle of degrees in knowledge and in reality alike. From this it was but a step to the relativity of knowledge, the main thesis of *The Reign of Relativity*.

The book went far beyond a study of the physical theory of relativity. Haldane said in his preface: 'the topics of this book are Knowledge itself and the relativity of reality to the character of Knowledge'. He set himself to examine the application of Einstein's theory to science, religion, philosophy, political science, and law. Before proceeding to his exposition of the metaphysical aspect of relativity he devoted four chapters of the book to an exposition of Einstein's theory. These chapters and the conclusions to which they led provoked a good deal of controversy. The mathematicians and the physicists doubted whether Einstein's theory, the value of which to mathematics and science most of them admitted, had any philosophical implications. Sir Oliver Lodge, who came to Cloan soon after the publication of the book, believed that Einstein's work would in due course be restated in terms of classical physics. Einstein himself had, confessedly, not looked beyond the purely scientific application of his theory. But he had said, 'if a thing is essentially unobservable then it is not a real thing'. Haldane's statement of his thesis was: 'The final and fundamental fact appears to be the fact that I know. For it is in terms of Knowledge that all existence is expressed. Excepting for Knowledge nothing has any meaning, and to have no meaning is to be non-existent.'[1] He proceeded to develop the doctrine of the relativity of reality to knowledge from this view of knowledge. Such difference as existed between his view and that of Einstein was a difference of degree not of kind. The chapters of *The Reign of Relativity* dealing with the development of mathematics and science, and in particular with the physical theory of relativity, were written simply to show how the general theory of relativity is illustrated in this particular case. He concluded his review of Einstein's work:

'Einstein and his disciples have only entered an enquiry as to the answers science can give to the questions raised. So far they are able to do little more than reveal to us unlimited possibilities of truth attainable by reflection. But at least they have helped to emancipate our minds from the deadening effect of conventional ideas.'[2]

Thus emancipated he went on to a general survey of the field of knowledge, and this led him to conclude:

'The final and complete truth cannot be less than a systematic whole of Knowledge within which all particular and partial outlooks have their places as levels and degrees in Knowledge. It is therefore from above and not from underneath, from what is concrete and individual, and not from abstractions only derivative from it, that we must seek to enquire if we would strive to realize the ideal of bringing the whole under a final and adequate conception and of so attaining to full truth.'[3]

[1] *The Reign of Relativity* (1st edition), p. 30.   [2]*Ibid.*, p. 117.
[3]*Ibid.*, p. 419.

The book is in fact not, as it was taken by some of Haldane's critics to be, an amateur's exposition of Einstein's work, it was a development of the faith in which Haldane lived and died, that 'the more things are interpreted systematically the more they are found to be real'. In *The Pathway to Reality* he had quoted Emily Brontë's 'Last Lines' as summing up his faith:

> O God within my breast
> Almighty ever present deity!
> Life—that in me has rest
> As I—undying life—have power in Thee.

In *The Reign of Relativity* he returned to Emily Brontë as summing up his statement of his faith:

'The time has come to enter upon a further question. What significance are we to attach, for the purposes of the accidents and limits of ordinary life, to the ideal of self-completion implied in our knowledge of God as immanent in us? Is it a significance that in an intelligible fashion discloses that ideal as any sort of fact actually attained and present?

'There are obviously many points of view from which ideal self-completion is not accomplished in particular experience. Still it may be a present and shaping end. It may mould our experience in a fashion such as that in which in organic life the impulse to fulfil an end preserves continuous form amid change of materials, or in a fashion such as that in which the universal gives meaning to the particular in what is actual only in their union. There we find reality attained in individual shape; in an activity that, because of the movement in it of what is general, is ever stretching beyond what it has set up as its own limits. Our experience, in our consciousness of self in its relation to the world, is always revealing to us the ideal as at all events an immediately present and compelling power. At a degree even higher than that exhibited in organic life it is there, and always as dynamic and continuous in its process of self-accomplishment. In knowledge the ideal has a yet higher place than in mere life. For it appears as an entirety within which falls, distinguishable as if self-subsistent only for abstract reflection, every standpoint from which mind directs itself. Relativity arises from the differentiations so made, and it is the ultimate character of mind to establish within its all-embracing ambit these differentiations and the reasons for them, as its degrees or as levels attained in its own progress towards self-completion in a perfect entirety. It is so that the principle of relativity in knowledge seems in ultimate analysis to find its justification with the solution of many problems of consequence. If the ideal is never present as a self-contained and finally accomplished fact, it is not the less the foundation and meaning of finite activity. Just on that account truth and freedom from limitation by what is lower are attained in the very quality of a sustained effort towards that ideal.

'We do more than we are aware when we thus conceive and dare. We do not stretch out our hands in vain, moved merely by love of the shore from which we are divided. We are conscious, dimly, it may be, but sufficiently, in feelings and metaphors that spontaneously fashion themselves, of a transcendence of our own selves. The real is within and not apart from us.

> *With wide-embracing love,*
> *Thy spirit animates eternal years,*
> *Pervades and broods above,*
> *Changes, sustains, dissolves, creates and rears.*

> *Though earth and man were gone,*
> *And suns and universes ceased to be,*
> *And Thou wert left alone,*
> *Every existence would exist in Thee.*

> *There is not room for Death,*
> *Nor atom that his might could render void,*

Thou, Thou art Being and Breath,
And what Thou art may never be destroyed.

Our words, when we utter as Emily Brontë thus spoke,
express what we really mean by God.'[1]

He concluded with this statement of his faith:

'The survey endeavoured in this volume now approaches
its conclusion. There is a final question that the reader may
ask, since the end is in sight. Assuming the principle of relativity to mean all that has been said, what guidance does it
offer for the conduct of our individual lives? I do not think
the question is a difficult one to answer. The real lesson which
the principle of the relativity of knowledge teaches us is always to remember that there are different orders in which
our knowledge and the reality it seeks have differing forms.
These orders we must be careful to distinguish and not to
confuse. We must keep ourselves aware that truth in terms of
one order may not necessarily be a sufficient guide in the
search for truth in another one. We have, in other words, to
be critical of our categories. As an aid to our practice, the
principle points us in a direction where we may possess our
souls with tranquillity and courage. We stand warned against
"other-worldliness" in a multitude of concealed forms. We
are protected, too, if the doctrine be well-founded, against
certain spectres which obtrude themselves in the pilgrim's
path. Materialism, scepticism, and obscurantism alike vanish.
The real is there, but it is akin in its nature to our own minds,
and it is not terrifying. Death loses much of its sting and the
grave of its victory. For we have not only the freedom that is
the essence of mind, but we are encouraged to abstract and
withdraw ourselves from the apparent overwhelmingness of
pain and even of death itself. Such things cease to be of the
old importance when they lose the appearance of final reality.

'There may come to us, too, contentment of spirit, and a

[1] *The Reign of Relativity*, p. 401 *et seq.*

peace which passes our everyday understanding. We grow in tolerance, for we see that it is in expression rather than in intention that our fellow-men are narrow. We realize that we are all of us more, even in moments of deep depression, than we appear to ourselves to be, and that humanity extends beyond the limits that are assigned even by itself to itself. Our disposition to be gentle to those who may seem to misinterpret us because of dissent from our outlook on life grows with the recognition that, as Spinoza wrote two hundred and fifty years ago, in his answer to the letter offering him refuge in a chair at Heidelberg from his theological persecutors, "religious dissensions arise not so much from the ardour of men's zeal for religion itself, as from their various dispositions and love of contradiction, which leads them into a habit of decrying and condemning everything, however justly it may be said".[1]

Professor Whitehead, whose work Haldane had used freely and appreciatively, was not amongst those who disclaimed any connection between the theory of the mathematician and philosophy. He wrote to Haldane:

'I do not believe in the disconnection between science and philosophy, though often it embodies a sound practical counsel in the particular circumstances of a short life, or of a special occasion. The complementicity of things impresses itself on one. I am distrusting ruthless simplifications, neglecting half the plain facts of existence. It is intolerable arrogance to assume that what we cannot immediately fit into our petty systems must be non-existent. The problem of time seems very fundamental, in some respects it extends beyond nature. It expresses the fundamental activity of existence. This activity governs the general character of nature, which is an abstraction from the concrete totality of fact. Thus time in nature is a special aspect of a grand problem of philosophy.

[1] *The Reign of Relativity*, p. 425.

'Space in nature takes its origin in this time-impress arising from the general character of fact. I would put it thus:— Time "spatializes" nature—namely, the moment of time is simply the instantaneous aspect of nature as specially inter-related, three-dimensionally. There is not both "a moment" *and* instantaneous three-dimensional space with its varied physical content, but this space *is* the moment exhibiting the form of nature necessary for the expression of the activity of existence—namely activity is analysable into a subject in a passage of states—each more abstract than the concrete acti-vity. Now the spatialized nature exhibits the subject under the guise of one state (the moment), and the temporal succes-sion of moments is the passage, completing the representation of activity.

'Now it does not seem to me that the general notion of activity requires that spatialization should necessarily be thinking activities of mind, then (as it seems) the mental grasp of the relation of *A* to the rest of nature is one unique spatialization of nature selected out of the group of spaces containing *A*, so as to exhibit the relevant group of objects (i.e. the body) as in a maximum relation of "repose"—i.e. with the minimum of irrelevant detail of motion. Thus our minds so grasp nature in respect to its spatialization as to express the relations of the body the passage of nature with the maximum simplicity. Hence the unique time-series of actual experience.'

In the seventeen years that have passed since the appearance of *The Reign of Relativity* thought has moved on and now there are many physicists who are coming to hold that the development of the Theory of Relativity and of the Quan-tum Theory are carrying them over the border-line between science and metaphysics. I cannot produce better evidence of this than the concluding words of the Haldane Memorial Lecture delivered by Professor Sir Arthur Eddington last year: 'I have often been asked, How far did Lord Haldane understand Einstein's theory? I will try to answer that. To say that he understood it better than any other British pure philosopher at that time, would, I am afraid, be a poor compliment. For what it is worth it is undoubtedly true. Nor is it much of a testimonial to say that he understood it better than many who are perfectly familiar with the mathematical calculus, and can manipulate tensors as easily as numbers. As I have already said, the heart of the theory is not in the mathematics, though the mathematics is very necessary in working out its physical consequences. It is all too common to see the formulae misapplied because the conditions which determine their applicability are misunderstood. Perhaps we may come to the point this way: if you think that Lord Haldane, who (as he tells us) had been a philosophical relativatist for forty years, jumped at the superficial resemblance of the new physical theory and distorted it to support his views, you are profoundly mistaken. In the first place, that was not Lord Haldane's way—I am sure those who are familiar with his other activities will bear me out. He had a wonderful power of concentration which enabled him to get to the essentials of an unfamiliar subject. In the second place, that was not his approach. He discussed Einstein's theory not for the purpose of claiming its support, but to see whether he could conscientiously support it himself. If you read the long fifth chapter of his book, you will see that it is the Einsteinians who are arraigned and cross-examined to see whether, beneath their unphilosophical language, beneath their glib use of the word "relativity", they have any true perception of the relativistic outlook.

'Lord Haldane not only had a good understanding of the theory; but, what is equally important, he knew just how far his understanding went. I cannot find any point on which he *misunderstood* the scientific theory—except perhaps that it is not clear in his exposition that there is a law governing the curvature of space, as well as a law prescribing the motion of a particle in space; he limits his remarks almost entirely to the latter law. There are points which he finds himself unable to understand, and says so; but he makes us feel that it is our inconsistency of expression that is at fault, and that this in turn is the result of an insufficiently deep understanding on our part. Let him speak for himself.

' "What I have ventured to say must be taken as pretending to record no more than it does, the impressions of a non-mathematician about what the mathematicians are saying to one another when they enter the borderland of philosophy and speak about it among themselves. The impression is that of a stranger in whose presence they talk, but who, though keenly interested in learning from them, is but imperfectly acquainted with a language which to them is one of second nature. They may, therefore, be gentle with him if his accent seems strange and his capacity to do justice to their words appears inadequate. His reason for listening and in his turn making comments does not appear to be an irrelevant one. They are in a territory that is occupied in common, and forbearance on both sides is therefore necessary. I do not believe that the fundamental conceptions are as obscure as some of the mathematicians take them to be. The reason they seem so is that they are concerned with matters which involve considerations of a more than merely mathematical character. For the rest I am not lacking in admiration for the splendid power of the instruments the mathematicians possess, and the wonderful results they have achieved with them; instruments which impress me not the less because it is beyond my powers to wield them." '[1]

The Einsteins, who were in the United States when *The Reign of Relativity* was published, came to England in the middle of June at Haldane's invitation, and stayed with him at Queen Annes Gate. Haldane had arranged with Dr. Ernest Barker, the Principal, that Einstein should give an address at

[1] *The Reign of Relativity*, p. 100.

HALDANE AND EINSTEIN, 1921

King's College, University of London, on his theory, and at this address Haldane presided. He gave a big dinner party at his house in honour of his guests and showed them round London. His talks with Einstein were not quite as easy as he had hoped. It was nearly ten years since he had spoken German and he found he was not as fluent as he used to be and he also found Einstein to be sceptical of any metaphysical application of his theory. At the dinner party the Archbishop of Canterbury[1] had asked Einstein whether he thought that his theory had any religious application and Einstein had bluntly replied 'None.' Still the visit was a great success. The two men went carefully through the chapters dealing with the theory in *The Reign of Relativity* and as the result Haldane made some important alterations in the third edition of his book. On leaving England Einstein wrote to Mrs. Haldane a letter of which the following is a translation:

'One of the most memorable weeks of my life lies behind me. Visiting this country for the first time I have learned to marvel at its splendid traditions and treasures of knowledge. One of my most beautiful experiences was the intimacy with your two children, the harmonious hospitality of their home, and the wonderful relations which unite them with yourself. For the first time in my life I have heard of a prominent public man who converses by letter every day with his mother. The scientific talk with Lord Haldane has been for me a source of pure stimulation, and so has the personal intimacy with him and his remarkable knowledge.'

The ferment in politics which marked 1922 began early in the year. The Coalition Liberals had decided to form themselves into a distinct party and the Asquithian Liberals at once arranged a counter-demonstration. Asquith wrote to Haldane on January 18:

'You will, I expect, have seen the announcement in the Press that following immediately upon the meeting of the

[1]Archbishop Davidson.

Coalition Liberals which the Prime Minister is to address on Saturday, January 21, a big Liberal Demonstration, at which Lord Grey and I have promised to speak, will be held in the same hall—the Central Hall, Westminster—on the evening of Monday, January 23. It will be a great pleasure to Lord Grey and myself if you can be with us on this occasion.'

To this Haldane answered:

'MY DEAR ASQUITH

'Your letter has come to me, with its invitation to be present at the meeting which you and Grey are to address on the 21st.

'I need hardly tell you that, so far as individual feeling is concerned, I have the fullest desire to be by your side. Intimate association in public affairs during many years and deep regard for you personally naturally make me anxious to be with you now.

'But there is a question of principle which for me is one of vital importance. My public life has for long been bound up with the cause of Education, more than with anything else. It is now so bound up more than ever.

'I am in deep sympathy as fully as in old days with the great spirit and tradition of Liberalism. I wish to see reforms of high quality carried out, and great standards maintained. Now I have observed for some time past that, with the vastly extended electorate, the inspiring power necessary for the attainment of these things is hopeless unless a systematic and far reaching policy of enlightening the people and developing their minds is given a highly prominent place. Experience in meetings all over the country and the demands that are pouring in this year for more of such meetings satisfy me of the new wish that is springing up all round. And I feel that except by invoking the ideal of an enlightened democracy we cannot hope for the public insight which is the indispensable preliminary to progressive enthusiasm and so to reform in every direction. Nothing short of such an ideal is likely to move or consolidate a majority of the new electors. Divorced from it programmes seem to them mechanical. In its absence we seem likely to be governed at the level of the present administration. The people will get the only government they deserve.

'It was for this reason that three years ago I decided for the future to work with whatever party was most in earnest with Education in the widest sense. I came to the conclusion that whichever of the existing parties are really most in earnest about the general enlightenment of the people would in the end get their confidence.

'I observed then, as I observe now, the almost complete lack of harmony between my strong conviction on this subject and the programme of official Liberalism. Sir Donald Maclean alone seems really to care about the matter. In the official programme, and even in your own speeches, I can find no response about the thing I care for before any other at this moment, and regard as the key to reform generally. That is why I am driven to seek it where I see a chance of finding it. And that is why I feel I ought not to accept an invitation which in other aspects I much appreciate. For I am with you in all else.'

Asquith replied repudiating the suggestion that Sir Donald Maclean was the only Liberal leader who was interested in education, and referred Haldane to a speech of his at Bristol on March 10, 1921, in which he had condemned the proposals of the Government 'to cut down and curtail in every possible direction our expenditure on education'. But Haldane would not be moved. A letter to his sister dated January 12 explains his reason more fully:

'Things political are moving, in what direction is at present uncertain, but it is certain that there will be changes before long. Ll. G. is trying hard to establish a permanent centre party under his leadership recruited from the progressive elements of conservatism with such reinforcements as he can attract from Liberals and Labour. He is not likely to succeed. His prejudices are far too violent to make him the leader of a centre party and the taste of autocracy which he enjoyed during the war has not made him any fitter for the task. I have been approached to know whether I would join the Coalition Government and have replied with a firm negative. Asquith and Grey are making an effort to stage a Liberal revival, but the Liberal party as we knew it has been killed and there is, I think, very little chance of its being galvanized into life. If there is to be an effective Liberal party it must be reborn with new ideals and fresh outlook. Old fashioned middle-class Liberalism is out of touch with Labour and its ideals. I am too old to attempt to recreate a party and I don't mean to try.'

While watching political developments with a detached but interested eye, Haldane returned to philosophy. He had in the previous year been invited by the Provost of Trinity College, Dublin, to deliver the Donaldson lectures there. These lectures he published, with some additions, in the same year under the title *The Philosophy of Humanism*. This, his third considerable philosophical work, was a continuation of *The Reign of Relativity*; as the latter had been a continuation of *The Pathway to Reality*. It is a striking testimony to the man's unflagging industry in keeping himself abreast of every important development in scientific and philosophical thought. The popular success of *The Reign of Relativity* and Einstein's visit to England not only greatly increased the interest in Einstein's theory but was bringing more and more people to the view that there was something more in that theory than a new statement of a problem of mathematical physics. During the year that had passed since the publication of *The Reign of Relativity* a number of notable books had appeared, chiefly in Germany, extending or modifying the application of the theory of relativity. Haldane had made a careful study of these and *The Philosophy of Humanism* was the result. It is much heavier reading than *The Reign of Relativity*, 'a dull book', he called it to his mother, but it is a cogent defence of his theory that philosophy would fail in its duty if it did not face and tackle the problems which the principles of relativity presented. 'In *The Reign of Relativity*', he says in his Introduction to *The Philosophy of Humanism, 'I was concerned mainly with the fashion in which knowledge enters into and fashions reality. Want of space prevented me from doing more than deal with the question as one of principle and from following the principle into its application in detail in science. In this volume I have sought to add what is concerned with the application in detail. Not the whole of it, for I have restricted myself to mathematical physics, biology, and psychology. But even in these domains alone the ground to be covered is so extensive that I am well aware that it is only a few of the main features that I have been able to deal with. These features, however, are indicative of certain root conceptions, and these I have tried to bring to light. The whole task for its completion would require the investigation of other fields, such as those of ethics, the theory of the state, jurisprudence, art and religion. How a proper inquiry has to be fashioned for these I have indicated, but only indicated, in the chapters of the earlier book in which their treatment is approached. I have not tried in the present volume to revert to these subjects again. The task would be an enormous one. Indeed, the task of the present and limited inquiry is a great one, and requires in reality a much closer training in the special subjects than I have the privilege of possessing. No one knows this better than I do. But then I am not setting myself to attempt a series of expositions of special sciences. What I am concerned to do is to endeavour to bring out the relations of certain sciences to each other and to knowledge, relations which depend on the principle of relativity in its most general form. Now this is work which lies beyond the limits of any single science. It is a task which is that of philosophy, and in these days philosophy fails if it shirks the effort to grapple with it. More and more philosophy is becoming dependent on materials which the sciences alone can provide for its work, and more and more it becomes plain that immersion in particular sciences is apt to bring with it a tendency to some form of dogmatism, based on the assumption, usually made quite unconsciously, that the method and conceptions employed are adequate for the description of reality in its entirety, and not merely in special aspects.'

He got Professor Whitehead to help him with the chapters concerned with mathematical physics, and his brother John with the chapters on biology, but the book was not a further discussion on Einstein's theory. This was put in its place amongst other subjects. The book was what it professed to be, a study of Humanism, and the interest of it to his biographer lies in the evidence which it presents that during a year, crowded as I have described with many activities, he somehow found the time to study closely some half-dozen important and closely reasoned works in foreign languages, and to produce the results in a volume of some three hundred pages. This is clear evidence that, just as he never failed to devote some time to the daily letter to the mother he loved, so also he can rarely have failed, if it was only on a railway journey, to a meeting on education, to have given some of his day to the philosophy he loved. He never professed to be a creative philosopher, he never tried to found a school. His philosophy was his guide to life and he was at extreme pains to see that it was equipped to be the best possible guide. He believed that the best way to this was to submit to the discipline of formulating his thought and prescribing it for criticism. This and his desire to interpret life and knowledge by a study of the greater philosophers, as well as by a study of the work of the physicists and the mathematicians, was the purpose of *The Philosophy of Humanism*, which he concluded with a restatement of his case for an alliance between science and philosophy:

'On what principle then are we to fashion our abstractions? Surely by considering first the sort of fact with which we are dealing. If that fact is life, we ought not to assume that we can render our conceptions of it into those of physics. We may have to do this in order to describe certain aspects which living organisms present, but these may be neither the only nor the dominant aspects of the actual in such a case. The criterion required is that we should satisfy ourselves by observation of the actual as to the categories required in its study. Thus the relativity of knowledge gets a further significance, for it is only relative knowledge that we have when the standpoint is one that is not such as to cover the full reality.

'A view like this does not affect the accepted criterion of truth in science. It rather insists on that criterion being applied in more thoroughgoing form than is common. The various branches of inquiry relate to special domains, and we fall into error if we apply general conceptions appropriate only to the character of one domain to the description of what is of the order of a different domain. It is observation that tells us in each case with what character we are really concerned. We are not in difficulty over this if we are careful to start in our study with what is concrete, and not with some abstract distortion of its nature, due to insistence on a special standpoint arbitrarily adopted. There may be many standpoints from which we can view an individual fact. The question is which of these can account for fact in the starting point, the actual as experience shows it to be.

'The variety of order in which knowledge presents itself, if we do not distort but observe it in its self-development, gives us the key to the variety of its standpoints. Its universals are not difficult to find. But it is one thing to find them and quite another to hold fast to them when found. Most of the confusion that has characterized the history of reflection has been due to the assumption that a particular set of universals would prove sufficient for the description of objects differently characterized in facts disclosed in nature. The inquirer has again and again pursued in consequence a path which has led him away from these facts.

'If there is a service which philosophy can render with more advantage to science than any other, it is probably to keep reminding men of science never to forget to criticize their categories before employing them.'

I have mentioned Haldane's devotion to his dogs. It was a great grief to him when a very old favourite, a great St. Bernard, named Kaiser, passed away. There was much correspondence between him and his mother before a successor was installed. Eventually the choice fell on a big black Labrador retriever. The Prime Minister of Newfoundland was called in to advise. 'He says we are doing right in our choice. The smooth haired Labrador, such as this one, is a true aristocrat. The curly-haired, so called Newfoundland, is not the pure breed. Dogs like Bruce assist the fishermen in Labrador by drawing wood for them.' In the letters to his mother at this time there were daily inquiries as to the behaviour of the newcomer, and great satisfaction when he proved to be as great a gentleman as his predecessor. Bruce became a great favourite with Barrie, who was a regular visitor to Cloan, and the two used to romp together on the lawn and on the drawing-room hearth-rug.

During the summer Haldane was much troubled with a return of his rheumatism, but he managed in June to get down to Nottingham for the realization of a scheme in which he had long been interested, the provision of new buildings for the University College of that city. He wrote to his mother:

'The reception was wonderful. The Duke of Portland came over from Windsor and took me to it. There was a luncheon of 500 people to whom I spoke by request for an hour, explaining the plan for the new University. Sir Jesse Boot has

HALDANE AND BRUCE AT CLOAN, 1925

provided £250,000, the bulk of the money required. My dramatic surprise was when I took out of my pocket cheques for £110,000 which had been given me by enthusiastic admirers to help in the good work. The students insisted in drawing me on an improvised throne to the hall. I am not sure, however, that I drank a tankard of beer. I probably accepted it and handed it back. Had I not done so I fear that my top hat would have been damaged. The procession was very orderly and dignified. I laid the foundation stone of the new buildings and then addressed the large crowd standing in the open air. So another provincial University is launched.'

During the late summer and early autumn of 1922 the political developments which he had been expecting came to a head. On the collapse of the Turkish Empire the Greeks had established themselves in the Ionic settlements of Asia Minor. In this they had been encouraged by Lloyd George. But Greek opinion was divided between Venizelists and Royalists and political division led to military weakness. When in August Kemal Pasha led a recreated Turkish Army to the attack, the Greek defence collapsed, and the Greek armies were speedily driven back to the sea. Kemal then turned his eyes on Constantinople, which with the Dardanelles and the surrounding country was occupied by an Allied force, composed of British, French, and Italian troops under the command of General Sir Charles Harington. Kemal began a rapid advance towards the Dardanelles and the Bosphorus. Neither the French nor the Italians were at all anxious to quarrel with Kemal, and we were left to deal with the problem alone. Lloyd George was eager to fight it out and prevent the Young Turks from regaining Constantinople, from which the Sultan had fled. Reinforcements were hurried out and the Prime Minister appealed to the Dominions for help. There was a very cold response to this appeal and it became evident that the country at home was in no mood for a war with Turkey. Eventually, thanks to the tact and firmness of General Sir

Charles Harington, a provisional agreement, by which the Turks were permitted to cross the Bosphorus and enter Thrace, was concluded and the danger of war disappeared. The immediate result of this was a revolt of the Conservatives against Lloyd George's leadership, which came to a head at a meeting at the Carlton Club on October 19. Of this Haldane wrote to Gosse:

'Yesterday's vote at the Carlton Club came as a surprise to me. It means that young Conservatism thinks that its hour has come. It means also that Lloyd George's plan of creating and leading a centre party has come to nought. He will find his future a difficult one. He has destroyed the Liberal party and Labour won't have him. His inherited prejudices are too strong for him. He hates landlords, soldiers, Roman Catholics, and Turks, and each of his hatreds has led him into trouble. I suppose we shall now have two years of Bonar Law as King Log.'

The election of November resulted in the return of 347 Conservatives, Labour 142, National Liberals 53, Independent Liberals 64. Haldane's comment on this was: 'The election has gone very much as I expected. Labour has emerged as the second party in the state. The National Liberals will gradually merge with the Conservatives as the Liberal Unionists did, and the old-fashioned Liberals have ceased to be an effective party. It will be some years yet before Labour will be in a position to form a Government, but their time will come.' Events in the world of politics were to move faster than he anticipated.

Soon after the election he had as senior bencher to receive the King and Queen when they visited Lincoln's Inn on the occasion of the completion of its 500th year. Of the banquet which followed he wrote to his mother:

'I was seated between the Archbishop of Canterbury and the Lord Chancellor. We had as our guests the Allied ambassadors, great foreign jurists, and some 300 judges, Cabinet

Ministers, etc. Sir Edward Clarke had been chosen to propose the toast of these our guests. But he did not appear, why we do not know. Anyhow the Treasurer came to me in the middle of the dinner and said that I must get them out of the difficulty. My distinguished neighbours left me little time for thought, so I was really quite unprepared when I rose to speak. I am a bad after-dinner speaker, except on serious subjects which I know well, and on which I have been asked to hold forth. Therefore I was immensely surprised when my speech was a tremendous success. All the ambassadors came and shook hands with me and I was overwhelmed with congratulations. Moral—midnight oil doesn't mix well with after-dinner wine.'

His nephew Graeme Haldane had in the previous year visited Göttingen and had been very warmly received. He brought back news of several of his uncle's old friends at the university, and in particular of his old hostess Fräulein Schlote, who was in failing health. Haldane had kept up a regular correspondence with her, interrupted only by the war, and hearing that she was eager to meet him again before she died, he went to Göttingen with his nephew in December. The visit was a great success. Haldane gave a dinner to some of the professors and Fräulein Schlote was overjoyed to see him. At the end of the visit the mark was cascading downwards, and Haldane, who could never master the simplest arithmetic, was much puzzled by German money. The Haldanes were travelling with diplomatic passports and were received at the German frontier station with the greatest courtesy and attention. Wishing to make a good impression on his first return to Germany since the war, Haldane presented to the station-master, with an air of princely generosity, a note of the value of something less than a penny. Fortunately Graeme Haldane saw from the station-master's face that something was wrong and applied the needful remedy.

Chapter VI

A RETURN TO PARTY POLITICS

1922 to 1923

Haldane's letter of January 1922 refusing to take part in Asquith's Liberal meeting was taken, as it was meant to be, as a severance from the Liberal Party, and while he was still constantly in touch with the leaders of the Labour Party, more particularly on educational policy, he had not joined that party. So for a period of some two years he was without any definite party affiliation. He became, once more, a general factotum for causes or problems in which he was interested, whether they were patronized by the Government or by the Opposition. The smoking-room at Queen Anne's Gate was the resort of any of the Conservative or Labour parties, philosophers, educationalists, soldiers, sailors, and airmen, who came to seek or to give advice, while, when he was in London, hardly a week passed without a dinner party to one or other of these groups, followed by a talk over his long cigars.

When the Scottish Churches Bill became an Act there remained to consider how the objects of the Act should be applied to the property and endowments of the Church of Scotland, and at the urgent request of Mr. Robert Munro, then Secretary for Scotland, Haldane agreed to become chairman of a committee, in April 1922, to inquire and report on the adjustments required to facilitate Church union, which was the prime object of the Act. The other members of this Committee were Lord Maclay, Sir George Adam Smith, Sir

James Dodds, and Mr. John Prosser, the Crown Agent. The work of the Committee was complicated and arduous. It involved an intricate knowledge of Scottish Law relative to land tenure and titles, and, for Haldane, many journeys to Edinburgh, where most of the meetings were held, and many discussions with Scottish theologians. Finally, after a full year's work, the Committee was unanimous in its conclusions. These were cordially received and were embodied in a further Act, which completed the opening of the door to Church Union in Scotland.

While he was still busy with this important inquiry he was asked by Lord Derby, then Secretary of State for War, in January 1922, to take the place of Lord Cave, who had become Lord Chancellor in Mr. Bonar Law's administration, as chairman of a War Office committee appointed to consider the methods of obtaining and educating officers for the Army. He accepted and this brought him back to the War Office, for the first time since he had entered it to order the mobilization of the Army in August 1914. He was welcomed very warmly and the subject with which he had to deal was one which interested him very deeply. The Committee conferred with the head-masters of public schools, visited Oxford and Cambridge, and the military colleges, and as a result recommended some important changes in the courses at the military colleges, which included the admission to the colleges of selected men from the ranks.

Lord Derby in acknowledging the report wrote: 'The recommendations of your Committee will, I know, carry all the more weight as they are signed by a Chairman who, as Secretary of State for War, did so much to ensure the efficiency of British military organization.'

Finding that there was little prospect, owing to the preoccupation of the Government, of official consideration being given to the report of the Machinery of Government Committee, he determined to organize voluntary support for his campaign for the application of scientific methods to administration, and, in consultation with Sir George Murray, Sir Robert Morant, and others he founded the Institute of Public Administration, of which he became the first President in 1922. The object of the Institute was to bring together those concerned with public administration, both in the Civil Service and in the boroughs and counties, to collate experience, provide opportunities for research, and to develop and co-ordinate the work of the universities in the teaching of the science of administration. In his inaugural address as President, which he entitled 'An Organized Civil Service', he set out his aims:

'In all organization, whether it be of bare scientific knowledge or of that knowledge embodied in the practical direction of business, there is a cardinal phase which is indispensable if a maximum standard of efficiency is to be attained. What is done, be it purely theoretical, or be it the realization of plans in the transaction of everyday affairs, must be based on clear thinking. Such thinking must take the form of objects and principles lying at their foundation. It is by taking thought and by that alone that we can accomplish what the unreflecting mind cannot accomplish, add cubits to our mental stature. . . . What would be an ideal Civil Service and what should it always set before its eyes? Its first and dominant common object ought to be the service of the public in the most efficient form practicable. Virtue is its own reward here as elsewhere. Yet if the public realize that they are receiving such service they will pay for it freely. Ignorance may be often the cause of extravagance, but it is not less frequently the cause of niggardliness. A prolonged experience of the minds of my fellow-countrymen has made me a believer in their fairness in this matter, and an optimist about it. Seek ye first the Kingdom of Heaven and all things shall be added unto you, is a maxim of wide application. But if efficiency is to be the key principle it is necessary to be clear as to what it means. Not extravagant expenditure. The Duke of Wellington is said to have laid down that if an army was to be made and kept efficient there must be no expenditure of more than was strictly essential. A prize-fighter is not the better trained by being made heavy. Fat must disappear and developed muscle take its place. To secure this kind of economy there is a first thing needful. There must be a plain reason for the presence of every official employed. The organization must be treated as a whole and the members must be there simply because they are needed. The existing sloppiness about requirements in personnel must give place to requirements which are founded on exact reasons. Otherwise not only economy but efficiency are in peril. It is only by having his definite duty within a whole the structure of which is not less well defined, that the Civil Servant can live his life with satisfaction to himself and to the State. Much depends on really intelligent supervision and appreciation by the permanent heads, and not less on co-operation with them in the execution of a common purpose on the part of the whole staff. That is one reason why the organization and its provision for pay and promotion must be such as to admit of general contentment right through the Service. For the reason I have indicated, the great saving which is always effected when there is a sufficiently good organization to exclude useless branches and members, I do not think that this is an ideal of extravagance. Well carried out it ought to result not only in a more efficient but in a more economical Service.

'The spirit, then, is everything, for it will in the end carry with it science of this kind in organization. And the spirit can only be at once real and reliable if it is based on adequate knowledge. I do not think that either the members of the public or of Parliament realize how difficult and delicate a problem organization is and how much thought and knowledge it requires. Of course, an organization may only gradually develop itself, and may grow into a very efficient form.

When this is so it is always because of unceasing stimulus from some strong motive which is always operative. That is the advantage which private enterprise has over State enterprise, and it is a very real one. I often marvel when I enter the office of my bankers at the apparently wonderful organization which I see around me. To create it by the stroke of a pen would seem impossible. It has grown up simply because the bankers have required what it is and nothing short of what it is in the interests of their profit-making purpose, and, by the standard which this purpose demands, they have for generations been testing and improving it.

'But profit-making is not the only or the most powerful motive. I doubt much whether it is the most real source of inspiration. If you look, for example, at that wonderful living structure, the British Navy, you find a set of motives more dominant, in so far as self-sacrifice for the sake of public duty is accepted as more important than life itself. Right through the Navy, as our great wars have shown, there has been continuity of this spirit from generation to generation. The cause comes first, the individual second. And in general this is so with the men as much as with the officers. It is a tremendously strong impulse to conduct, not the less strong for rarely being explicitly stated. In this last respect Englishmen stand in some contrast to Japanese and Germans. But the motive is not the less potent because it rarely comes to expression. I have seen the same spirit in the Army, and I have seen it in the Civil Service itself. But on the whole the Navy seems the best field in which to study it. For it is there as the outcome of a long tradition, and of a natural aptitude which was as marked in the days of the Armada as it is to-day. The spirit is one which is at least as efficient as that of profit-making, and it is the result of tradition and education. It is the outlook and attitude of the best naval and military officers which make their leadership welcomed by the men, men who are trained to look for it and to expect it.

'This attitude is the result of tradition based on the preference of duty to the State, extending to the sacrifice of life itself of the individual concerned. It is a motive which has shown itself to be potent and dominant. It is the outcome of training and habit of mind based on it. I do not believe that the practicability which experience has demonstrated of encouraging it, is any monopoly of the fighting services. I have seen something analogous, but hardly less marked, in the refusal of civil servants to exchange modest salaries for lucrative employment in commercial and industrial profit-making concerns. Such a refusal when it is made comes generally from a deep sense of duty to the State as the higher choice. It is the result of a habit of mind which I believe we might see yet more of in other departments if we took the proper steps to stimulate it. It is most common amongst those who have cultivated the high ideals based on that larger outlook which is the result of knowledge of the meaning of life.

'Such knowledge seems to me, therefore, to be something which the State and the Civil Service itself should realize as a great aid to progress. Education, even of the widest type, cannot guarantee the habit of mind of which I speak, but it can render its prevalence increasingly probable. The education question in its most extended sense is therefore vital. It does not mean mere capacity to pass examinations. It means rather life in an atmosphere where knowledge has shown that, because of the complications of human affairs and of human nature, nothing is sufficient that is not of the best quality. Of this outlook our Universities are the guardians, and it is only if they can extend their influence to the democracy generally that it can be sufficiently extended to make the best result probable. As I have said, I would not wish to see an extensive record in education made the sole test. There are many individuals with unusual natural aptitudes for whom we must provide in a proper organization because we require services from them which we can only have if they are given full chances. But in the main a high standard of education is, I believe, one on which we shall do wisely to insist. The Civil Service itself, if it has the desire to do so, can accomplish much in the way of making this apparent. How it is to be done in detail is a problem of practice on which this is not the occasion to enter. The democracy as it becomes better instructed is likely to insist on its solution. For it has itself much at stake in seeing that those to whom the administration of many of the most important of its concerns are entrusted are fit for their work.

'One or two things seem plain. The general organization of the Civil Service must be based on the carrying into effect of some such simple principles as those to which I alluded earlier. We may hope that this method will in the end be applied not less to the local public services under town and county councils. A distinguished public person, who had been engaged in making an investigation of the subject, said to me recently that he believed that the country could, if proper reforms were made, be governed at two-thirds of its present cost. That may have been too sanguine an estimate. For there is an ever increasing number of new services required as standards rise. But I think that there is underlying it a firm substratum of truth. There is to-day waste everywhere simply because we have not thought out our real requirements.'[1]

He watched carefully over the growth of this, his latest child, succeeded in obtaining for it funds for that research which he always required as the essential foundation for sound development, and brought it into touch with the London School of Economics and Political Science, of which he was a Governor.

While these were his major activities in the first six months of 1923 he still managed to find time for educational propa-

[1]The whole address from which this is an extract is published in volume I of the *Journal of Public Administration*, Jan. 1923.

ganda. On March 4 he went down to Liverpool to open the new Research Laboratories of the university, where he was, as usual, welcomed as its father. In his speech he renewed his appeal for closer co-operation between science and industry, and he challenged the view that the late war, unlike other wars, had not produced any intellectual stimulus. 'The war', he said, 'has brought great change. It has given a new keenness. Our young men and young women are alert and desirous of developing their minds in a way unknown before the war. Out of its misfortunes there seems to me to have come something good and great, a new profusion of ideas, a new prescience of spiritual activity. The conclusion of Ernest Renan, in his little-known book, *The Future of Human Knowledge*, that great wars and great periods of oppression are always followed by an outburst of fertility and of new ideas, is still true. In the days in which we live all development depends more or less on knowledge, and the result is that new developments are becoming as important to trade as to the world of science. No business in these days dare stand still, because if it did some new invention or discovery would sweep it away. Processes have constantly to be revised in order that liquidation may be avoided. Therefore these are perilous days because science is advancing with great rapidity. The theories of Einstein, the discovery that what is called mass is simply energy in another form, the possibility of startling developments in the study of the atom, and its electrons, are examples of what I mean. Discoveries may be made in Germany, in America, or in France, but I would rather see them made in this country, because experience shows that the practical application of a great new scientific principle is likely to take greater hold on the country of origin than elsewhere. We are face to face then with a state of things in which scientific knowledge is going to be, as far as can be foreseen, at the very foundation of industry. Therefore it is not on the score of benevolence that we appeal to the great industrial world and its magnates. If they wish to ensure the future and to provide themselves against surprises, which are not only possible but sure to come, in one direction or another, they had better regard gifts to such institutions as ours not as benevolences but as an investment of capital which would produce compound and more than compound interest.'

In the midst of these activities he kept a close eye on political developments. Mr. Bonar Law's Government was confronted almost immediately after taking office with the problem of the French occupation of the Ruhr. Of this Haldane wrote to Lord Knutsford in February 1923: 'I do not pretend to understand what Poincaré is aiming at. Gosse, who has recently been in France, tells me that the feeling of the people whom he came across was pacifist and anti-military to a degree which is not realized in England, and that they are willing to submit to almost anything rather than fight. And yet Poincaré is engaged in sticking banderillos into a weary and exhausted bull. France seems to have forgotten completely her own experience after 1870, which should have taught her something of the strength of national feeling and the impossibility of stifling it. I can understand that there are French soldiers who think this is a golden opportunity for stifling the hereditary enemy, but I can't understand how any statesman can allow himself to be made the tool of such a policy. With lack of logic these people are at one and the same time proposing to crush Germany to the dust and wring thousands of millions of pounds out of her. France can no more obliterate Germany than Germany could obliterate France in 1871. The two have got to exist and they have to be neighbours. Therefore the occupation of the Ruhr and the quartering of black troops on the Rhine is sheer crass stupidity. The Government is, on the whole, taking a sensible line and has the country behind it in protesting to France. The trouble is that our protests have no power behind them and therefore have no influence.'

This last sentence is evidently a reference to another problem which was much in his mind. He had, as I have said, always been in favour of an Air Ministry and of an independent Air Force. He was now much exercised about the weakness of our Air Force, and he had a number of consultations with Sir Samuel Hoare, then Secretary of State for Air, and with Sir Hugh Trenchard, then Chief of the Air Staff. The occupation of the Ruhr had produced a strong anti-French feeling in England and there was a very general opinion that we were being dragged at the tail of French policy into measures of which we disapproved and which were against our interests. But in considering how we were to release ourselves from unpleasant entanglements we were faced by the plain fact that France had a very strong and efficient Air Force, and we, a very vulnerable air target, an Air Force so weak as to be quite incapable of giving us any protection against attack. It seemed to Haldane and others that the time had come to press for a remedy to this state of affairs. Lord Birkenhead raised the question in a speech in the Lords on March 21, 1923, when he asked for information as to the relative strength of the British and French Air Forces. The Duke of Sutherland, Under-Secretary at the Air Ministry, in reply said the strength of the British Air Force was 34 squadrons of 395 machines, of which 5 squadrons were available for home defence, while France had 140 squadrons with 1,260 machines, of which 111 squadrons were in France. When the Duke sat down Haldane rose and said:

'The position in which we are seems to me to be inadequate, so far as home defence is concerned. I am talking of the Air Force now, and in a few sentences I will tell your Lordships why I think so. I found myself, on some points, very much in agreement with the noble Earl who opened this discussion. In the first place, you will never see far ahead with foreign relations. When I listened to the noble Duke referring to the General Staff proceeding on the footing that there will be no great war for ten years, I remembered that the last thing that the General Staff wishes to do is to meddle with political questions of that kind, and that what it means is: "If you tell us there is to be no war for ten years then we will prepare plans and estimates accordingly." The General Staff, fortunately, has not, as part of its business, to deal with questions for which it is very ill-prepared. It is for the Government of the day to forecast these things, and the Government of the day cannot forecast them very much better. Anybody who has followed, with any attention, the history of Europe for the last quarter of a century, and more, will see that the situation has varied from year to year. At times we have been on terms of great friendship with the Central Powers. At other times we have been on terms of great antagonism with them. We have gone from one side to the other, and we have done so because we could not help ourselves. Not we, but the changing situation, brought it about. Before the war it had ceased to be true that we had the advantages of splendid isolation. I had always thought that the real justification for the *Entente* was that British Naval supremacy had ceased to be possible while we stood by ourselves. Continental fleets were growing up, and a combination might very easily have come about, in which we should have been out-matched. Therefore it was necessary that we should have some friends, who at all events would be neutral. It may be that is one of the reasons for the adoption of the principle of the balance of power. I do not agree with the balance of power, for if other people set it up then a counter-balance of power proceeds to establish itself.

'Fortunately we are nearer a position of splendid isolation than we were before the war, but we have not reached it, nor has France reached it. It would, I think, be a very great misfortune if our relations with France became bad. France and ourselves depend on each other mutually for security. France needs our friendship for her security. We need the friendship of France if things are to remain peaceful. I am not sure that we do not need the friendship of France less than France needs our friendship, but on that question I am not speculating, nor attempting to measure the relative needs. I do say, however, that the situation is profoundly different from what it was before the war, and that it is the task of the Committee of Imperial Defence, if it does its duty, to estimate the real risk we have to face, and to deal with it.

'My noble friend who opened the discussion very properly said that in considering this question you cannot take one arm in isolation from another. It is your grouping of arms, determined by your strategic necessities, which determines your strength. That is particularly true of some of the subjects which we have been discussing, and I think that this consideration has dropped a little too much out of sight. Supposing we were threatened by a Continental Power at this moment, what would be our weapon of defence? The first weapon is one which is never sufficient to prevent war, but which generally in the end decides it. I mean the economic question. It is very potent in the long run, but not at first. The second weapon is the Navy. The great terror of the Navy to a Power which encounters a Power with a stronger Navy, is that the stronger Navy will not only destroy its trade and commerce but block the routes to its Colonial possessions, and make those possessions impossible to hold. There we are very strong, because, notwithstanding the reduction of the Fleet which followed the Washington Agreement, the British Navy is still a very powerful organization, and it is permeated with the spirit of Victory which is worth very many ships. Will that remain? I do not think it would be prudent, so far as I can judge, to reduce any further. I think we have got the Navy to a comparatively low point, but I agree that relatively to other Powers we still possess what is probably considerably the strongest Navy in the world.

'I come to the Army. The Army is smaller than it was before the war, but there is reason for that. Before the war it was necessary to have a small and highly organized Expeditionary Force, because of the need of defensive operations which you might have to undertake. We could not defend the Northern ports of France unless we had that Expeditionary Force. But that is over now. Germany is no longer in the field, and the Expeditionary Force, although required for other parts of the world, is not required in the same way for a Continental war. Therefore I am not troubled by the Army reductions as I am by other things.

'It is really when one comes to the Air Force itself that doubt arises. I do not agree that the Air Force takes the place of the Navy; it is only to a very small extent that it can. To a considerable extent it takes the place that the cavalry used to hold with the troops. That has to be borne in mind in estimating what the real strength of our Air Force is compared with that of France. The noble Duke made a point which I thought was a good one, when he called our attention to the fact that a good deal of the French *personnel* was Army *personnel* which was employed for aircraft purposes. The French keep up a large standing Army, and that standing Army, according to modern requirements, necessitates the provision with it of an Air Force which will accompany it. That swallows up a good deal of the French *personnel* and *matériel.* Of course, that is so with us, too, but to a much smaller extent; and therefore I suspect that if you investigated the figures you would find that a good deal of the difference is due to the difference in the size of the standing Armies of the two nations.

'But that does not touch the other question of home defence, to which my noble friend alluded. With a large superiority in bombing squadrons a foreign Power might come and work enormous destruction. For that, which is perhaps quite a small part of the general problem, a nation like this ought to be prepared. I do not say that I can form any opinion or offer any advice, as to what the Defence Force should be for that purpose, but at least the problem is a special one; and as in itself it is not one which entails enormous cost, I think it is one of the points to which the Committee of Imperial Defence should give the closest attention. What chances have we of defending ourselves against a short-range expedition from the Continent, the purpose of which would be to attack, say, London? It is all very well to say that war is not likely. I do not for a moment think that France dreams of war with us; I do not think that the least probable. But at the same time I am keenly aware that the whole course of history is a record of constant changes and sudden situations emerging, and that you cannot afford to leave out of account what the possibility of those situations may be. Therefore, just as we have always felt it necessary in times of perfect peace to keep up a strong Navy, so I think we require a Defence Force for that particular emergency which I have spoken of—a short-range attack of a destructive character on the shores of this country.

'I have always noticed that there is a good deal of danger in making isolated reductions. I think armaments could be reduced very substantially on one condition, that is that all the nations would agree; but if one country says: 'We are going to reduce our armaments,' and does so, such is human nature that it is not altogether a useful plan in its results. In international affairs the level of morality has always seemed to me to be below the level of the morality of individuals. There is not a very gentlemanlike spirit between the Chancelleries as a rule, and you cannot rely upon people not taking advantage of you, even when your intentions have been of the best and purest. The result is that, if you make sudden and rapid reductions, without seeing that your neighbours are prepared to make their reductions on the same footing, and at the same time, you are not making for peace. It is a paradox that it should be so, but reduction of your necessary defences may be the way of leading to the greatest extravagance in bringing

about situations where you have suddenly to recover yourself, and to resort to extravagant expenditure to do so.

I am not one of those who think that the problem is as
difficult or as black a problem as has been suggested. We have
emerged from a great war with an enormous number of
highly trained men. Before the war we had not anything like
the number of highly trained men that we have now—and
they are there. What we have to provide for them is the
matériel and the plans for using that *matériel*. The rest probably could be organized in an emergency comparatively
rapidly. That is true even as regards the Army. Although it
has been reduced, everybody who knows about the Army is
aware that there is available—and their services could be got,
as the National Reserve were got before the late war—an
enormous number of people of the highest quality who are
prepared to take their places in new formations, or to make
up wastages in the old formations. Therefore I do not worry
about the Army or the Navy; nor do I worry myself about
those Air Forces which are required to go with the Army and
with the Navy. But I do worry about the Defence Air Force,
and that is why I am most anxious that in the coming enquiry
concentration should take place on this subject.

'The people of this country are not easily terrified; they
will endure. But we do not want them to have to endure, and
we do not want to have a situation where we may, all of a
sudden, have to create a Defence Air Force of this kind under
circumstances which may look as if we thought war was
actually on us.

'It is far better to do two things; first of all, to work out
your plans very diligently and carefully, with the best military
talent you can bring to bear on the problem; and then, in the
second place, to go slowly to work in the way of building up
reserves even more than in building up the actual machines
and *personnel*. Before the war we were short of aircraft. They
had not been thought of so early as they were thought of

in France and Germany. I was faced with the difficulty of providing them, and I remember well what happened. The manufacturers came crowding forward and said: "Let us build; it is only a question of money, and we will produce plenty of aircraft." I saw admirable people, of great energy and great enterprise, the brothers Wright and others; but a little conversation with them satisfied me that, able as they were, they were mere empirics. And we found it better—it was done by the Government to which I belonged—to establish a branch of the National Physical Laboratory at Teddington, at which the late Lord Rayleigh presided over the best experts we could get in the country, to work out the plans. We set up a construction factory at Farnborough, close by, where these plans were translated into actual models to be issued to the manufacturers for them to build from. The manufacturers did not like it, and there was great criticism of the Government for its apathy. But we were not apathetic at all, and we got the benefit of our arrangements afterwards.

'I am sure this is the right plan, and that it is the plan to follow now. Do not rush into giving an enormous lot of orders for what you call standardized air machines. They are standardized to-day; to-morrow they are obsolete. There is no machine which changes more quickly than aircraft. If that is so, it is your study of these things and your determination of the plans you really want that are vital to you for building up your reserve of strength. That reserve of strength will never be determined until you concentrate on that which is your real danger and the real point at which you are to avert danger, and, if I am right, that is the shortage in home defence. Therefore, my Lords, I conclude by saying what I said at the beginning, that it is on that one point, and almost only upon that point, that I feel the necessity of action, and that I think that we owe substantial thanks to the noble Earl who has introduced this subject, for having put it before us.'

Haldane returned to the same subject later in the session. There was a debate in the Lords on July 11 on air policy. The Government had announced its decision to proceed with the construction of a naval base at Singapore, the estimated cost being £10,500,000. On this Haldane said that he agreed that it was very desirable to have a naval base at Singapore, but we were short of money and in these circumstances it was a question of the relative urgency of our defence requirements. He was suspicious that money which ought to go to the Air Force would be diverted to the new naval base. He went on:

'By a great misfortune we have simply destroyed our organization as far as the Air was concerned since the war. We put an end to it. I do not know how or why, but I suspect that it was that people did not stop to think. Anyhow the organization of the Air Force has gone and it has to be developed *de novo*. I believe it is being developed with the utmost thought and concentration, and that the Government have the advantage of earnest and able men who are giving their assistance in this matter. But my point is that it is not a quick business, nor a cheap business. To have a proper Air Force you have not only to have your first line but some sort of second line. I do not care for the name 'territorial' in this connection. You will have to have skilled people who will develop and expand the first line when it is suffering the fearful depredations which a first line always suffers in case of attack. This will have to be built up and it is going to cost money. I want to hear something in the way of figures how the Government propose to provide this money and yet raise these millions for Singapore. The Air Force is the urgent, Singapore the second consideration.'

To-day in 1938 we are engaged upon a hasty expansion of our Air Force primarily with the object of obtaining air parity with Germany. Fifteen years ago the first impetus was given to the recreation of our air power by the general desire that we should be less dependent upon the changes and whims of French policy. As Haldane had said on March 11, 'We have gone from one side to the other and we have done so because we could not help ourselves.'

At the same time as he was a protagonist in the cause of air expansion he was busy preparing his evidence for the Salisbury Committee on the question of a Ministry of Defence, so he was once more immersed in the problems of defence policy, yet with his amazing capacity for finding time for any job which wanted doing, he became chairman of a Home Office Committee on Vivisection.

In May Mr. Bonar Law's health broke down. He resigned and the King sent for Mr. Baldwin. Of this Haldane wrote to Gosse: 'I do not envy Baldwin his job, but I am glad that it is he and not Curzon. I think that B. is a shrewd manager of men and that Curzon certainly is not. I met Lord Younger in Edinburgh and had a talk with him. He is strongly anti-Curzon as indeed are almost all the Conservatives I meet. G. C. with all his ability is strangely inhuman and has never managed to make a following. It is a bitter blow to him.'

With the change of Prime Minister political events began to move swiftly. A settlement with the French over the occupation of the Ruhr was in sight and the major problem was now labour unrest and unemployment. An Imperial Conference assembled in London and was followed by an Imperial Economic Conference at which Mr. Bruce, speaking on behalf of Australia, came out strongly on the side of Imperial Preference, a policy as strongly supported by Lord Beaverbrook. The demand from a large and influential section of the Conservatives for protection became vocal, but even so the dénouement took everyone by surprise. When Parliament rose for the summer Haldane wrote to his mother: 'Baldwin has established himself. He is out to develop a democratic conservativism, and has a great deal of sympathy with the aspirations of Labour. Liberalism is full of excellent things but as a political creed it does not satisfy current aspirations. My impression is that Baldwin will last his time.'

This was the general impression, but within a few weeks there came a dramatic change. Speaking at Plymouth on October 22, Mr. Baldwin said that in his opinion protection was the only remedy for unemployment. In the general election of 1922 Mr. Bonar Law had given a pledge that he would not have recourse to protection, beyond certain measures for the safeguarding of industries. Mr. Baldwin's pronouncement therefore made a general election inevitable. When Parliament reassembled on November 13 he stated that 'he would not attempt to steer the country through the winter of 1924 without an instrument which was not permissible under the Bonar Law pledge', and he announced an immediate dissolution. Just as in 1905 Mr. Joseph Chamberlain's campaign for protection had united the two wings of the Liberal Party, which had been divided over the South African War, so now the call to the defence of Free Trade united the Independent and the Coalition Liberals, and Mr. Lloyd George and Mr. Asquith joined in a manifesto on behalf of an historic Liberal cause. But Labour refused to have anything to do with Liberalism and fought resolutely for its own hand. Haldane now came out definitely on the side of Labour, and addressed several meetings on behalf of Labour candidates. The result of the election was the return of 255 Conservatives, Labour had gained 191 seats, and the two Liberal sections together 108. No one party could command a majority of the House.

'The general result of the election was very much as I anticipated,' wrote Haldane. 'Labour has increased its power as it was bound to do and Liberalism has as inevitably declined. Now a new and difficult problem arises—how the King's Government is best to be carried on. It is possible that Baldwin may come to an arrangement with Asquith which would enable him to carry on. But I feel that this would be a blunder, and that any attempt to keep Labour out by a combination would be deeply resented and might have very serious consequences.'

As late as December 12 he still believed that the Conservatives would come to some arrangement with Asquith which would keep them in office. On that day he wrote to his mother:

'I think that Mr. Baldwin is going to go on. This averts a crisis. But your little dog has come into sudden prominence. When I went to the House of Lords yesterday the Lord Chancellor told me frankly that it was my duty to save the state by taking office, and all the officials I found expecting me to resume the Chancellorship. Later on Ramsay MacDonald telephoned urgently for a meeting. In the evening he offered me anything I chose if I would help him; the leadership of the House of Lords, the Chancellorship, Defence, Education, and the carrying out of my plans. He will be in opposition, but possibly very powerful, and it may be my duty to advise and help him, and be prominent in the Lords. But I shall remain independent. The Press is in full cry and Williams[1] is keeping them off. Last night I made a speech which was broadcasted, and on Sunday I am to publish a manifesto.'

The manifesto, which appeared in the *Sunday Times*, ran:

'We live on an island. In order to avoid being no better than a densely populated country, underfed and feeble, and isolated by the northern seas, there are two things that we do invariably. We maintain a Navy so strong that it can police the ocean and keep it clear for our trade, and we import freely the food and raw materials which are essential for our growth. By adhering to these things, we have attained in the past to greatness. Whenever the people have suspected either of them of being put in jeopardy, they have protested stoutly. They have just added another instance to those in which in days gone by they have done this, and a great Government

[1] His butler.

137

majority has as a result disappeared. But its disappearance was stimulated by yet other causes. Political conditions never stand still, and there has of late been a growing change in these conditions. A vastly extended franchise has led to increased aspirations after equality in social status, to which our democracy is more and more asserting a title. The general demand has moved, and it is still moving. Social distinctions are being held in less account than before, and the hand labourer is claiming to be given the right to an improved position, like that which the brain-worker has established for himself. It is becoming evident that until a similar title to chances of mental and moral development are conceded there will remain a deep sense of unrest in a society of which the hand worker forms by far the larger part. We have emancipated women from the disabilities of their sex, but we have not emancipated the vast numbers in society generally who are, in point of status, unfree in a yet deeper sense, inasmuch as the conditions of mental freedom have not yet been put by the State within their reach.

'In other words, one thing that appears essential, if social and industrial co-operation and tranquillity are to be attained, is that democracy should feel itself better provided with chances of enlightenment. This is not the occasion to state in detail how the thing can be done. Fortunately the problem has been worked out in a good deal of detail, not only in books (including even Blue Books), but in experiments, which, if restricted, have been none the less illuminating. The ideal is that of a workman who, with decent wages and a decent home, will be well content to produce willingly and intelligently, that he may earn the leisure required for the stimulation of his soul by direct contact with the best teachers —including those who teach in books.

'To-day few have had the chance of having their minds so trained as to possess this capacity. Indeed, at the best, it will be only a minority who will prefer society of this intellectual order to lower things. Even among the well-to-do people, who have been trained to this end in the Universities, only a minority take full advantage of their chances. But, on the whole, that minority contains the leaders of the rest of the middle classes. They are conscious of freedom and power of a kind that their neighbours do not know. And the reason of the thing points to the conclusion that, as it has been growingly with the middle classes, at least since the days of the first Reform period, so it should be in the end with the working classes if we will only let them have a better standing.

'Should this diagnosis of a good deal of the origin of unrest be correct, we must recognize that, in the upheaval which took place during the General Election, there were motive forces working at a deeper level than even questions regarding fiscal and foreign policy or capital levy. It is not difficult to find some direct evidence of this. A powerful Labour Party is a phenomenon of recent growth. Do not let us misinterpret its appearance. The new party is no mere embodiment of demands for capital levies and the nationalization of certain classes of undertaking. These things are but ripples on the surface. Their real signification is to be looked for in the concluding words of the manifesto of November 17 with which Labour entered the election contest. That manifesto ended with "an appeal to all citizens to make a generous and courageous stand for right and justice, to believe in the possibility of building up a sane and ordered society, to oppose the squalid materialism which dominates the world to-day, and to hold out their hands in friendship and good will to the struggling people everywhere, who want only freedom, security, and a happier life".

'Observers who had some opportunity of being present at Labour meetings during the Election and witnessed the overflow which then thronged the streets, and the spectacle of the people contributing almost unbrokenly from their scanty purses towards the expenses of the contest, and volunteering with enthusiasm to do election work unpaid, could hardly but see that the moving ideal was ultimately of the kind expressed in these words. It was not the notion of any single item, a capital levy or anything else, that seemed to stir the people. It was the ideal of a better social order in which there should be equality for themselves and fairer chances for their children. And those who had been previously in contact with the men in the day-time, and had only too often found dread in factories and workshops as to whether there would not be wholesale dismissals, cutting down of wages, or the imposition of hard conditions, saw one at least of the motive forces that have been at work.

'Some employers are admirable, but there is still a very large number who have not yet realized that human labour is not a thing to be bought freely in the cheapest market with the object of producing what is to be sold in the dearest. The idea is taking root that the principle under which capital exclusively, and often selfishly, dominates industry, ought to be replaced so far as is practicable by the different one, that the produce of industry should wherever practicable, be distributed on the basis of the services rendered in producing it, including remuneration—it may be of necessity high—for the services which capital itself has afforded, and for those of the inventor and the leader. It is not without having closely reasoned conceptions before them that the most brilliant writers of the Labour Party, men like Mr. Tawney, have produced their books on social economics and the right to educational chances.

'Now if this be true, and a new party has arisen which is rapidly growing in numbers and power, with an ideal before it for accomplishment which is hard to gainsay, it is well to consider whether the time has not come to put our house in order. Such a putting in order does not mean the introduction of revolutionary Socialism. It is rather a counsel of moderating conservatism. It signifies a steady effort to avert revolution. Heroic remedies are only called for where evils are being left to operate unchecked. Remove the evils and the remedies cease to be interesting. What we need above everything is a Parliament setting itself to deal with the mischief in a really intelligent fashion. Mere surface treatment, such as the two older political parties used to think enough, is insufficient. It is not by treating the spots on his skin that the fevered patient can be cured. What is needed is the mitigation of the underlying causes. The demand is for equality of chance, and particularly for an enlightened people.

'Last year it fell to me to address more than fifty meetings in various industrial centres in different parts of Great Britain in an effort to promote the work that is being done unofficially by the Workers' Educational Association, the British Institution of Adult Education, and other bodies. The object was to establish local centres of higher University teaching outside the walls of the various Universities. The Universities, out of their slender resources, have made a splendid response to the appeal to them to do this work for the nation. The State ought certainly to develop their capacity and strengthen their influence. What impressed me at every turn was the eagerness of the men and women at the meetings to have systematic evening courses of a high quality established among them. They seemed to be searching for a new sense of freedom, arising from heightened capacity to think and know; and to seek to reap it from contact with teachers of a high order, and from books which they had been taught how to read.

'This is one thing that could be furthered by a Parliament which was ready to act. The cost would be small. At the meeting which Lord Grey and I were privileged to address on the subject in London last month, during the Election, that cost was put at under half a million a year. The price is little for a first step towards the mitigation of a general sense of injustice. Enlightenment still is in the main the monopoly of the few.

'There are other topics under that of general enlightenment the systematic examination and treatment of which is called for. One of them is recognition of that principle of fair payment for the value of services rendered to which I have already referred. Some publicity as regards profits made is a cognate one. Care in the interests of industrial growth may well be required in the introduction of these and other ideas, but it would tranquillize those who suffer from the want of the principle were they satisfied that impartial enquiry into it by Parliament was taking place.

'We have to recognize that a great change is in progress. Labour has attained to commanding power and to a new status. There is no need for alarm. All may go well if as a nation we keep in mind the necessity of the satisfaction of two new demands—that for the recognition of the title to equality, and for more knowledge and its systematic application to industry and to the rest of life. We have not yet fully awakened to the necessity for recognizing and meeting either of these demands. The result of the General Election may prove a blessing to us if it has awakened us to our neglect of something momentous which has been slowly emerging for years past. The old Conservative Party had hardly awakened to it, and the Liberals were, in point of fact, just a little soporific over the problem. Much more than middle class professions of an abstract faith are wanted. Labour may not know clearly what it is really summoning us to recognize, but at least it is using a powerful trumpet, and is calling us from our couches of repose.

'Three-quarters of a century since the old Whigs, wise in their limited way, refused to meet the Chartist movement merely with a blank refusal. Thereby they earned our gratitude. For while most of the nations of Europe were plunged into revolution as the result of turning deaf ears to their violent progressives, we were saved, and remained in comparative quiet. The six points of the Charter were gradually conceded—all of them excepting one, annual parliaments, a demand now recognized as unnecessary. We had spoken with the enemy in the gate, and he had turned out to be of the same flesh and blood as ourselves within the city. Social peace was re-established. There is no reason why it should not be again established to-day if the new Parliament will explore the reasons of unrest, and deal with them. We had better see whether we cannot accomplish this now at a comparatively small sacrifice of our prejudices.'

The question of how the King's Government was to be carried on was settled by Asquith, who in an address to the Liberal members of the new Parliament on December 18 said: 'The days of the present Government are numbered. It seems to be generally assumed that as the second largest party in the House of Commons the Labour Party will be allowed to assume the responsibility of Government. Well this may reassure some trembling minds outside: if a Labour Government was to be tried in this country it could hardly be under safer conditions.'

The next day Haldane wrote: 'Asquith's pronouncement makes it evident that the Liberals, or the bulk of them, will join with Labour in defeating the Government on the Address, and Ramsay MacDonald will be sent for. The City is in a panic at the thought of a Labour Government and is cursing Baldwin for bringing on this election. All the old ladies are writing to their brokers beseeching them to save their capital from confiscation. I venture to prophesy that Snowden will be the most orthodox Chancellor since Gladstone. I have had a message from Baldwin begging me to join the Labour Government and help them out. I will come in on my own terms and have not yet told MacDonald what these are.'

The formal offer came on Christmas Eve. MacDonald wrote from Lossiemouth on December 23:

'MY DEAR HALDANE

'I have been having some preliminary trials in making up a Government, but I may have to face the task in earnest and I wonder if you would be disposed to help me by taking an office like Education. I must have a good man, earnest, efficient, and yet not extravagant. I have also been thinking of the Admiralty, but that presents some difficulty. I venture to hope that if you took Education you would have a fine field. I should find little difficulty with the Lord Chancellorship and I should like to increase my representation in the Lords. India might also be available and that would help me to get over the difficulty that all Secretaries of State must be in the Commons.

'Perhaps on this you would express your views generally. I have several awkward corners to get round.

Yours very sincerely

J. RAMSAY MACDONALD.'

To this Haldane replied at once:

'MY DEAR RAMSAY MACDONALD

'I realize how exceptionally hard at this stage you must be finding an inherently difficult task. Those who believe in the underlying ideal of the Labour Movement cannot but feel an obligation to do their best to be helpful to your purpose.

'But the first thing needful is that you should have a chance of succeeding with it. The conditions of success are not obscure to any one of your experience of our miscellaneous and slightly conservatively minded democracy. I do not think, however, that all your supporters, judging from their speeches, recognize what difficulties confront you. Labour may be forced by its adversaries into forming a Government within a month from now. With only a minority in Parliament to support it, they calculate on its being discredited within a few weeks later by inexperience in administration, and also by artificial adverse combinations. Having regard to the numbers against you, I seem to see only one way in which

144

the difficulty can be averted. If the Labour proposals to the country are so well thought out and so reasonable that sufficient fair-minded people are likely to be of opinion that Labour ought to have its chance, all may shape itself well. Labour may then hope to justify its claim. But if the new Government does not commend itself Labour will be out for a long time.

'This creates a very delicate situation. As I have said before now, I hope to support you, not the less if myself out of office than if I were in it. I am not troubled by capital levy or by any mere ripple on the surface. What counts as the underlying current is a great purpose. It is for the sake of the broad purpose that I should care to be of use in office, as I believe I could be. But to office I have no personal wish to return. I have spent ten years of my life in Cabinets, and pomps and ceremonies and stipends are nothing to me. But I do care for my ideals having a chance, and to secure that chance there are things that have to be seen to. Without security for this it would be hopeless for me to join you. Defence, to take an example, is a vitally important subject. I do not wish to return to the Army, or to go to the Navy or Air Force. There is something more fundamental, the general policy guided by the Committee of Imperial Defence. We wish to reduce armaments and expenditure. But we cannot get anything accomplished with a diplomacy that is impotent for want of power behind it. I have worked for successive Governments, ever since the war, in trying to improve the existing organization. It is a very complicated one, depending on supervision under the Prime Minister by a colleague in the Cabinet with time to give to it but without special office, and selected for his knowledge. He has always other duties. But he is supposed to have time, and also to have learned what it takes years to have learned about. At present the organization is only nascent. It is under Lord Salisbury, who is doing his best. But close handling, by a Minister with sufficient position, would give confidence right through the Services and the country, and strengthen the position of the new Government.

'Then there is Education itself. On this I have been concentrated for years past, and there are definite reforms coming into sight without which my life-work would be thrown away. They do not require my presence at the Board of Education, but they do mean a definite Cabinet policy and some, though not a great deal of, money.

'There is, besides, Justice. Here reform is called for more urgently than is generally known. What is required is described in the "Machinery of Government" Report of the Committee where Morant, Mrs. Webb, and Sir George Murray were my colleagues. They all concurred in the Report, which I, as Chairman, drew up myself. It was the outcome of long study and strong conviction. The task is as delicate as it is extensive. In the same connection there arises the question of the Judicial Committee of the Privy Council, over which I have been presiding through nearly the whole of ten years. Certain of the Dominions watch this closely, and their aspirations have to be studied.

'These and other points make me feel that I must have close talk with you before answering the practical question of your letter. I do not wish to part with an independent, if outside, position, in which I feel that I am of general use, without the prospect of being able to do some good.

'If you can come to Cloan, we shall be in a position to consider these things.

'It is therefore not practicable that I should respond to your question affirmatively without thought. But I none the less sympathize deeply with you in difficulties which are, I imagine, certainly not less than you have hinted to me. I should add that I think that the management of the House of Lords will be a very delicate task indeed. It cannot turn a Government out, but it can indirectly create a far-reaching opinion adverse to it. For there are certain men who understand every form of the machinery of the Constitution, and they will not be friendly.

'I leave for Cloan, Auchterarder, on Wednesday morning,
Believe me, yours very sincerely,
HALDANE.'

Ramsay MacDonald came to Cloan, and there Haldane stated his conditions. He was prepared to join the Labour Government as Lord Chancellor, but with a modification of the work of his predecessors. He had sounded Lord Cave and had found out that the outgoing Lord Chancellor was willing to continue to preside over the legal business of the House of Lords and of the Privy Council. Haldane proposed that Lord Cave should continue to use the Lord Chancellor's quarter in the House of Lords, and resigned £4,000 a year of the Lord Chancellor's salary. The time saved from legal work he proposed to devote, firstly, to the reorganization of the Committee of Imperial Defence, in accordance with the recommendations of the Salisbury Report, and he asked for the chairmanship of the Committee of Imperial Defence; secondly, to the reorganization of the Lord Chancellor's department on the lines recommended in the report of the Committee on the Machinery of Government, over which he had presided. Ramsay MacDonald, who, it is evident, was willing to bring him in on any reasonable terms, accepted these conditions. When Parliament met the Government was defeated on the Address, the King sent for Mr. Ramsay MacDonald, and Haldane again became Lord Chancellor.

In 1925 he wrote a note explaining the conditions on which he had agreed to take office:

'I have been often asked why, seeing that I had devoted myself to the cause of Educational reform since I left office in May 1915, I did not ask for the Board of Education, which in fact Ramsay MacDonald offered to me. I was pretty certain that Labour was now sufficiently interested in Educational reform to carry through as much as was practicable, but I knew that my full programme would need a great deal of money and that with the demands that would come from the rank and file of the Party for other social reforms there would not be a great deal left for Education. I was satisfied that my advice on educational policy would be as effective from outside as it would have been if I were President of the Board. But there were two other questions, which I regarded as of the first importance, and I was certain that Ramsay Mac-Donald could get no man else to tackle them, as I, with my experience, could.

'I remembered what had happened in 1906 when the Liberals came into office after ten years in opposition. The Committee of Imperial Defence had been created during that period by Lord Balfour, and none of us had had any experience of its working. The military conversations with France, which resulted in our plan of campaign of 1914, originated in a letter which Grey wrote to me, enquiring whether the Army was ready to support France in case of need. In the same letter he told me that Fisher had his plans ready for naval co-operation with the French. I consulted the Prime Minister and he agreed that the British and French General Staffs should get into touch, on the understanding that neither Government was committed. It was only some years later that I discovered that the War Office and the Admiralty were preparing two different and divergent plans. Further, in watching the progress of the war I was conscious that the way in which we had prepared our plans had hampered our conduct of the war. I was convinced, and am convinced that the military advice given me was right and that our military problem in 1914 was to send the largest possible expeditionary force to support the French in the shortest possible time. For that I prepared. But for France the vital thing was her Army, and her Generals, particularly Joffre, had great influence on French Statesmen. Joffre and the others measured our help in terms of our military contribution, which was at first small. The consequence of this was that we exercised little or no influence on the preparations of the Allied plan of campaign, and we accepted a French estimate of German strength which was in fact wrong. If our plans had been made, not in the War Office and in the Admiralty, but in the Committee of Imperial Defence, and had been presented to France from that body, still with the same proviso that this implied no precise commitment of the Government, I believe that France would have been more impressed by the extent of our contribution and our influence would have been correspondingly greater. At no period during the war was the Committee of Imperial Defence used as it ought to have been used, and in fact it was not then effectively organized for its task.

'In 1924 a Labour Government was coming into power for the first time, and it, like the Liberals in 1906, knew nothing of the Committee of Imperial Defence. The Salisbury Committee had recently reported and I was in complete agreement with its recommendations. I was fearful that if there were not someone in the new Government who understood the problem and realized its importance, the recommendations of the Committee would be pigeonholed and an unrivalled opportunity for getting the machinery for the formulation of defence policy effectively at work would lapse.

'This was my main reason for putting to MacDonald the conditions on which I would join his Government. The other was that I had set my heart on reorganizing the work of the Lord Chancellery and I was sure that he would not be able to get hold of another lawyer who knew as much about that as I did.'

On the eve of taking office Haldane wrote to Asquith:

'MY DEAR A.
    'To-morrow I take office under a Government of which you are not the head.

'It is with a very real sense of sadness that I realize that. My mind goes back to the evenings before either of us contemplated Parliament for ourselves, evenings in which we were none the less concentrated on ideas. And I think of old days at Cloan, and at Auchterarder, and in London. Nor do I forget how you stood by me, of how you fought for me over the Chancellorship in 1905, and how you put me there in 1912. Believe me I am not oblivious of these things. Now it is a new period, and the adventure is both difficult and uncertain. It is not without misgiving that I face it. But I do not consider that I have the right to stand aside in this hour.

'None the less the old sense of personal affection and of gratitude remains with me. But for you I should not have been where I am—whatever that may stand for.

'And so to the end I shall continue to describe myself as
Yours ever affectionately

H. of C.'

To this Asquith answered:

'MY DEAR H.

'I was greatly touched by your letter. The memories to which you refer are, and will remain to the end, fresh in my mind. They are associated with the best days of my life.

'I share in the fullest degree your regret that after so many years of close co-operation and almost unbroken agreement we should now be called upon to part company.

'You are a far better judge than I can be of what, in these strange conditions, is your duty. I confess to a profound distrust, not of the good intentions, but of the judgement of your new associates. I sincerely hope I may be wrong.

'And for yourself, as you know, my old feeling never has, and never will be the least abated.

Always your affectionately

H. H. A.'

Chapter VII

THE FIRST LABOUR GOVERNMENT

1924

Haldane found interest and amusement in settling the new Government into office. His first official connection with the Labour Party occurred before Baldwin's administration was defeated on January 21 in the Commons by 72 votes on the Address. Ramsay MacDonald had asked him to have the dinner for the Labour Party on the eve of the new session at Queen Anne's Gate, and the Address, a copy of which had, as is customary, been sent to the leader of the Opposition, was read and discussed by the prospective cabinet in his dining room. With this indication that he was to act as host to the Labour Party he brought in his sister to help him. His wine and cigars were famous amongst his friends, but on his sister's advice on this occasion he made a change in the liquid refreshment. He wrote to his mother: 'The King's speech dinner went off remarkably well. At Bay's suggestion I provided both lemonade and orangeade. The unofficial cabinet meeting which followed was a remarkable display of competence and also of conservatism. I never attended a better cabinet meeting. We agreed to take a firm line about the railway strike.'

On the day after the King had sent for Ramsay MacDonald he wrote: 'Bay is invaluable. She has already made friends with Miss MacDonald and is helping her in taking over No. 10, an awkward rambling house for a girl to manage. She says that Mrs. Baldwin is being very kind and helpful and that my old friend Berry the office keeper at No. 10 was very fatherly and promised Miss MacDonald to see her through. "You must be very careful, Miss, not to speak to reporters, or you might say something your papa would not like you to say." '

A little later he wrote: 'Bay and I have had a number of consultations with Lord Stamfordham. The King and Queen are anxious to get to know the new Government and their ladies and to make things as simple and easy for them as possible. Finally it was agreed that an afternoon tea-party at Buckingham Palace would be the best form of introduction.' The tea-party came off. 'You may have heard from Bay about the King's tea-party to the Labour ladies. Every thing was very well done and the King and Queen took great pains to make things easy for everyone. Beatrice Webb refused to go. She fears the Court will wean Labour from the strait and narrow path and suspects Ramsay MacDonald of a partiality for duchesses. Stories of the new Ministers are becoming the common talk of London dinner parties and about ninety per cent. of them are apocryphal, but I believe it is true that Thomas introduced himself to the heads of departments of the Colonial Office with the statement, "I'm here to see that there is no mucking about with the British Empire." I hear that our new war minister, Stephen Walsh, who is a very good fellow and a diehard trade-unionist, created an excellent impression on his generals by announcing that he stood for loyalty to the King. The Foreign Office is simply delighted at getting the courteous MacDonald in exchange for the autocratic Curzon, who has a way of treating his officials as if they were serfs. Altogether the departments have given the new Government a very friendly, even cordial reception. But these strikes, which are being handled with a firmness which surprises everybody, do not make our task easy.'

The new Government had inherited a series of labour troubles and a railway strike was actually in progress when they took office. No sooner was this settled than it was fol-

THE FIRST LABOUR CABINET, 1924

Back row: Mr. Sidney Webb, M.P., Mr. John Wheatley, M.P., Mr. F. W. Jowett, M.P. *Second row:* Mr. Charles Philips Trevelyan, M.P., Mr. Stephen Walsh, M.P., Lord Thomson, Viscount Chelmsford, Lord Olivier, Mr. Noel Buxton, M.P., Col. Josiah Wedgwood, M.P., Mr. Vernon Hartshorn, M.P., Mr. Thomas Shaw, M.P. *Front row:* The Rt. Hon. William Adamson, M.P., Lord Parmoor, K.C.V.O., Mr. Philip Snowden, M.P., Viscount Haldane, Kt., O.M., The Rt. Hon. James Ramsay MacDonald, Mr. John R. Clynes, M.P., The Rt. Hon. James Henry Thomas, M.P., The Rt. Hon. Arthur Henderson

lowed by a dock strike, and in quick succession by a miners'
strike, and by a strike of the London bus and tramway men.
The last of these troubles was settled by March 31, and on
April 2 Haldane wrote: 'The Government has gained a good
deal of credit over its handling of the strikes, and without
making any unreasonable concessions it has got settlements
much quicker than any Conservative Government would
have done. Shinwell in particular has handled the coal miners
with tact and firmness. It is a great advantage to have influential trade-union leaders in the Government, who have been
able to influence the Trades Union Council and get it to stick
to principles and refuse to be led away from them by extremists. But our experience shows that there is a pretty strong tail
which is trying to wag the dog, and the real problem of the
Government is to educate a large section of its supporters in
the problems of government. This I had always foreseen
would· be the case and it is the chief reason for my educational
campaign.'

As was the case when he was a member of the Liberal
Cabinet of 1906 to 1914, Haldane devoted himself much
more to the subjects in which he was interested than to the
routine of party politics. His normal day was to spend an hour
or so in the Lord Chancellor's office in the morning with Sir
Claud Schuster, working out his plans for the reorganization
of the Lord Chancellor's department, then to go to the offices
of the Committee of Imperial Defence, where he busied himself with Sir Maurice Hankey in developing the organization
of that Committee, and he used to preside at the occasional
meetings of the new committees of the three chiefs of Staff,
the prime purpose of which was the co-ordination of defence
policy. This was not an easy task, for at this time both the
Army and the Navy were insisting on complete control of
those portions of the Air Force which they regarded as indispensable for their tasks, while neither had much use for an
independent Air Force. Haldane, as a convinced advocate of

the policy that the Air Force should be allowed to develop freely on its own lines, did much to help the youngest service through its teething troubles, and he consistently upheld its claims against those of the Navy and Army.

The Government accepted Haldane's advice on national defence. MacDonald, in coming into office, had adjourned the House until February 12 to give the new ministers time to make acquaintance with their offices, and on the resumption of Parliament on that day it fell to Haldane to make a statement of policy from the Woolsack. After announcing that the Government had decided to recognize the Soviet Government of Russia and was endeavouring to do everything possible to improve our relations with France, he went on:

'That brings me to security. I believe that security is that which, in their hearts, the French desire most. I do not wonder. Can anybody who reads the lamentable record of how she was stricken in 1870 and what has happened since, while she was under the menace of the sharp sword, wonder that France should desire security? We wish her security almost as much as she wishes it for herself, and the only difference is a difference as to methods. Grave considerations come in here. After 1870 there came a period when Germany made up her mind as to the means by which security should be preserved. Prince Bismarck himself wanted nothing more than security for Germany. He had waged three wars successfully, unified the German Empire, and his advice to the German people was: Do not try to expand, do not embark on a policy of prestige; it is the most deceitful of all policies; and do not listen to admirals and generals when they give you advice on foreign policy. That was Prince Bismarck's strongly expressed view, but it developed in the hands of men with less clear and resolute vision into a policy by which Germany went on developing her armaments with the intention of keeping the peace by the sword. That turned out to be a most disastrous plan. . . . We believe that if these armaments are piled up now in the same way, if we cannot get rid of the notion of keeping the peace by the sword, a similar catastrophe will happen—perhaps not to-morrow, perhaps not in the lifetime of your Lordships or of myself—but it will happen inevitably if a false policy is pursued. That being so, what is our policy? Of course it is plain that until other people begin to reduce their armaments we cannot do so. We should be left in a weak position. But so soon as they accept this better method of security, this method of obtaining some sort of common mind among the nations of Europe, then comes a chance for the reduction of armaments. For my own part I will never believe in reducing armaments until the people with whom we are likely to come into conflict are ready to reduce armaments as well, but when those, who, like ourselves, possess great armaments will agree with us, when we can obtain what I have called one mind upon the subject, it will be a great advantage for the whole world, and a great burden may be removed. . . .

'That brings me to the cognate question of our own defences. Your Lordships will observe that I have not suggested any breach in the continuity of policy by which we have for years been organizing our defences upon an improved basis. This does not necessarily mean that which is called piling up armaments or competing in armaments. If you bring science into your organization, naval, military, or air, if you insist that nothing should be there that has not its definite place in the organization of defence as a whole, you make yourself by that very fact considerably stronger, and when you do act, as you must act in these days, you add immensely by this very process to the strength of the whole, because each addition falls into its place. Our predecessors in office also realized this fact, and they effected a reorganization of the Committee of Imperial Defence. The noble Marquess, Lord Salisbury, became Chairman of that Committee, a new position which gave him something of the authority of the Prime Minister, as I have sometimes thought, and in any case more authority than a mere individual Minister who is one among many. That was the view which I ventured to express at the time, and it was a view which the Government adopted in the Memorandum which they published. Lord Salisbury worked very hard and made considerable progress. It has been my good fortune to succeed to the position which he occupied. I, too, am working very hard; and, more than that, I find myself able to keep up the spirit of what he did in our attention to the national defences at this moment; and I think that in the main there has been no desire to do anything else but to keep up that policy, subject, of course, to questions of little consequence as to which there may be difference of view. In the main the policy of the Government is to keep up the defences in order the better to negotiate—if I am right in what I said to your Lordships a minute ago—in a happier state of things in which those nations who have no armaments will not wish to have them and in which we shall gradually find ourselves in a position of increasing security without the strain of the present time.'

This announcement that there was to be no marked change in defence policy produced a sigh of surprised relief in Service and Conservative circles, which had expected that the Labour Party would insist on drastic cuts in the expenditure on armaments for the benefit of social service. When the estimates for the three defence services were presented it was found that the plans for the expansion of the Air Force initiated by Sir Samuel Hoare in Baldwin's administration were to be carried out, that there was to be no change in the Army, while to the consternation of the left wing of the Labour Party it was decided that five new cruisers should be laid down for the Navy. The Admiralty had for some time been pressing for these and the Government announced, as a sop to its followers, that the reason for this new construction was to provide employment in the dockyards.

On another problem of defence the Government made a decision which surprised most people by its conservatism. As soon as the Labour Government came into office the advocates of the Channel Tunnel looked hopefully to it to reverse the previous decision not to proceed with this enterprise. The same thing had happened in 1906 when the Liberals came into power, and Haldane, as Secretary of State for War, had taken an active part in the investigations which led Sir Henry Campbell-Bannerman to decide against the scheme in 1907. Now, in 1924, the propagandists of the tunnel had enlisted much more support and had presented to the Prime Minister a memorandum in its favour signed by more than four hundred members of Parliament. A good many of these had added the rider that their support was subject to the proposal being approved by the Committee of Imperial Defence. The Prime Minister referred the question to the Committee for investigation and report and it was examined in the first instance by a sub-committee over which Haldane presided. The evidence obtained was far from being exclusively naval and military. The naval and military experts established their case that a certain element of risk, which would add to the anxieties of those responsible for national defence, was unavoidable if a tunnel were in existence. The soldiers agreed that the existence of a single tunnel in 1914 would not have increased appreciably the rate at which we could have delivered troops in France, while the French end of the tunnel would almost certainly have been a magnet to the Germans. The issue turned on whether the commercial advantages of the tunnel would outweigh the risks. On this the evidence was decisive. It was found that the only commercial advantage would be increased facilities for passenger traffic at the expense of the steamship services, that the diversion of traffic from steamer to rail would throw out of work a great many more than an increased railway service could employ, and that these men were of a type particularly valuable in a national emergency. The findings of Haldane's sub-committee were reported to a full meeting of the Committee of Imperial Defence, which endorsed them, and the Prime Minister reported to the House on July 7 that the Government felt bound to accept the advice of the Committee.

The only item of defence policy on which the Government reversed the policy of its predecessors was the postponement of the construction of the Singapore base. It was necessary to do something to reconcile the rank and file of the Labour Party, which was insisting on some economies in the expenditure on armaments, to the programme for the defence services which the Government had presented. In particular the additional cruisers had come as a nasty shock to many of them. Haldane had expressed his views on the Singapore base before he had decided to join the Labour Party, and he did not change them now. He never denied that from a purely naval point of view the base was desirable, but he was of opinion that the base would cost a good deal more than the £10,000,000 allotted to it and that in view of our financial position there was the danger that money would be diverted from the Air Force, the expansion of which he put first of our defence requirements, for the benefit of a less urgent naval need. He engaged in a protracted correspondence with several distinguished naval officers. To one of them he expressed his views more strongly than he ventured to do in the House of Lords:

'I have never denied that a base at Singapore is a desirable and convenient thing from a naval point of view. But this question is but one more example of the wrong way in which we have set about our problems of Imperial Defence. These cannot or ought not to be considered from the requirements of any one service. The first question to ask when the Navy, the Army or the Air Force presents a particular proposal is what is the policy of the Government and how does this proposal affect that policy. The next question is how does the proposal react upon the other services, and the third is how does this proposal affect our action in war. We are at long last now getting into effective operation an organization of the Committee of Imperial Defence which can examine these problems from these points of view.

'Now as regards policy, the Foreign policy of the Government is to do all that is possible to promote peace, and in this the major and most urgent task at the moment is to improve conditions in Europe. In that our diplomacy is hampered by the fact that after the war, because, as I think, of lack of fore-thought and planning, we almost abolished our Air Force. To-day the Navy is in European waters relatively far stronger than it was before the war, thanks to the disappearance of the German Navy. Therefore the most urgent problem from the point of view, both of policy and of security, is to strengthen our Air Force. I know of no problem in the Pacific of com-parable urgency.

'The base at Singapore is intended to be used to protect our interests in the Pacific. It is intended to be used in war, if we are involved in war in those waters. That is to say it is to be a sally port from which the fleet can act if our interests are threatened, and it is obvious that if those interests are threat-ened they are more likely to be threatened by Japan than by any other power. Therefore the construction of the base can-not be regarded as a purely defensive measure. It will be regarded by Japan as a threat, and as such it is not calculated to make the Government's policy any easier. We are not in a position at present to go out of our way to create friction. Finally if the base is to be used by the fleet in war it must be adequately defended. This means the construction and arming of land defences, the provision of an adequate garrison, the building of barracks and stores, and the provision of a suffi-cient air force to co-operate with the fleet and the land de-fences. We are, as I have said, very far short of our require-ments in the air for more urgent problems of security. I do not think that the whole of the implications and requirements of the Singapore base have yet been sufficiently worked out. I therefore agree with the decision of the Government that the general requirements of policy, of our economic situation, and of security, make it advisable to postpone further work on the Singapore base.'

At the end of April Mr. Snowden introduced the first Labour budget and this was as much a pleasant surprise as the Government's defence policy. It was a Free Trade budget, and therefore it pleased the Liberals, the City was relieved to find that there were no increases in income-tax and surtax, and delighted with a substantial increase in the provision for the reduction of debt, while Labour was pleased with a substantial reduction in indirect taxation.

Haldane wrote: 'I told you that Snowden would prove to be an orthodox financier. There is nothing socialistic about this budget. Our stock is going up. Gosse writes me that he was at Grillion's the other night and that Asquith was very chatty about the political situation. A. said that he would never raise a finger to turn MacDonald out, that he could enjoy his little hour of office, but that he was hanging by his finger tips to the edge of a cliff and would be dragged down by his wild men and never come back again. He is wrong. This is certainly the most businesslike Cabinet I have sat in. It is a great advance having a Cabinet secretary with an agenda and minutes and Hankey does his job to perfection. MacDonald is a better chairman than Asquith was, which may be due to the new system. He keeps us to the point and gets his decisions. In the old days we often rose with a very vague idea of what had been decided. I think that unless there is some unexpected turn in Foreign affairs, we shall last for another year, which will give me time to get what I am working at done. I long to leave the Constitution of Britain better than I found it and to perfect the machinery for the organization of defence and I seem to have been given a chance!'

In writing of Foreign Policy as a possible danger to the stability of the Government Haldane had in mind Mac-Donald's efforts to create a better understanding with France and to come to an agreement on the problem of collective security. M. Poincaré's government was defeated in the May election, and he was succeeded by M. Herriot. M. Herriot came to London and was entertained at Chequers. He agreed to a much more liberal policy towards Germany, and a definite term was put to the occupation of the Ruhr. In return for these concessions the British Prime Minister agreed to support at Geneva the French proposals for increasing the power of the League of Nations to provide security against aggression. From the very earliest days of the League France had insisted that the Covenant did not provide adequate security for its members against aggression, and had made repeated efforts to fill what she considered to be a gap in the Constitution of the League. In 1922 the Third Assembly had, under French influence, adopted the principle that disarmament and security must go together. In order to implement this decision a draft treaty was prepared, known as the Treaty of Mutual Assistance, and this treaty was, in this country, strongly supported by Lord Robert Cecil. The Labour Government was unable to accept this Treaty, on the grounds that it involved us in too vague commitments. Instead MacDonald offered to Herriot to support at the Fifth Assembly of the League, in 1924, an alternative treaty which became known as the Geneva Protocol. Haldane was aware that the Admiralty was strongly opposed to the terms of the Protocol, for much the same reasons as had proved fatal to the Treaty of Mutual Assistance. The Admiralty maintained that by the terms of the Protocol Great Britain as the principal naval power might be called on to apply the sanction of blockade to any power which, in the eyes of the League, was guilty of aggression, and that such a task, added to its existing responsibilities, would be altogether beyond the power of the Navy. Haldane, who was presiding regularly over the meetings of the three Chiefs of Staff at the Committee of Imperial Defence, had a good deal of sympathy with this point of view, and he rather expected that the Protocol would bring about a political crisis which would overthrow the Government. In fact the Protocol was rejected by Baldwin's second administration, but ere that the Labour Government was toppled over as the result of another development in foreign affairs, which Haldane had not foreseen.

In 1924 memoirs of distinguished persons who had taken a prominent part in the war appeared, some of which did not err on the side of discretion, and there were reports that there were more in preparation. The King was in some anxiety as to his control over his correspondence, and at His Majesty's request Haldane gave him the following opinion:

'The cases put by His Majesty in the course of conversation on Tuesday last were two:—The Sovereign writes a confidential letter to a minister, and the letter passes at the Minister's death, or in some other way, into different hands. Again the Minister has written to the Sovereign and has kept a copy of the letter, and this copy gets into the hands of some third person. The question is what power the Sovereign possesses to restrain publication.

'By the law of England the letter and the writing upon it become in each case the property of the recipient. But the copyright remains in the writer, and the Sovereign, or his personal representative, could obtain an injunction in the Courts of the land restraining the publication of letters by him. It is obvious that this remedy is unsatisfactory from a practical point of view. However, it has no application to the case of the letter written to the Sovereign, for the copyright and the consequent title to publish will be in the Minister or those to whom it has been transmitted from him, and the law gives the Sovereign in this case no power to interfere.

'It would therefore appear that a remedy adequate to the

case must be sought in the Criminal rather than in the Civil law. Now there is no provision in the existing Criminal law which touches the matter unless it be in the Official Secrets Act of 1889. The provisions of that Statute which are relevant to the present questions are those which enact that where a person holding an office under the Crown, while holding that office, or afterwards, publishes or even communicates, contrary to his official duty, any document or information acquired by him in his official capacity to a person to whom the same ought not in the interest of the State or the public to be communicated he shall be guilty of a breach of official trust and punishable by imprisonment or fine.

'It is obvious that the Act is of limited application. It covers the case of a letter written by the Sovereign to a Minister as such and relating to public affairs. It may also cover the case of a letter of a more private character provided the communication is such as could not have been communicated to him but for his position as a Privy Councillor or holder of office. It also covers the publication of a letter written by a Minister to the Sovereign provided the letter contains information acquired by the Minister in his official capacity. But the Act equally clearly does not cover certain other cases; for instance that of a servant stealing the documents from the Minister, or the case of the executors of the Minister publishing documents which would have been within the Act, if published by the Minister himself. Moreover it is somewhat doubtful whether the scope of the Act extends to matters the publication of which, though improper having regard to the position of the persons concerned, yet does not amount to publication of an affair of State in the strict sense. It would be of doubtful expediency to amend the Act by creating new offences at present not known to the law, and of a different character from those which it is the object of the Act to prevent. Something substantial would, however, be gained by amending the Act so as to cover the case of publication, not merely by an official himself, but by any one into whose hands the document had come from him. The Act if so amended would make it an offence for the executors or servants of the official writing or receiving a document to publish it whenever it would have been an offence of the official himself to have done so. Careful consideration of the general principles on which the law proceeds has not removed my impression of the difficulty of making such a change as would give a really adequate protection against the mischief which His Majesty referred to, but I think that such an amendment of the Official Secrets Act as is above suggested would, while not difficult to make, have a deterrent effect in cases where correspondence with Ministers was concerned.'

In the middle of July Haldane had a busy time. As a sequel to his visit as Lord Chancellor to Montreal in 1912 to welcome the American Bar Association, on the occasion of its first meeting outside the United States, a Canadian Bar Association had been formed. Now, in conjunction with the American Bar Association, it came to London to visit our Bar. It was a formidable gathering of guests, as the American and Canadian lawyers with their ladies numbered some 700, and there was an equally formidable programme of entertainment arranged for them. The present and past Lord Chancellors gave a reception in their honour in the Palace of Westminster, there was a formal and stately welcome to them in Westminster Hall, which Mr. C. E. Hughes, who led the American Bar Association, described as the shrine of the Common Law of both countries, another formal reception at the Law Courts, and banquets at the Inns of Court, Haldane presiding at that at Lincoln's Inn. The ceremonies concluded with a Royal Garden Party at Buckingham Palace. When they were over Haldane wrote:

'All has gone very well. I have made innumerable speeches and shaken innumerable hands. Our guests were duly impressed with our ceremonies, which were admirably arranged. The gathering at Westminster Hall was hushed with awe as the Lord Chancellor's procession, all in full fig, entered and took its place. There is no doubt that the Americans and Canadians love a display of historic ceremony. There were some rather comic scenes at the Garden Party. Some one had told the Americans, I suppose it must have been the American Embassy, that they must wear top-hats. Quite unnecessary, for the King had the Labour Party told that they could come in lounge suits, if they had not got top-hats. As we did not get the full list of the Americans until they arrived the invitations were sent out at short notice. London was ransacked for top-hats, but there were not enough and some of them came in opera hats. As one distinguished American was being presented to the Queen his hat shut up with a bang, to his great embarrassment, and the Queen's great amusement. Many of my old friends of Montreal days greeted me with enthusiasm and expressed their particular pleasure that I should again receive them as Lord Chancellor. Bay has been invaluable and has worked very hard, she had to preside at a banquet to the Canadian ladies at the Savoy Hotel, and I hear made an admirable speech.'

Just before the House adjourned for the summer recess two clouds appeared on the horizon, which portended storms. Under the terms of the Treaty with Southern Ireland a boundary commission was to be appointed to fix the frontier of Northern Ireland. Now Northern Ireland refused to appoint a Commissioner and a Judicial Commission had reported that under the terms of the Treaty nothing could be done if one of the parties refused to appoint a Commissioner. President Cosgrave immediately demanded legislation to bring the Boundary Commission into being, and the Government, supported by the Liberals, agreed, and it was decided that the House should assemble in September, four weeks earlier than had been intended, for this specific purpose. The Government was charged by the Conservatives with submitting to dictation from Southern Ireland, and there were angry protests, and as it happened they were soon presented with other material for attack. On August 5, just before Parliament rose for the summer recess, Mr. Ponsonby, Under-Secretary of State for Foreign Affairs, announced that a treaty had been drafted with Soviet Russia and would be signed next day. One of our chief concerns with Russia was to obtain a settlement of our debts and security for British holders of Russian bonds. On these points the treaty was very vague. It proposed that when at least half of the bond-holders were satisfied with the payments they received, and the Government was satisfied with the payments made on other claims, these agreements should be embodied in a subsequent treaty in connection with which the Government would submit a proposal guaranteeing a loan to the Soviet Government. This treaty was at once denounced by the Conservatives as offering a very substantial *quid* for a very vague *quo*. Government stock went up, however, when MacDonald brought to a successful conclusion the International Conference on Reparations, which following on his negotiations with M. Herriot he summoned to a meeting in London.

On August 18 Haldane wrote:

'Ramsay deserves all credit for his handling of the Reparations Conference. Hankey tells me that he has run it entirely in his own way, which is not the traditional way of the Foreign Office. There is no doubt that our relations with France are better now than they have been at any time since the war, and this has been brought about not by yielding to France but by bringing her round to our point of view. Herriot at least understands that he has to live with Germany as a neighbour and the arrangements for the evacuation of the Ruhr are now in train. But Ramsay has the defects of his qualities and is so convinced that he is the heaven-born Foreign Minister that he keeps foreign affairs too much in his own hands. I am not easy about his Geneva policy, the implications of which I don't think he has really worked out. It is a matter which must be linked closely with Defence policy, and the C.I.D. has not yet been consulted, and I find that the sailors in particular are uneasy. I think too that he has been rushed over this Russian business, and that there is trouble ahead. None of us knew anything about it until Ponsonby made his statement in the Commons. I am pretty sure that public opinion is on our side on the general principles of the treaty with the Soviet Government, but the terms proposed seem to me to be calculated to create the maximum of opposition.'

Haldane was feeling rather sore when he wrote this, and with good reason. On August 5 Curzon, who was leader of the Opposition in the House of Lords, got news of Ponsonby's announcement of the Russian treaty and the proposed loan made that afternoon in the Commons, and at the conclusion of business in the Lords he rose and asked the Lord Chancellor whether he could give the House any information on the subject. To his humiliation and the delight of the Opposition Haldane had to confess that he knew nothing about it. This was a clear indication that an important treaty had not been considered by the Cabinet, as was the fact, and the Conservatives produced this as evidence that the Government was being run by irresponsible extremists, a line of attack which they used very effectively during the General Election.

The Conservatives organized a political campaign during the recess against forcing a boundary commission on Northern Ireland and against the Russian treaty, and it soon became clear that the period in which the Labour Government had been treated with amused tolerance had come to an end and that it would have to fight hard for its existence when Parliament reassembled. The assailants were quickly supplied with fresh ammunition. In July the Director of Public Prosecutions had called the attention of the Attorney-General to an article in the *Workers' Weekly* exhorting sailors, soldiers, and airmen not to use their weapons against their fellow workers either in a military war or in a class war. The editor, Mr. R. J. Campbell, appeared before the Magistrate on August 5 on a charge under the Incitement to Mutiny Act. When a week later the case came up for a second hearing counsel for prosecution announced that no evidence would be offered, because it had been represented that the object of the article in question was not to seduce men in the fighting forces from their allegiance, but that it was a comment on armed forces being used by the State for the suppression of industrial disputes. Mr. Campbell's release was followed by a statement in the *Workers' Weekly* that the withdrawal of the charge was made by the Labour Government under strong pressure from Labour members. The Conservative Press naturally made the most of this and Sir Kingsley Wood announced that he would raise the matter when the House reassembled. Haldane wrote: 'There has been a very sudden change in our position. This Campbell case has been badly handled, and I don't think many Liberals will support us on the Russian Treaty. I think we shall be out before the winter. However I have done most of what I wanted and I shall leave office with no regrets.'

The end came a good deal sooner than he expected, but his view of the attitude of the Liberals was proved to be correct almost at once. Mr. Lloyd George began by thundering against the treaty and was followed by Lord Grey, who expressed his disapproval in less emphatic, but equally clear tones. On September 20 Asquith in a letter to a correspondent declared that the part of the treaty that related to the loan 'settled nothing, left the whole future to the chapter of accidents, and provided no security worthy of the name either for the just treatment of British claims or for any advance of British credit'. He did, indeed, drop a hint at the end of his letter that a revised treaty might be less unacceptable. Without Liberal support the Government was doomed and Parliament met on September 30 with all three parties prepared for decisive battle. Members had been recalled from the recess for the specific purpose of dealing with the Irish Free State Bill, the object of which was to set up a Boundary Commission. This the Government successfully steered through the Commons and the normal procedure would have been for the House to adjourn for the remainder of the recess. But on September 30 Sir Kingsley Wood asked his question about the dropping of the prosecution of the editor of the *Workers' Weekly*. Both Conservatives and Liberals expressed themselves dissatisfied with the explanation of the Attorney-General, and Baldwin asked that a day should be set aside for the discussion of the matter when Parliament reassembled. To this MacDonald replied that he preferred that the matter should be dealt with as soon as the Irish Bill had gone up to the Lords. Sir Robert Horne then tabled a motion on behalf of the Conservatives 'that the conduct of His Majesty's Government in relation to the institution and subsequent withdrawal of criminal proceedings against the editor of the *Workers' Weekly* is deserving of the censure of the House'. The Liberals for their part did not consider the matter worthy of a vote of censure and put up an amendment that the matter be referred to a select committee for investigation and report. The Cabinet met on October 6 and decided to make both motions questions of confidence. Asquith on October 1 had come out decisively against the Russian treaty, without any such saving clause as had appeared in his letter of September 20, and it was more than ever clear that the Government would be defeated when the House reassembled.

On October 7 Haldane wrote: 'Yesterday we had a decisive Cabinet. We are going to fight and refuse to accept the motions on Wednesday in any form. I pressed hard that this should be so and the P.M. agreed. Asquith's pronouncement had settled the fate of the Russian Treaty and we should only hang on with loss of dignity and prestige to be slain in November. If, as I expect, the Commons decide against us to-morrow we shall ask for a dissolution.'

When the House met on October 8 Sir Robert Horne moved the Conservative motion and Sir John Simon the Liberal amendment. After a few more members had spoken Baldwin intervened and said that it was obvious that the Government was hoping to defeat the Conservative motion with Liberal votes, and the Liberal motion with Conservative votes, that his party did not propose to let themselves be the dupes of such procedure and would support the Liberal amendment. That settled the matter and the Liberal amendment was carried by 364 to 198. The next morning Mac-Donald went to the King, who gave his consent to the dissolution. In the election campaign the Russian treaty became the main issue. The Conservatives urged that the Soviet Government was not one with which a self-respecting country could negotiate a treaty, and declared that MacDonald had been rushed into it against his better judgement by the extremists of his party. Labour maintained that a treaty with Russia, which would open up trade with that vast country, was the best practical solution of the problem of unemployment. The Liberals wobbled between the Conservative and Labour lines of attack and defence and suffered accordingly. While the campaign was at its height an unexpected and as it proved decisive turn took place in the struggle. On October 10 a copy of a letter purporting to have been sent on September 15 by Zinovieff, head of the Third International, from Moscow to the Communist Party in Great Britain reached the Foreign Office. This letter contained instructions to British Communists to work for the violent overthrow of existing institutions in this country and for the subversion of His Majesty's forces to that end. After the letter had been examined in the Foreign Office, where the letter was believed to be genuine, it was sent to MacDonald, who was engaged in the election campaign at Manchester. It reached him on October 16. He replied to the Foreign Office that the greatest care should be taken to ascertain if the letter was genuine or not; but if it was genuine it should be published at once with a strong letter of protest to M. Rakovsky, the Chargé d'Affaires of the Soviet Union in London. This draft letter was sent to MacDonald, who received it on the 23rd and returned it the next day with some amendments, expecting that nothing further would be done until he had received proofs of the authenticity of the Zinovieff letter. Mr. Gregory, of the Foreign Office, who clearly believed the letter to be genuine, took MacDonald's revised draft of the protest to Rakovsky as his final approval, and sent the document to the Press. Rakovsky at once stigmatized the Zinovieff letter as a clumsy forgery, and this was accepted by the majority of the Labour Party, though not by MacDonald nor by Haldane. The publication of the Rakovsky letter undoubtedly made the treaty with Russia for which Labour was contending impossible and caused a large number of Liberals to vote Conservative. The result was that 413 Conservatives, 151 Labour, and 40 Liberals were returned. Asquith was among the fallen. On October 30, when most of the results were in, Haldane wrote:

'The elections are going as I anticipated. The country appears to have turned Conservative. Our poor Liberal friends are being annihilated. I am vexed about Asquith, we should all have liked to see him end his time in the Commons, which he has adorned for long years. I don't think that the Zinovieff letter affected the ultimate result. The Conservatives would have come in in any case, but with a smaller majority, and by a strange freak of fate it is the Liberals who have suffered most from this document. No one yet knows for certain whether the Zinovieff letter was genuine or not, but the Foreign Office thinks it was genuine and I am inclined to back their judgement. Ramsay has asked me to be a member of a committee of enquiry into the authenticity of the letter, but I doubt whether we shall find out much more.'

The Committee consisted of MacDonald, Parmoor, Henderson, and Haldane. It had only a brief time for its investigation before the Government left office, and it reported that after hearing the departments concerned it was impossible to come to a definite decision. The original letter had not been found and action had been taken on what was not claimed to be more than a copy. MacDonald resigned on November 4 and the King sent for Baldwin the same day.

MacDonald's handling of the incident was severely criticized by Conservatives both during the election and after it was over. There were suggestions that he was trying to put the responsibility on the permanent officials of the Foreign Office, while Labour maintained that the letter was a forgery used unscrupulously by the Conservatives to influence the election. On November 9 Haldane received from Sir Eyre Crowe, the Permanent Under-Secretary of State for Foreign Affairs, the following letter:

'DEAR LORD HALDANE

'Your letter, the kind words, the friendly and generous feelings which I find in it, have made me more glad and more grateful to you than I can say. Let me thank you very warmly.

'You will, I feel sure, be interested, perhaps even gratified, to learn (what I tell you in strict confidence) that we have now proof that Zinovieff has admitted to the Soviet government in Moscow having sent the letter of September 15. In the discussion on the subject he advised that the only line that the Soviet Government could take was to deny the whole story! —which was accordingly done.

'We got this piece of information on Thursday evening, and I had just time to tell MacDonald before he went off to make his speech that evening. He thanked me, and I believe that in his heart of hearts he was convinced, though he—perhaps naturally—did not say so. At any rate he allowed me to warn him against committing himself any further as to the alleged forgery of the letter.

Believe me

Yours very sincerely

EYRE A. CROWE.'

This of course made it quite clear that the Foreign Office had obtained definite proof of the authenticity of the Zinovieff letter after the Labour Government had left office. Haldane was therefore surprised to read in *The Times* of November 14 the report of a speech by Austen Chamberlain at Glasgow the previous day. Chamberlain said:

'The episode of the Zinovieff letter has been left in a very peculiar position by our predecessors.

'In pursuance of a minute written by the late Prime Minister acting as Foreign Minister, a note to the Soviet representative in London, largely written by the Prime Minister himself in his own hand, and everywhere where he altered the original draft strengthened and made stronger, was delivered to that representative and published in our newspapers. It charged the Soviet Government with a breach not merely of old, but of recently renewed undertakings. It was a very stern document. Having caused it to be delivered and published the last act of the late Government was to express their inability to determine, whether the Prime Minister had any foundation for the charges which he made. I will express no opinion on the matter.'

On reading this Haldane rang up Crowe, who replied the same day:

'I was much annoyed and distressed on reading this morning the report of Chamberlain's speech at Glasgow yesterday. I have this morning at once seriously remonstrated with him for the way in which he referred to Mr. MacDonald's having "caused" (his very stern document) "to be delivered and published". I said this looked like a definite charge that he deliberately fired off and published the note to Rakovsky, and then allowed his Cabinet to disavow it. At the same time, by laying stress on Mr. MacDonald's having refrained from blaming his permanent officials, Chamberlain created the impression that all the blame fell on Mr. MacDonald.

'I reminded him that in a memorandum which I wrote for him and which he circulated to the Cabinet I had expressly explained that the whole trouble arose from a genuine misunderstanding and from my failure to interpret correctly what had been Mr. MacDonald's real intention when returning to me his corrected draft note.

'I have explained how desirable it would be in the interest not only of the Civil Service generally, but of the political and party situation, that this genuine misunderstanding, which has already caused so much unhappiness, should not be further exploited. And I added that Mr. MacDonald himself had intimated to me that unless his political opponents persisted he would do his best to let the matter peter out as quickly as possible.

'I am now perturbed that Chamberlain's unfortunate speech may make him suspect that I or someone in this office had in some way inspired it. The reverse is the case. Mr. Chamberlain has now promised me not to pursue the matter in this way. Moreover he proposes to see Mr. MacDonald and explain to him personally that he had had no intention of opening or aggravating controversy.

'I hope therefore very earnestly that whatever harm has been done will not lead to further trouble.

'Meanwhile I feel impelled to tell you this, as I value your friendship too much to allow you to remain yourself under a false impression which you might have gained from Chamberlain's speech, that someone here has not been playing the game. Please forgive my indiscretion, which I trust you will not consider importunate.'

On November 5 Haldane wrote to his mother:

'Yesterday we resigned and we are in partial repose. I am very glad that I joined the Labour Government. One of the reasons which influenced me was that I was confident that we could do much to allay the wild and unreasoning alarms which prevailed as to what a Socialist Government would do, and so help to kill class prejudice. This letter business has I fear destroyed much of the good we had done. It was just bad luck, and the way it appeared was due to a genuine misunderstanding between MacDonald, who was absorbed in the election campaign, and the permanent staff at the F.O. However, I have got masses of things done by not advertising them and so bringing on attacks. But they are done and slowly they will come to light. Yesterday I finished my work at the Committee of Imperial Defence, the decks were greatly cleared and Hankey told me that the Committee was in a state in which it had never been before. Thanks to Schuster's quick intelligence we have done much in the Lord Chancellor's office for which future Lord Chancellors will bless me.'

The administration of the law, like much else in our administration, had developed in a haphazard way without any clear idea as to what machinery was required or how it should be used. There was the usual intermingling of functions of different departments of State, which resulted in waste of time and energy, the Home Office, the Treasury, and the Lord Chancellor's office were all concerned with day to day legal administration. For example the pay and expenses of court officials was the business of a department of the Treasury, while the appointment and discipline of these officials was the concern of the Lord Chancellor. The appointment of County Court judges rested with the Lord Chancellor, but the Treasury controlled County Court administrative finance. The Home Office was concerned with much legal business for which the Lord Chancellor's office was also in part responsible. The Lord Chancellor was himself a member of the

Cabinet, and as such had his share of responsibility for the general policy of the Government, he was a member of the Supreme Court of Appeal and was expected to take his part in the exacting work of those courts, he was Speaker of the House of Lords, and was head of a great administrative department, which was responsible for as much or more patronage than any other department of State.

All this was pain and grief to Haldane's orderly mind, and he endeavoured to resolve the tangle by applying scientific principles of organization. His own solution was the creation of a Ministry of Justice, which should take over all the administrative functions exercised by the Lord Chancellor's department, the Home Office and the Treasury, and he maintained that the political head of this ministry should be a member of the House of Commons, and be responsible to that House for the patronage which he administered. In short he envisaged a separation of the judicial and administrative functions hitherto the responsibility of the Lord Chancellor. In the brief term of his second Lord Chancellorship he had not the time to work out his plans fully and there were objections and consequent opposition to his scheme for a Ministry of Justice, but he did a great deal to simplify and co-ordinate the work of the administration of the Law. It had long been a grievance of the Labour Party that it did not receive its fair share of consideration in the appointment of justices of the peace. Lord Cave had begun work upon a scheme for the appointment of Justices' Advisory Committees, which should be representative of all parties, and should in making recommendations see that a reasonable balance of political opinion was maintained. Haldane to a great extent completed this work and he saw to it that women were represented on nearly all the advisory committees.

But the work that he found most congenial was that of the Committee of Imperial Defence. He had expanded the principle recommended by the Salisbury Committee that there should be a permanent sub-committee composed of the three Chiefs of Staff to advise on the co-ordination of problems of defence, and had arranged for additional sub-committees to advise on problems of supply in war and on the provision and distribution of man-power between the three Services, industry, and agriculture. The treaties of peace had left us with new commitments in Palestine and Mesopotamia, and there was the prospect of a further commitment at Singapore. These meant that the whole question of the distribution of our forces had to be reconsidered, while the new machinery of the sub-committee of the three Chiefs of Staff had to be got into working order, which was not an easy task, owing to the friction between the Army and Navy on the one side and the Air Force on the other. The general question of India's part in Imperial Defence came up for consideration, and there were strong representations from that country that she was being overcharged, and that the Indian tax-payer was being required to shoulder what were in effect Imperial responsibilities. Lord Rawlinson, then commander-in-chief in India, came home to discuss these questions with the Committee of Imperial Defence, and in particular to fight a War Office demand on India for £1,000,000 for money spent during the war. Rawlinson had a number of interviews with Haldane, who took his side, and on his way back to India he wrote:

'MY DEAR LORD HALDANE

'Before I left England I had not time to write and thank you for helping me with the Million claim that has been put forward by the War Office against India so I send a line now to express my gratitude. I saw Lord Birkenhead the morning I left London and told him briefly what had occurred. Perhaps if you also could say a word to him it would help matters for I am sure the War Office financiers will be pressing us again at an early date. Could you also speak to him on the subject of an Imperial reserve being maintained in India for

Imperial purposes, but at the expense of the Home Treasury? I went into the question fairly fully with Cavan[1] before I left but the subject is one that should be brought before the C.I.D. at an early date, and I do not know who has taken over the chairmanship from you under the new Government. I am entirely in favour of at least one Indian division being held as part of the Expeditionary Force in India for I see no other way of preventing in the not very distant future a further reduction of the British garrison in India.

'I have read your book *Before the War* with the deepest interest. Much of it is of course quite new to me though I had always suspected that the Great General Staff at Berlin had got out of hand and precipitated hostilities for their own swollen headed ends. And what a mess they made of it! There were at least three occasions on which they ought to have won the war. Thank goodness they had not the old von Moltke at the head of affairs.

Yours sincerely
Rawlinson.'

One plan on which he had set his heart he was unable for want of time to bring to a conclusion. His experience on the Committee of Imperial Defence had led him to the opinion that it would add greatly to the efficiency of the machinery of Government if the Prime Minister had at his hand a body organized on the same principles as the Committee of Imperial Defence to advise him upon civil problems of a technical nature. His first note on the subject written in March 1924 he called 'a plan for organizing a body in civil affairs, to occupy a similar position to Balfour's Defence Committee for Naval and Military Affairs'. Haldane had a number of consultations with Sir Maurice Hankey and Sir Warren Fisher, and an outline of the scheme was presented to Mac-

[1]Field-Marshal the Earl of Cavan, then Chief of the Imperial General Staff.

Donald, who told Haldane to go ahead. The complete plan for a Committee of Civil Research, to be a Standing Committee reporting to the Cabinet, was not ready until August. The committee was to be advisory with the Prime Minister as its president and a minister nominated by him as its chairman. All the other members were to be chosen by the Prime Minister for their expert knowledge of whatever question was referred to the committee for examination. Its terms of reference were to be to give connected forethought from a central standpoint to the development of economic, scientific, and statistical research in relation to civil policy and administration. This was clearly a child of Haldane's Machinery of Government Committee. When the complete plan was ready the Prime Minister was fully occupied, first with his International Conference on Reparations, and then with the political crisis which followed. So he had no time to consider the complete plan, and the Labour Government went out of office before it was approved. When the Conservatives came in the plan was submitted to Baldwin and taken up with enthusiasm by Balfour. It was adopted with little change in Haldane's scheme. Balfour became its first chairman and he invited Haldane to become a member for one of its first inquiries. The committee remained in being for five years, and did some very valuable work, but in 1930 its functions and title were changed and it became the Economic Advisory Council.

All this was very exacting work, and besides all this, when Parliament was in session Haldane had to spend most of his afternoons on the Woolsack endeavouring to get Government business through with the aid of a mere handful of Labour Peers. He was in his sixty-ninth year and the strain was beginning to tell. Even if the Labour Government had lasted longer it is doubtful whether Haldane could have continued much longer to work at such a pace.

Chapter VIII

A LEADER OF THE OPPOSITION—THE GENERAL STRIKE

1925 to 1926

It had been Haldane's practice to dictate from time to time notes of his impressions of the men and events of his time obviously intended to guide his biographer. When he got away to Cloan after the fall of the Labour Government he added to these, and in one dated January 16, 1925, he concluded:

'Ramsay MacDonald was a man of remarkable ability. He travelled so much and had seen so many foreigners that he had acquired that rare gift—an International Mind—and in the Foreign Office and in his general conduct of affairs he inspired foreigners with the sense that he understood them as his predecessors had not done. He was not passionately devoted to the details of his office in the way that was my old and intimate friend Edward Grey, who in character, sincerity, industry in his office, and in dignity, was almost a unique figure, but Ramsay MacDonald understood the Continent as none of his predecessors had done and the results have been good. Where he failed with his Ministry was in this that he did not care about other matters. He left them to us with the result that they seemed not to have the attention of the Prime Minister.

'I think he could have done the work he set himself to do in foreign affairs as well as that at home, but he did not do it and the result was that the Labour Government of 1924 went out without receiving sufficient credit for the work it had done. The Russian policy, which was premature and the result of inefficient control from himself, ruined it. I made personal friends in the Foreign Office—men like Sir Eyre Crowe and Sir William Tyrrell and with these I went as closely as it was possible to do, but I have regretted that I did not have as full opportunities as I could have wished for working at foreign affairs during the MacDonald Government.

'I am glad that I joined the Labour Party. It has made mistakes but its reality rests on this, that it is the Party that is most in contact with the democracy of this country. That democracy does not include the whole of the Labour leaders, but it includes a very large part of them, and with the growth of education that part is likely to increase. The mistake Tories and Whigs alike made was in failing to see that as the franchise was extended, and as Education permeated further and further, it became vital for any political party which desired to remain effective, to be in the closest contact with the people and to break down the gaps which separate class from class unjustly. Labour is the only Party that has so far succeeded in giving this faith to its supporters, and I think that it will prove in the end to be the Party that has really averted upheaval in this country. It may progress slowly but it seems to me to be progressing surely. The Labour Government has now gone out, but at its request I have accepted the Leadership of the House of Lords of the Opposition there. MacDonald wished it and the Conservative Government also wished it, and the House of Lords has acquiesced. I sit on the front Opposition Bench, provided by the State with a comfortable room and attendance. It remains to be seen whether I shall be able to carry out my purpose, which is to induce the new Conservative Party with its large majority to act and not merely to talk. If it does this we may get a great deal done, however slowly. We may also by degrees build up a progressive party more wide in its scope than any we have yet seen.'

Haldane had been disappointed that MacDonald had not consulted him on foreign affairs as Grey had done. It is very probable that Haldane's well-known friendship with Grey was the reason for this, for MacDonald was firmly convinced that if Grey had handled matters differently the Great War could have been prevented. It has been suggested with some authority that MacDonald authorized the publication of the Foreign Office documents, which have been so admirably edited by Messrs. Temperley and Gooch, in the expectation that they would bring this to light. It is a little odd that in this note Haldane should have accused MacDonald of the very fault with which he was so often charged himself, that of concentration on the problem which interested him to the detriment of his share in the general business of the Government, though, of course, this was a more serious defect in a Prime Minister, responsible for the direction and co-ordination of Government policy, than in the head of a Department of State.

As the note says, Haldane agreed to lead the Opposition in the House of Lords. There was a skirmish with the Liberals before this was settled, for they had a good many more Peers than had Labour, and they put in a claim to the Leadership. But Baldwin decided that the claims of Labour, as the second largest party in the State, should be upheld. Haldane did not take on the job with any joy: 'I won't run away,' he wrote, 'but, as you know, I take but a mediocre interest in the routine of party politics.'

His first appearance in his new role was not such as to give much satisfaction to the Tadpoles and Tapers of his party. As was his duty he rose to reply to the mover and seconder of the Address in the Lords, when Baldwin's second administration first met Parliament. He then said: 'I have never thought that the business of an Opposition was to oppose. I have always held that the business of an Opposition is to criticize; to examine and study and to get what good it can out of the

Party in power; to be ready to criticize severely if there is any deviation from what it thinks ought to be, and to bring to the fore points of view which are apt to be neglected.'

One of the achievements of which the Labour Party was particularly proud was the Geneva Protocol, which was designed to strengthen the sanctions of the League against an aggressor, or would-be aggressor. It had a very warm advocate in MacDonald, who was responsible for a part at least of the design. It had been adopted unanimously by the Fifth Assembly of the League for reference to the several governments for ratification, and had been ratified by France, who had ardently supported it from the first. There was a reference to it in the King's speech saying that it was under examination. On this Haldane said:

'About the Geneva Protocol I will only say this, that it is a very important document, the terms of which have to be very carefully examined. The condition of things in this Empire is such that we depend very much on the freedom of movement of the Fleet as a police force, and we have to see that it is not interfered with in any international document that we enter into; on the other hand the Protocol is a document of immense importance embodying as it does an idea which has been brought within sight by the agreement and its main terms. The Government have the problems to work out, and I hope that they will keep the second consideration as well as the first before their minds.'

This was very faint praise for one of his Party's favourite children and there were grumbles from its members. In the subsequent debates on the Protocol Haldane took no part, probably because his party felt that this lukewarm advocacy was of no service, while Haldane himself was well informed as to the way things were going and knew that there was no need for him to intervene. Eventually Baldwin's Government refused to ratify the Protocol for the very reason which made Haldane suspicious of it, namely that it would turn the British Navy into the policeman of the world, a task which, added to its heavy Imperial responsibilities, would be beyond it.

Very shortly after Baldwin became Prime Minister he invited Haldane to continue to be a member of the Committee of Imperial Defence. There was precedent for this, for on previous occasions leaders of the Opposition had been invited to join the Committee, notably when the question of the Channel tunnel came up for consideration, but this was the first time an invitation had been issued to an Opposition leader to join the Committee to take his share in its day to day work, and not as a temporary member for the study of a specific problem. Haldane accepted joyfully, but his leader did not see eye to eye with him, and MacDonald wrote:

'After I left you last night I was turning things over in my mind, and it occurred to me that as Leader of the Opposition in the House of Lords you might find it awkward, and so might we in the House of Commons, if you were responsible for decisions come to by the Committee of Imperial Defence. Should not this be very carefully considered before finally making up your mind to accept Baldwin's invitation to continue upon it? It may be said that it is a purely technical body, but the Cabinet will have to communicate to it matters of policy, and technical decisions will also very frequently affect policy.

'The way that Austen Chamberlain is using my name in his dispatches (for this I understand there is no precedent) shows that they are not going to scruple to drag us into their activities wherever and whenever they can, and we might find ourselves in a fix at any moment if either in your House or in ours the Government could say "Oh but Lord Haldane is a member of the Committee and has agreed to what we propose". Had you thought that aspect over, and are you quite satisfied about it?'

Haldane, who had always maintained that defence policy

should, at least in its major aspects, be removed as far as possible from the sphere of party politics, stuck to his guns, and resumed his work under the chairmanship of Lord Curzon.

Upon another major problem of the day he was not in agreement with the majority of his party. On March 25, 1925, the Duke of Sutherland moved a resolution in the Lords on the reform of that House. On this Haldane, after reviewing previous proposals for reform, said:

'What does all this amount to? It amounts to this: that your Lordships have tried your hands three times and have wholly broken down in the effort, notwithstanding the "grey-haired" wisdom to which the noble Duke referred, to find a solution of this problem. The House of Lords did not come here as the result of any Statute or as the result of any plan fashioned in modern times. You must go to the historical method and you find that it has grown up and has become what it is by slow degrees. A body like that can only be dealt with in one of two ways. You may sweep it away; you may put a Second Chamber in its place which is in the nature of a Senate. It is very difficult to construct a Senate, but it can be constructed in one way. You can make it a Senate which accords with the opinion of the times as manifested by the election of the House of Commons, and which will change as the House of Commons changes. That is a perfectly feasible plan, but I do not think we have reached that stage yet. Nevertheless it can be done. I myself have put a plan in a Bill on which I have expended a good deal of time and trouble and which I think would be quite workable, but I do not propose to bring that Bill to your Lordship's attention now. Possibly I never may. But there is another fashion in which things work. Ours is an unwritten Constitution, and because it is an unwritten Constitution it is a Constitution which develops and varies as decade succeeds decade. The position of the House of Lords to-day is not the same as the position of the House of Lords fifty years ago. It is no longer a body that is irresponsive to public opinion. Your Lordships have shown in recent years great readiness to acknowledge the force of public opinion and to respect it. During the days of the late Government you were very good to us, you recognized that we stood for a good deal in the country and that it was not expedient there should be conflict between you and us. You met us handsomely on every occasion. That is a spirit which in itself goes a long way to get over difficulties. You do not reduce anything to writing, you do not lay down any rigid propositions or attempt to define, nor do you deal with abstractions. You deal with the concrete situation that arises, and your Lordships take up the position that whenever you see clearly that public opinion is supporting the lines taken by the other House you will not stand in the way.

'As I have said, that state of things is different from the state of things fifty years ago. In those days the House of Lords did throw out and mangle Bills. It even parted with its right to deal with Money Bills very reluctantly. Now unless there is some passing eccentricity this House does not attempt to interfere with Money Bills, nor have we any experience to show that it is necessary it should. It is not my business to give advice to His Majesty's Government nor would they thank me for it. But if I did I think it would assume the form of a single sentence: Let well alone. Things are not worse than they were; they are better than they were, and I doubt whether anybody elected from outside, anybody nominated by the Crown, or nominated by a selection from among your Lordships' members, which might not always be a selection of great wisdom, would do better than your Lordships' House as constituted at present has done. As I have said, we are not dealing with a written Constitution. It is not necessary to go to the Senates in the Dominions, nominated as they are in Canada and New Zealand by the Crown, or as they are in Australia through direct election, or as they are in France through a very different system of local government to which we have no analogy in this country. It is not by going to these analogies that you will get light.

'We are the only country in the world which has a thoroughly unwritten Constitution, a developing Constitution. That quality is the quality that has enabled us to surmount many difficulties and which as generation succeeds generation, more and more closely shows itself as expressive of the opinion of the day, whatever that opinion may be. I am not pretending that the constitution of this House, as it is to-day, can be defended upon abstract principles. If you must go to abstract principles, then I have indicated to your Lordships that I know another way which it is possible to consider. But if I interpret the sentiment of this House aright, it is not a sentiment which requires or calls for any violent changes. Let us, rather than attempt anything rash, remain as we are, carefully watching and accommodating ourselves to the opinion of the time. It will not avert changes which some of your Lordships would not like to see, but then you cannot avert them whatever machinery you set up, because when these changes come, as they have come and will come, they come as the outcome of a tremendous democratic opinion in this country which you could not resist even if you would—a public opinion which is more potent than Kings and more potent even than Parliaments.'

His own specific to which he had referred was a simple one. Having no belief in reforming the Upper House root and branch, he wanted it to develop in its own way, but to improve its efficiency and bring it into closer touch with public opinion. His view was that the efficiency of the Upper Chamber was hampered by the fact that it often happened, when questions of the first importance were debated, that the minister concerned was not a member of the House, and the duty of reply to debate fell to a junior member, often a Lord-in-Waiting, who had no connection with the department concerned. Haldane's proposals were that when questions were debated in the Upper House the minister concerned should attend and take part whether he was a peer or not.

On April 9 Mrs. Haldane celebrated her hundredth birthday. This became almost a national celebration. There was of course a great family gathering, and delegations and presentations from Auchterarder and from the estate. Letters and telegrams poured in from the King and Queen, from Queen Alexandra, from both archbishops, the Lord Chancellor, the Prime Minister, Mr. MacDonald, and hundreds of others. In celebration of the event an institute for young men and women was opened in Auchterarder, and a tea, the chief feature of which was a cake with one hundred candles, was given in the poor-house near the town. At the party this conversation was overheard between two of the inmates:

'Eh! wumman! She must be a proud wumman this day with such a son.'

'Na! I warrant she'll no' be that. But she'll be what she's been a' her days, and that's a prayin' mither, and that's what's made him the man he is. An' God bless them both! Mither and son all their days.'

Six weeks later Mrs. Haldane passed peacefully away and again there was a nation-wide outpouring of tributes to her life and character. His mother had been such an influence in his life that I feel I must repeat here a little tribute to her which he wrote for a short memoir edited by Miss Haldane.

'I wish to try to set down my impressions of my mother in the last years of her life, the years in which she was physically too much of an invalid to leave her room, but was mentally at what seemed to me her highest. Apart from her inability to move about, partial deafness was her only hindrance in the freest communication with her children.

'To me the striking feature through the dozen years of which I write was my mother's steady growth in mental stature. This seemed to increase in every year. She was not what would be popularly called a learned or very clever

HOUSE PARTY AT CLOAN ON THE OCCASION OF MRS. HALDANE'S 100TH BIRTHDAY

Front row: Professor J. Haldane, Lord Haldane, Bruce, Miss Haldane, Sir W. Haldane. *Second row*: J. B. S. Haldane, Lady Haldane, A. R. B. Haldane, Miss M. E. Haldane, T. G. N. Haldane, Miss A. Chinnery-Haldane, B. Chinnery-Haldane, B. Chinnery-Haldane (of Gleneagles). *Back row*, T. G. Bullough, Mrs. Bullough, General Sir Aylmer Haldane, A. Chinnery-Haldane, Mrs. Chinnery-Haldane

woman. But her outlook and mental grasp were widening to the end steadily. She read extensively, in various languages, and her reading included difficult philosophical books, as well as memoirs and histories. Whether she took in all the details in those books, sometimes intricate, it was not easy to tell. But is was clear that she had grasped the substance not only of what she read, but of the things that had been said to her by remarkable visitors to Cloan with whom she delighted to hold conversations. She conveyed the sense that she was genuinely looking at things from a high point of view, which reached not only to the things set down but over them. Her mental activity was great and its range wide.

'Deeply religious, she was never narrow. The old doctrines with which she was familiar were for her symbols in which she approached what she grasped as being higher than what the symbols could express. She was not troubled by speculative doubts. Above these she seemed to have risen to a standpoint from which the substance of things unseen appeared to introduce itself unhindered by difficulties. Death had no terrors for her. It was but an event essential to the completion of life. She did not dwell on pictorial imaginings of another life. What she sought for was rather to hold fast to the highest quality in this one, where the human and divine were never for her shut off from each other. The presence of God was foundational. But her faith in Him was a living faith. Her's was no abstract mind. In the person of Christ she had always an intense sense of God and Man as one. This was constantly before her, and no doctrine was of value if it did not express this, which was a supreme fact of her experience.

'Thus she was intensely religious, with expressions for her religion that were characteristic of her mind. Of what these expressions meant the children were keenly conscious. But her views were never thrust on them. She claimed liberty of thought, and she accorded it equally freely. No apparent aberrations in her children from tradition surprised or distressed her. For from the widest point of view she saw the truth present notwithstanding the form of its expression.

'All sorts of people used to come to the house, and she was always anxious to see them. They used to leave her room impressed by her grasp of realities. In return she estimated them by their possession of this kind of grasp. She never judged harshly. In the learned and in the humble she looked for the same sort of quality. She was a fine judge of whether it was present. She liked to see much of her children at her bedside, and to know all they were trying to do, great or small. Their pursuits were varied, but into these various pursuits she loved to enter. She was a perfect mother; our only anxiety was to appear before her as worthy of her great love for us. Whether we were engaged in country life, or in household matters, or in public work, or in philosophy, or in science, she always seemed equally interested in our efforts. She did not fail to discriminate between our visitors, but she was never contemptuous in her criticism. But I used to feel that for some of them she was a formidable person to encounter, whether they fully realized it or not.

'In the people round about, in Auchterarder, for instance, she maintained an interest which had been keen when she could go about, and which never flagged after she ceased to be able to move. She delighted in summoning them to consultations. Her day was rarely unbroken by interviews. These did not seem to tire her. She found in those who came what she wanted, and if they asked her for counsel or help it was freely given. Her old servants she watched over affectionately and kept up her close friendship with them.

'In her attire, whether there were visitors or not, she was neat and exact. She had always cared for beauty, and she liked her clothes to look well, even when she could only sit up in bed. Even with her children themselves she never liked to be found untidy. She wrote as well as received a great many letters. Over the composition of what she wrote, and her own handwriting, she took much pains. Everything in her life was ordered, even the arrangements for her own simple funeral she herself had made, and she had insisted on discussing them with us, long before the end came. No one treated more thoroughly death as a natural and necessary part of life, to be prepared for like every other event. When it came to her it came as a profound sorrow for her children. For them much of the basis of life was swept away. But the sorrow was lightened by the preparation of their minds for it through the years before it descended. She wished this to be so, and, if there was no trace of anything morbid in her language about it, she had succeeded in making her passage one to be looked for as the completion of her life. "I rest in God" were her favourite words. They were the words uttered by her mother when she was dying, sixty years before our mother herself died.

'For me to talk with my mother was not always a simple thing. For she liked to direct the conversation to the past, rather than keep to the present, and to bring back pictures which might not easily fit into the period in which we lived. But the difficulty of appreciating this desire on her part quickly diminished as she brought out the identity of the best ideas of those early days with the substance of those of to-day. For her father, who was a profoundly religious man, she had a great reverence, and she used to speculate on what turn his mind would have taken had he been born just a few years later and remained under the influence of his contemporary at Oriel, Keble. The story of the Oxford Movement was always deeply interesting to her, and she read and re-read Dean Church's book on it. She had no narrowness. The Church of England, the Presbyterian Church, the Baptists, and Plymouth Brethren, among whom she had been brought up, all appealed to her in different ways. They were the aspects which a general spiritual organization presented to her.

'Thus she grew to have many friends, and very real and

attached friends. With many of these she corresponded regularly to the end of her life. They felt in their different ways that whether she agreed with them or not she understood them. But it was not only on the religious side that she attracted people. There came to Cloan and talked with her a variety of those who held foremost places in literature and in public life. Meredith, Barrie, Gosse, Whitehead, Hume Brown, Pringle-Pattison in literature, and Lord Roberts, Sir Ian Hamilton, Lord Ypres, and many other soldiers knew her well. Among public men, Asquith, Edward Grey, John Dillon, Morley, Ramsay MacDonald, and a variety of those occupying high places used to visit her. Of the archbishops, bishops, and eminent divines of the other churches the list is long. I think that each felt that she had as much that was real to say to him as he had to say to her.

'She was accessible, too, to all the neighbours, and they liked to talk with her over local affairs. Of these she had a wide knowledge, which she was keen to keep up to date. Her sense of humour in her intercourse with them and with her children was strong. She said good things when we were least looking for them, and she looked out for comedy more than for tragedy. Everything came to light with the background of her own character to make it stand out. That character did not change, and it always appeared. It showed itself in a clear view of every situation and in a strong will. A decision once come to was not easily shaken. Her mind was never doubtful even about where the things in the house were. She had a marvellous memory for where they could be found—books, articles of furniture, clothes—she remembered when she had last been able to move about and look at them, and she seemed in her old age to visualize what she had known of her possessions.

'Of character she was an acute yet not unkindly judge—both in women and in men. She had a strong sense of what a "lady" ought to be like, and she recognized the natural-born lady as readily among the humble as among the great. As to men, she had an instinctive sense of whether their knowledge was real or superficial. I rarely knew her to be deceived in an estimate. To talk with and to understand those of foreign nationality was congenial to her. Of insularity she had no trace.

'A long experience of daily and sustained personal intercourse has now come to an end for her children. The break is great, but it is not to be wondered at if a tradition had entered so deeply into their lives that it does not seem as though time could weaken it.'

Haldane had resumed his legal work in the Privy Council and became chairman of a sub-committee of the Committee of Imperial Defence appointed to consider the problem of anti-aircraft defence. He brought in his brother John as a member of this committee and was the first to enlist the resources of the Department of Scientific and Industrial Research and of the National Physical Laboratory in the investigation of this very vital matter. He was also chairman of another sub-committee of the same body on the emergency legislation required at the outbreak of war, and in the early autumn Balfour asked him to become a member of the newly created Committee of Civil Research to consider the question of Government support of the British Dyestuffs Corporation. This was an enterprise which had been started in the war, when it was found that Germany had what amounted to a monopoly of the production of dyestuffs, and that we were incapable of producing dyes effectively. This was a subject in which Haldane was deeply interested—not that he had any technical knowledge of dyestuffs, but he had knowledge of the methods by which Germany had built up the industry, and he maintained stoutly that if we used our scientific resources in the way in which Germany had used hers we could produce as good results in this or in any other industry. He maintained that Germany had built up her dyestuffs industry by concentrating first on scientific research, in which she had not neglected to make use of the work of British scientists, that we, in the emergency of war, had been forced to attempt to build up a new industry by supplying to it Government capital, but that this was beginning at the wrong end of the stick; that the right course now was to supply money for research and to leave the industry to apply the results of research.

Unfortunately a breakdown in his health prevented him from attending the final and decisive meeting of the committee. Haldane's proposal meant supplying more money and a good deal of it, both for research work and to keep alive the industry started under artificial conditions, and the demands for economy were so insistent that he was overruled. He sent Balfour a memorandum from Cloan, where he was convalescing, and Balfour replied:

'It is most unlucky that you were away from our discussion on Dye Stuffs; but a decision by the Committee had absolutely to be come to in the course of this week and delay was impossible. I feel confident that if you had been with us you would have agreed to the course we have taken.

'It must be remembered that we have no power to prevent the Dye Stuffs Corporation going into liquidation, and from a commercial point of view they would have some justification for such a course. They are undoubtedly hampered by limitations which apply neither to their German nor to their British rivals and they are losing heavily. I feel just as strongly as you do the necessity of encouraging the greater employment of organic chemists in our industrial processes, and there is no doubt that we are far behind both Germany and Switzerland and I believe America in this respect. But I do not believe it is possible to force a Company in which the investing public are largely interested to pursue a policy which (in their hands at least) is unprofitable. If they had the technical knowledge of the Swiss Company, which under a

British name (which I happen to forget) is doing extremely well, or if they were managed with the skill and enterprise of "Scottish Dye Stuffs", things might be different. As it is I do not believe any more than the Directors themselves that they would make a good job of their present undertaking. As things are the Government have no means of compelling them to encourage research on a large scale and they are without doubt subject to hampering limitations to which none of their rivals, domestic or foreign, have to submit. I doubt greatly whether the Scottish Dye Company would endure them for a moment.

'I shall not be present when the subject comes before the Cabinet next Wednesday, but I have had your memorandum circulated to the Cabinet.

'*P.S.* I understand that the great German Combine of colour manufacturers makes *all* its profits out of bye-products which the British Dye Stuffs Corporation are precluded from manufacturing.'

Throughout the first part of the year 1925 the dispute in the coal-mining industry had been simmering. A joint inquiry between masters and men had been instituted and the findings of the inquiry convinced most people that the owners were right in their contention that the economic position of the industry was such as made it incapable of meeting the men's demands. On this Haldane wrote: 'I have just been reading the findings of the joint inquiry of masters and men in the coal industry. I do not think that there can be any doubt that the facts and figures produced by the owners support their contentions, but the fact remains that the condition of a large number of the miners, I should say probably a majority, is gravely unsatisfactory. The real difficulty is to get the Government to face the fact that this is something more than an industrial dispute between masters and men. It is a question of stopping a grievous waste of vital national resources. We must, if this waste of power and energy is to be prevented, go back to the Sankey Report and work out a scheme which will lead up by well considered steps and adequate preparation to Nationalization of the industry. There is a general realization amongst Labour that something of this kind is required and that the Government is tinkering. This is producing a state of mind which will I fear lead to an explosion.'

The general stoppage in the coal industry did not begin until April 30, 1926, but it hung like a cloud over the country from the time when on June 30, 1925, the owners issued notices cancelling existing agreements, and announcing that they 'had not seen their way to agree that the state of the industry calls for an adjustment both of wages and of working conditions'. The miners refused to accept this decision, and in July a general stoppage was imminent. The Government then intervened and offered a subsidy to the industry and yet another inquiry into its conditions. This proposal was debated in the Lords in August, when Haldane described this proposal as more tinkering and repeated what he had said in the letter I have quoted above. He mentioned in this speech that Lord Milner had expressed the opinion that nationalization was the only real cure.[1] What he had in mind for coal was a system of national control similar to that he had long advocated for electricity. His Coal Conservation Committee of 1916 had unanimously recommended a large scheme of electrical development centrally controlled, and he had since then been in frequent consultation with experts, and with them had worked out the lines of a definite scheme. When the Labour Government came into office he persuaded his colleagues to take the question up and became a member of a Cabinet Committee which examined the scheme under the chairmanship of Snowden.

The life of the Labour Government was too short, and in its last months it was too much occupied with other things, to allow it to present its proposals in the form of a Bill, but as

[1]*Parliamentary Debates, House of Lords*, vol. 62, p. 788.

soon as Baldwin's Government came in it took up the question where the Labour Government had left it. Baldwin appointed a committee, of which Lord Weir was chairman, to investigate the scheme as then formulated, and its report adopted the Labour Government's proposals with some important improvements. The result was the establishment in 1926 of the Central Electricity Board with power to borrow up to £33,500,000 and the beginning of the grid. Haldane took an active part in helping the Government, which had to face some determined opposition from a section of its followers who represented the private companies, to get the Bill through Parliament.

During the summer and autumn of 1925 Haldane was troubled with his old enemy, rheumatism, and, while nursing his health at Cloan, worked at the last of the philosophical books which he was to publish. This, which he called *Human Experience*, appeared in 1926. It was in its main structure a sequel to *The Reign of Relativity*, but was designed rather for those who were interested in philosophy than for philosophers. His experience of the adult educational movement had taught him that there was an increasing number of working men who had that interest and sought guidance, and *Human Experience* was intended to be an introduction, not only to his own philosophy, but to the works of those philosophers who had been his guides in life. 'The purpose of this book', Haldane said in his introduction, 'is to throw light on the real character of experience. The method employed for this purpose is not merely that which is familiar in psychology, but is the general method which is used in philosophy. For the solution of the problem raised turns out in the end to depend on an answer being found to a fundamental question with which psychology cannot deal, that of the ultimate character of mind itself, as distinguished from what seems to be its various appearances in nature. . . . For many centuries the problem of the nature of mind has been the subject of scrutiny by what are popularly called philosophical methods. What this really means is that the starting point, behind which such methods do not go, because they are forced to assume it as the starting point, is the full world, without and within, as it presents itself for our minds. The task of philosophy has been to disentangle the significance of this world and to discover what is implied in its constitution. That philosophers have differed in their systems does not detract from the fact that for many hundreds of years some of the greatest intellects in history have been concentrated on the task. Despite their differences I believe that they have succeeded in disentangling for us a good deal, and that we cannot to-day neglect the results of a sequence of efforts which have been gigantic. These efforts have generally sought to bring to light tacit assumptions, which have obscured the obvious nature of reality, and have led mankind into a region in which the true character of our actual world has been resolved into unsatisfactory and inadequate abstractions.

'The great problem of the ultimate character of the real remains as interesting to mankind as it ever was. It is the flood of unduly specialized inquiry into it that appears to have produced confusion and uncertainty about the possibility of any solution. And yet our belief in the necessities of a higher life than that of the mere animal demands the attempt at some sort of answer. That is why I have ventured to write, and it is in the hope that the book may not wholly fail to prove suggestive to those who are enquirers that it has been written.'

He returned to his old contention that a great deal of common-sense opinion about the mind and the world and a great deal of accepted scientific knowledge of nature are in reality metaphysics based on no better reasoning. 'We think', he said, 'of minds as things, looking out of boxes, called skulls, on entities which exist in themselves without any relation to knowledge.' He endeavoured to show in language to be understanded of the people that metaphysics was the complement of, and not the enemy of pure scientific research.

'But mind, even in its human form, has a quality that distinguishes it from other external objects. It has implicit in it actually an infinity of range and of forms, and the range of these forms appears implicit in every phase of its activity. Apart from mind as such we do not interpret and fix in even the crudest reflection the most rudimentary feeling. If such feeling is merely attributed by inference and not consciously experienced, we are in the region of what is only a feature of life as such. What biology and physics give us is what is so far inadequate that it does not reach the level of the individual experience in which mind knows itself as itself.'

He concludes the book with a passage more revealing of his attitude to poetry and religion than anything which he had previously written:

'Knowledge, for example, as even introspection discloses it, is not made up of sets of successive series of impressions which can be exhibited as a simple time and space relation of objects external to each other. Mere association is no principle that explains it. For knowledge is that through and in which such association takes place and becomes possible. Do not let us, then, take it to be sufficiently explained as the spatial and temporal association of the ideas which are its objects. Such a method seems to mean that knowledge is being brought under a conception that does not fit it. The result is inevitable failure to grasp what it implies. The universe rests on a foundation of a wider nature than this. To the understanding of that nature we are not helped by methods based on the analogy of those in mathematical physics, confined as these and the conceptions employed by them are to bare order in externally. Moreover the symbols in which the sciences are compelled to express the conceptions they employ are but abstract symbols, inadequate for other phases of the rich world to the interpretation of which in various fashions they are directed. We need not then disturb ourselves when we find in poetry and religion statements made that are lacking in this kind of precision. For it is not such precision we are in search of when we turn to them. What we seek is to have our minds lifted towards the consciousness of new meanings in what is actual, meanings that can only be expressed in pictures of individual form, but which not the less direct us towards the kind of truth we are in search of. That from other standpoints we must be critical of these pictures does not therefore destroy their value for us. The universe is a whole and the truths that it yields to reflection are of different kinds.

'It is of interest to illustrate this principle by reference to its neglect in theology, as much as in the sciences of nature. In current literature some examples of the distorting effects of this neglect are given.

'In his strenuously written book *Lourdes*, Émile Zola tells the story of the cure at Lourdes of the heroine, Marie Guersaint. The majority of the Paris physicians who had seen her had diagnosed a lesion of the marrow, believed to be the result of an accident. They thought the case hopeless, but raised no objection to her being taken to Lourdes. It could do no harm. But another Parisian doctor, who had also seen Marie, took a different view. Like his colleagues he had no faith in the miraculous interpretation by the Church of the processes of the Grotto there. But he differed from their diagnosis. He was of opinion that the case was one of no more than auto-suggestion, brought about by the violent shock of pain produced by the accident. If a sudden and sufficient determination could be induced in the patient to throw off the false idea of physical pain and paralysis, bringing about a will to breathe freely, and suffer no more, then a cure would at once take place. What was essential was the lash of an intense emotion. He therefore not only advised that Marie, who was very religious and capable of intense belief, should be taken to Lourdes, but predicted that if she was, and the emotional conditions were satisfied, she would recover. A devoted Abbé

Pierre and her father escorted her on her journey. She suffered much but became full of faith. At the Grotto, in the midst of a crowd stirred to intense emotion by the priests who addressed it, she suddenly rose and declared, what turned out to be the case, that she was completely cured. The Abbé Pierre, who knew of the dissentient diagnosis, unfortunately indeed for his own peace of mind, could not bring himself to regard the cure as miraculous. It was psychological and it had turned out exactly as the doctor had predicted. The mental bond was broken, but broken by a cause of which science could take account, and which fell within the ordinary laws of nature.

'Now this story of Zola's is an illustration suggesting how easy it is to misconstrue the field of experience by the application to phenomena belonging to one order in it of conceptions belonging to quite a different one. The ecclesiastical authorities at Lourdes had recorded the miracle as the cause where it seemed unnecessary to suppose that there was any miracle at all, or more than what was due to suggestion. A wide enough view of the phenomena of life would have found what occurred to belong to the sequence of these phenomena. But the priests at Lourdes had introduced in religious metaphors mechanical ideals of a cause which not only was outside that order, but was in conflict with it and therefore supernatural. Had they simply insisted on the meaning of religious faith and on its power over the mind, they would have had no need to introduce the idea of a non-natural cause, the direct interference by a physical act of the Virgin with the bodily condition of the patient. But apparently they fell into a paralogism, and into a mistake both of logic and of fact.

'This kind of paralogism is an example of what mankind is highly prone to fall into. People concentrate on a phase in an experience that is of more than one kind, and construe the phenomena which belongs to that phase with the aid of ideas that belong to other and distinct phases. We always tend towards mechanistic notions because they are the simplest, and belong to that domain of time and space as frameworks of the not-self which seems to confront and be independent of us. To turn to causes external to the events we meet with is thus natural, even in the metaphorical reasoning of religion, and we search for such causes in every field of experience, regardless of the question whether it is a field where the idea of externality applies. Even where such ideas are excluded by being superseded, as at times in poetry and in some of the language of the Bible, we find metaphor and simile with some physical reference breaking in; such is the tendency of the unrestrained imagination.'

His old friend and colleague in philosophy, Pringle-Pattison, wrote to him on getting the book:

'A copy of your "confession of faith" from Murray has just crossed my letter to you at Cloan about Berlin and Göttingen. Many thanks; I made it my Sunday reading yesterday. It is a good confession, and the last chapters bear a distinctly personal ring about them which strengthen their appeal. You have spoken frankly on important issues and I find myself in sympathy with what you say about the organism of the soul. Also, though I have "put the case" for personal immortality in my last Giffords—and had previously argued rather passionately for it—I understand your position there also. So far as my own feeling is concerned the question of personal survival does not occupy the place it once did. For the rest, the position you state in this little volume is the one to which you have been singularly constant ever since you began to write. But I think you have brought out more clearly for the reader precisely what you mean by "knowledge"—the abstract term which you have specially used in your recent books. The conceptions in which knowledge consists are shown to be functions of the universal self for which all experience exists. This of course you always im-

plied but I think it is an important help to have it re-emphas-
ized. All that you say on "particularity"—the necessity of
that element in finite experience should also be useful as an
answer in advance to the misconception of Idealism as an
"unearthly ballet of bloodless categories". Altogether it was
worth putting the position, as it is put here, in shorter com-
pass and with its important personal application.'

Haldane's health had sufficiently recovered when the session of 1926 opened for him to resume his place in the Lords
as Leader of the Opposition and to return to his work on the
Committee of Imperial Defence. He was again invited to join
the Committee of Civil Research, for the purpose of ex-
amining the recommendations of the Royal Commission on
the Coal Industry for the establishment of a National Fuel and
Power Committee, of which as we know he was a warm
advocate. He resumed work on this problem with enthusiasm
but with no result. The Government had its hands full and
was in no mood to take up a question which bristled with
thorns, and in fact the General Strike removed the problem,
for the time being, from the sphere of practical politics. The
General Strike was a heavy blow to Haldane. Every effort to
bring owners and miners together had failed. The men refused to accept the terms which the owners insisted were
essential in the economic condition of the industry, and on
April 30 the lock-out notice, which the owners issued, took
effect. There was a complete stoppage in the coal industry.
The Government thereupon issued a Royal Proclamation
declaring that a state of emergency existed and bringing into
operation the Emergency Powers Act of 1920. The general
Council of the Trades Union replied by ordering a general
strike to begin at midnight on May 3 if the owners' notices
had not been withdrawn by that time. Tempers were
strained, and while negotiations were still pending, on the
night of May 2 the compositors of the *Daily Mail* refused to
set up in type some sentences which they held to be insulting

to the workers. The Prime Minister took this to be a challenge and negotiations broke down. Haldane, who had maintained consistently that the Government was to blame because it had not tackled the problem of the coal industry as a whole, and had disregarded the recommendations of the Sankey Report, had a good deal of sympathy with the men, while he thought that the Trades Union Council had been foolish. He put this view in a speech in the Lords on May 4 in which he accused the Government of shutting and barring the door to negotiations. He quoted the last paragraph of a communiqué which the Government had issued the day before. This, after referring to the *Daily Mail* incident as gross interference with the liberty of the press, goes on:

'Such action involves a challenge to the rights and freedom of the nation. His Majesty's Government, therefore, before it can continue negotiations must require from the Trades Union Committee both a repudiation of the actions referred to that have already taken place, and the immediate and unconditional withdrawal of the instructions for a General Strike.'

'If any step', said Haldane, 'could have been chosen which was most likely to put an end to every chance of peace than the latter part of that communiqué which I have just read, I do not know it.' For once Haldane was wrong in his facts and the next day Lord Birkenhead had no difficulty in showing that the Trades Union Council had issued orders for the General Strike before the Government issued its communiqué, and in the discussion between the two Haldane had definitely the worst of the argument.

In spite of this 1926 was a happy year for him. In the summer volumes 30 to 33 of the series of documents prepared by the German Foreign Office relating to the Great War were published. This contained a full and accurate account from the German end of Haldane's mission to Berlin in 1912. These were reviewed at length in *The Times*, which had been one of

the leaders in the attacks on him, and now generously admitted that it had been wrong, while sticking to its contention
that the country had not been warned of the danger which
the failure of the mission made inevitable. He must have
chuckled when he heard a Conservative War Minister announce formally that the Territorial Army was henceforth to
be the recognized means of expansion of the Regular Army
in a national emergency, and was delighted to get two letters.
The first came from Lord Dartmouth:

'Owing to a breakdown in health I have had to give up a
good many of my Chairmanships, including the Chairmanship of the Council of the Territorial Association, which I
regret.

'In going through some old papers I came across the heated
controversy which took place when your scheme was first
brought forward. It makes interesting reading to-day. The
three principal criticisms were:

'1. That a force raised as the Territorial Force was to be
raised, and trained as the T.F. was to be trained, would in the
day of emergency, instead of an asset, prove to be an incumbrance, and possibly even a danger.

'2. That if it should ever become necessary to mobilize
the Territorial Force, which God forbid, the crazy structure
would collapse from its own weight.

'3. That it was absurd to think that in the event of war the
enemy would give time for the six months' intensive training,
which was a large part of Lord Haldane's Scheme.

'With regard to 1, events have proved that so far from
being an incumbrance the "T" that marked the Territorial
has become a badge of distinction instead of a mark of
contempt.

'With regard to 2, we know from Lord Ypres' despatches
that the mobilization of the T.F. made it possible to send out
the Expeditionary Force in the earliest days of the war, while
the mobilization itself, although of course there were hitches

here and there, was carried out with an efficiency that I look upon as one of the longest feathers in the cap of the Territorial Associations.

'With regard to 3, it is an interesting fact that the North Midland Division, when it left these shores, had had a full six months' intensive training and a little more besides. I do not remember any far reaching scheme so riddled with criticism when it first saw the light, that in the end so fully justified the intentions of its Inventor. I am glad to think that, personally, I had something to do with the raising of the Force, and have never wavered in the high opinion that I held and hold of the value of the Territorial Soldier, and I should like to conclude with a note of very sincere gratitude to you as Originator of the Movement.'

The second, which came to him on his seventieth birthday, was from Sir Herbert Creedy, the Permanent Under-Secretary of State at the War Office:

'The Army Council send you their cordial congratulations and best wishes on the occasion of to-day's anniversary. Even now it is not sufficiently recognized outside how much is owed to you for your administration of the Army during the eventful years of your Secretaryship of State, but all of us who have been behind the scenes remember your work with admiration and gratitude and think of you with regard and affection.'

Chapter IX

LAST YEARS

1927 to 1928

Parliament met for the spring session of 1927 with a general desire to forget the past and promote industrial peace, though there were a few of the Conservative right wing who wished to make the most of the defeat of Labour in the General Strike. It happened that one member of that group drew a lucky number in the ballot for private members motions, and on February 18 he moved the second reading of a Bill to make it illegal for trades unions or their members to invite or accept funds from foreign sources. The Government left the motion to a free vote of the House but put up the Home Secretary, Sir Joynson-Hicks, to oppose it. The Home Secretary said that the Government drew a sharp distinction between strikes for political and for industrial objects, and that if this motion were accepted they would be justifying the accusation brought by the Labour Party that Conservatives were the enemies of the trades unions and meant to strike a blow at their existence. It was, he said, the declared policy of the Conservative Party to do nothing to hamper the industrial development of trades unions.

The next day Haldane wrote to his sister: 'I was in the gallery of the Commons yesterday more by chance than by design. I went there to talk with a couple of people about the Institute of Adult Education. As we agreed, I have now to give up some things, and I am looking for a successor as President. I stayed to listen to an attack on Trades Unions by a

Tory die-hard. These gentlemen like the Bourbons never forgive and never forget. Joynson-Hicks made an excellent speech and the motion was heavily defeated. Baldwin is doing very well. He became the Conservative leader almost by accident, but they could not have found a better man for the times. He is very human and has wide sympathies, and he won't allow his wild men to exacerbate the Opposition. He understands that the Labour men who sit opposite him often put good cases badly and at the wrong time, but that the cases are good and that Labour is in earnest about things that are worth while. Besides this he has plenty of courage and won't be browbeaten by the Press Peers.'

A few weeks later, on March 16, there was a debate in the Lords on national economy, the Earl of Midleton moving a motion calling on the Government to take immediate steps to curtail national and local expenditure and to reduce the staffs of the public departments. This brought Haldane to his feet on behalf of a favourite theory of his, that the right way to get economies is not to impose it from above but to enlist the co-operation of the spenders:

'I remember very well that years ago when I was at the War Office it was necessary to effect a considerable reduction in the Estimates. I thought it ought to be effected. I brought it up to the Generals in the Army Council and was told: "It cannot be done; we have looked into it everywhere; we can get nothing down and we shall want £3,000,000 more." I then saw them one by one and said: "We shall never get anything done in this way. You do not know whether there are possibilities of reduction, not even all the heads of Departments immediately under you know, but set to work, see your heads of Departments individually, take them into your confidence, do not bully them, do not order them about, reason with them and ask them to co-operate in a common policy; they will do the same with the people under them and you will get down at last to surprising economies; at least that is my strong suspicion." They were doubtful at first. They went away and came back after an interval and said: "It has turned out exactly so, expenditure and extravagance are going on right deep down at places where we could not get to, the heads are now seeing that it is so and those under them are working to effect economies and the money that is wanted to come off will come off."

'The noble Earl, Lord Midleton, spoke of the number of troops being reduced. The number of troops is reduced as compared with the year of which he spoke, but then he said that the staffs have gone up very much. Yes, they have, and that is one reason why the number of troops can be less to-day than it used to be. War, like industry, is a matter of thinking and planning, of working out things in detail, and, therefore, it is necessary to think and to employ skilled thinkers to an extent that was never the case in the old days. That being so, the matter is not disposed of by Lord Midleton's suggestion that the staffs have gone up very much. Of course the staffs have gone up very much. There is an enormous deal more of work that has to be done by the staffs than there was in the old days. The conduct of war depends on that, and if we had not had these staffs and had not had Generals trained in the highest degree in these methods— Generals Lord French and Lord Haig—we should have been defeated in many of the battles that we had to fight in the late War. As it was our Generals, I think, were trained in the study of military science in a way which showed them to be equal to those German Generals to whom they were opposed.

'What is the moral of that? The moral is that if you are really keen about economy, if you want to bring about these things of which the noble Earl spoke, you cannot do it merely by doing sums, merely by arithmetical methods. What you have to do is to put your soul into the business of inquiry. You have to take people into confidence and work with them in confidence. I have had a good deal to do with the Civil Service. I was Chairman of an organization of the Civil Service for a good many years and I think I am still. I see their work and I see what they are doing just now. There is no body that is advancing more in its ideas and in its methods than the Civil Service. They meet, they read papers on this great question, their leaders come among them and talk to them. There is an intelligent spirit among the members of the Civil Service such as did not exist a few years ago. Why not apply the only method that is effective in getting economy to the Civil Service? Take their chiefs into consultation. Do not let the Chancellor of the Exchequer utter a ukase and say that the Expenditure of the country is to come down so much, only to be defeated. The far better course for the Chancellor of the Exchequer and the other Ministers is to take the Civil Service, or rather its heads much more closely into confidence, and to ask them to take their own subordinates into confidence until there penetrates right through the body of the Civil Service a desire to carry out the common policy of which I spoke.'

As he had said in his letter to his sister Haldane had at last agreed with his friends that with seventy years behind him and with failing health he could not go on working as he had been doing almost continuously from the time when he was a student at Edinburgh, and that he must hand over some of his children to others. He had for some time been suffering from diabetes, and his doctor was constantly urging him to rest. So in 1927 he resigned the Presidency of the Institute of Adult Education, in the foundation of which he had been the prime mover, and he induced Mr. Oliver Stanley to take his place. Since the days when, as a young lawyer, he had gone to the Working Men's College to give a course of lectures on philosophy, the Adult Education movement had developed out of all recognition. Then there had been a few thousand working men students in institutions founded and supported by a few enthusiasts, and the teachers were for the most part unpaid. There was no recognition or help from the State.

Now, in 1927, there were in the administrative county of London alone just under 12,000 organized classes dealing with just under 200,000 students over eighteen years of age, not being students of any university. The movement was officially sponsored by the Board of Education, which made grants on special conditions, and had established as part of its machinery a Consultative Adult Education Committee. The great majority of the Local Education authorities of the country had admitted adult education to a place in their educational programmes, and provided funds. Every university throughout the country had responded to Haldane's appeal that the universities should widen their borders to provide facilities for extra-mural students.

Apart from but contemporary with the development of part-time tutorial and other classes for men and women engaged in work in the day-time a whole crop of residential colleges for working men had sprung up; Avoncroft College in Worcestershire; Holyoake House in Manchester; Fircroft, which was due to the enterprise and benevolence of the Cadburys, at Bourneville; Holybrooke House, Reading; Ruskin College, Oxford, and Woodbrooke at Birmingham. The latest of these, Coleg Harlech, which had developed out of Haldane's reorganization of the University of Wales, and owed much to Lord Davies, came into existence in 1927, with Haldane as its first President.

All this was the result of real hard work. In his campaign for adult education he had in the course of some thirty years given more than a thousand addresses on behalf of the movement, and this in the midst of a vast deal of work of national importance. He had linked with this campaign his other campaign for the extension of university education, for he had seen that the two movements should go hand in hand and that the new universities would supply the tutors he wanted for his adult education classes. His one regret when he resigned from the Institute of Adult Education was that he had not been able to persuade the Board of Education to provide more than what he held to be a miserable pittance, for men and women who were doing work which he regarded as of the first importance to the nation. Of his work for and in the British Institute of Adult Education I cannot do better than quote the tribute of his enthusiastic fellow worker, Albert Mansbridge, in the number of the *Journal of Adult Education* which followed on Haldane's retirement:

'From the actual moment of its inception Lord Haldane became the vital head and leader of the British Institute. The details of its formation were thrashed out in his own study at 28 Queen Annes Gate. In effect it was part of a larger scheme put before him, dealing with education as a whole, some of the salient features of which it preserved. Directly the simple lines of construction were made clear and he approved them, no effort of time or thought on his part was lacking. That gracious hospitality, so characteristic of him, was extended to anyone likely to be interested and helpful. Most of those who assembled round his table became persistent workers in the cause of Adult Education. He sought out young politicians as well as old. Journalists were induced to believe, and to act on the belief, that Adult Education really counted. Round the fireside at Queen Annes Gate in the winter of 1920, the ideals of the Movement were expressed clearly and drew many to their service.

'He had been interested in the World Association also from its inception, and he used his influence to secure sufficient financial support from the outset. It was his own idea that the British Institute should be actually projected by the World Association, for his practical mind realized the great advantages of having, during its early years, the support and nurture which an existing institution could give.

'The formation of the British Institution, and his consistent support of the World Association and of the Workers' Educational Association are, however, small matters compared with the prophetic insight which he had into reality, the uniform self-sacrifice which characterized his attitude to those who desired the best he could give, the power of inspiration which he exercised, and the everyday common sense which he brought to bear upon all details.

'The philosophic temper of his mind prevented his ever being disturbed by transitory happenings, and he held steadily to the even tenour of his way. It was this that made him so supremely helpful to men and women dealing with wayward details and apt to be depressed when the burden and heat of everyday work beset them.

'Of the work of Lord Haldane for national education much could be written. To some it seems a national tragedy that he never was President of the Board of Education, but one thing is certain, that no one exercised a greater influence than he did on the public educational policy of recent years.

'It was not always that his ideas were adopted. His scheme of Provincial Councils never came to birth, but it was his unflinching and fearless advocacy of the necessity of developing reform that largely made possible the Education Act of 1918.

'His interest in Adult Education was lifelong. It was his teaching that helped to inspire the initial steps taken to found the Workers' Educational Association. A quotation from one of his books, *Education and Empire*, precedes the first public expression of the plan to unite Labour and Learning in a definite Association: "Educate your people and you have reduced to comparatively insignificant dimensions the problems of temperance, of housing, and of raising the condition of your masses."

'In common with Lord Balfour, Lord Oxford, and Mr. Ramsay MacDonald, he lent his support and assistance to the successful carrying out of the notable lectures on "Parliament" given to thousands of working men and women, as many indeed as could be admitted, on June Saturdays, in 1908 and 1909, in the Royal Gallery of the House of Lords, by Dr.

Masterman. His urbanity and persistence when afflicted by sportsmanlike suffragettes as he sought to speak about the Adult Education they actually approved and supported, were symbolic of his whole mental attitude, unruffled then by little things, but to be tried to the utmost by the catastrophic events which were even then casting their shadows before.

'It was in April 1913, that he expressed clearly the reality of his attitude to the whole matter—an attitude which remained unchanged to the very last of his days in London, when he met, feeble as he was, a small group of people eager to honour another consistent friend of Adult Education—the retiring Archbishop of Canterbury.

'A few sentences from reported notes of a speech which he made at the Working Men's College on April 22, 1913, will bring this attitude of his into clear light.

'Referring to a previous speaker, he said that it was not to the intellect merely, that he was seeking to appeal; it was to the real man and the best of the real man.

'"Ah! that is just it! Latent in everybody, reachable in very many, is a spark of idealism which you can touch, be it adult rural labourer or be it professor. You can rouse it, and you can get it to flame up. If you do that you have a great moving force in the individual, and if you get it in many individuals you have a great moving force in the nation.

'"It is possible if you have the genius to do it, to appea successfully to almost everybody; it is certainly possible to appeal successfully to a great many. Borne down though they may be by the weight of worldliness that rests upon their shoulders, indifferent as they may seem to the highest things of the spirit, yet these things are there with them, and if you can just break through the crust, if you can just get them for a moment, then you have awakened a great force which, if you can waken it sufficiently, will transform society. That is the secret of national education; to ask the highest, to ask the best, and to base your movement upon nothing short of idealism. That may seem a hard task, and it may look as if the quality was not present extensively. But it is not so really.

' "We are deeply responsible, I am responsible, you are responsible, all of us who have opportunities of appealing to people. It can be done; it is possible, and the fault is ours, or the defect at least is ours, if we are not capable of doing it. Yes it is a steep road that we have in front of us, and a pretty long road, but there are forces that can take us up to it and on to its very end, if we have only faith in these forces and can evoke it in the people themselves, and there is plenty of idealism in the people if we only know how to awaken it. That is why this Workers' Educational Association, since I came to know something of it, has appealed to me very much. National Education is a very wide subject; there is very little which it does not cover. It is not a matter of the intellect only; it is not a matter of the mind; it is not a matter of the religious side; it is not a matter of the physical side only, but it is all these phases of life, without which you do not get the perfect man or woman, which have to be called out and evoked and put together in their proportions and in their places in a great scheme by which what is best in everybody may have a chance of being called forth. It is a very great undertaking and will cost a very great deal of money. The work will only be done if the nation is behind the movement for its own education, and the nation will only be behind the movement for its own education if we do our work in appealing to the nation and if we put our appeals high enough. That is why I value the work of this Association so much, because it has appealed to the higher cause, it has put education not on merely utilitarian grounds—it has made it an affair of the spirit. Do not think that I neglect the utilitarian side of education. It is not the only side, nor is it the highest side, nor the most convincing side; the highest and most convincing side is the side which appeals to the best elements in people and which puts before them education as something not confined to this or that phase of spiritual life, which does not limit itself to training to this or that attitude, but which seeks to develop and to make them citizens of the highest type, men and women who take that large view which shows them to their neighbours as themselves, and shows them in the common life of the city something that causes them to put forward the utmost endeavour that is in them. I believe that a great time is coming to this nation, a time of awakening; there may be years to elapse, but the beginning of the twentieth century has seen a new standard brought before our eyes. Let us see to it, one and all, whoever we may be, and whatever our opportunities, that we realize our great responsibility, a responsibility to do nothing less than the utmost within us, each one who can influence those with whom he comes in contact." '

On hearing of his retirement Dr. Lang, then Archbishop of York, and now Archbishop of Canterbury, wrote to Haldane: 'I see that on May 6 you will address the British Institute of Adult Education for the last time as its President. I am very sorry that I cannot be present, but I am constrained to write this word as one who shares your faith in and your enthusiasm for the cause of Adult Education. To you all the comrades of the cause owe a debt which cannot be measured for the leadership, ideals, hopes and efforts which you have given to it. I only wish that my overcrowded life had been able to find more space for association with this great movement. But my heart is in it, and that is why I write. I am glad to think that your name as Honorary Life President will still be at the head of the movement.'

In June a three-power conference on naval disarmament between Great Britain, the United States, and Japan, with France and Italy as interested observers, had met at Geneva. It resulted in a complete deadlock between Great Britain and the United States, which, soon after the conference broke up, announced a formidable programme of naval expansion.

Lord Cecil, who as Chancellor of the Duchy of Lancaster was a member of Baldwin's Cabinet, resigned as an expression of his disagreement with the foreign policy of the Government in general and in particular with the way in which the Naval Conference had been handled. Haldane's criticism of the Government was that there had not been sufficient diplomatic preparation with the United States before the Conference met and insufficient use made of the Committee of Imperial Defence. He said so in a debate on the failure of the conference which took place in the Lords on November 10.

'When the noble Earl opposite[1] went to Washington, where he negotiated with such conspicuous success in 1921, the ground was to a considerable extent known before he got there and when he got there he was able to use his materials. But at Geneva one has the impression—at least I have the impression—that the naval proposals were too much thrown at the heads of the people with whom we were dealing. The question of disarmament is a very difficult one, because it depends on the special circumstances of several Powers—circumstances which may be different in each case. There was no difficulty here, I gather, with Japan. Admiral Saito was able to concur in the proposals which were brought forward by Mr. Bridgeman,[2] or at least it appeared so. The difficulty came from the United States, and why did it come from the United States? I think very largely because there had not been nearly enough of that preliminary discussion which is essential if you are to have a good chance of getting an agreement. To my mind, as I have said, the proposal of the noble and gallant Lord,[3] that we should withdraw from the Declaration of Paris, would have been fatal to any chance of getting American acceptance of our proposals, but I go further than that. I think that these proposals have to be put forward on a wider

[1]Lord Balfour.   [2]Then First Lord of the Admiralty.
[3]Admiral Lord Wester Wemyss.

basis than that of merely naval efficiency. Naval efficiency, yes. You want the guidance of the Navy in your specific proposals. You want the guidance of the Navy to tell you how far you may go and why you may go no farther; but when you have got these technical details—and they are very technical—they have to be turned into another form. What I would have wished to see done before we raised this question at Geneva at all was that our plans and our necessities should have been fully described in a document prepared, not by the Admiralty—prepared with the assistance of the Admiralty, if you like, but prepared by the Government of the day, and, by preference, with the aid of the Committee of Imperial Defence, and that document should have gone into all the wide questions of policy, which proposals of disarmament raise. For instance there was the question of 8-inch guns on cruisers. We probably could have given good reasons both for thinking that we wanted a number of cruisers more than were to be willingly conceded to us and that we could do with smaller guns, but I should have liked to see that reasoned out, and I should have liked the Americans on the other side to have reasoned out their case for having 8-inch guns instead of smaller guns. I do not mean that these things should be merely technically set out, but I do mean that they should be set out in a document of a diplomatic character having such persuasive powers as there could not be if it was merely a departmental matter. The misery of Geneva was that it was an Admiralty affair, and in saying that I am not reflecting in any way on Mr. Bridgeman, who, I think, showed great temper and tact, or on Mr. Gibson.[1] It is simply that if you are going to hope for an agreement on a matter so complicated as relative disarmament it seems to me to be essential that you should negotiate it out beforehand and negotiate it out diplomatically as well as technically.

'It was a mistake to go to Geneva until you had come to a

[1] The representative of the U.S.A. at the conference.

preliminary agreement. If the noble Earl opposite could have taken himself to Washington and with his persuasive powers put these things forward, I think it is possible we might have come to a basis which could have been turned into an agreement at Geneva, but I am not at all surprised when I read of the way in which the thing was, as it were, in the most polite and persuasive and kindly manner thrown at the head of the Americans, that they should not have agreed. The Americans on the other hand did not give us any materials on which we could say whether we differed or not. The result is that until the matter is taken in hand in another way I am not very hopeful of getting disarmament of any consequence at Geneva. That does not mean that I am hopeless about the situation. Mr. Bridgeman ended in a really good temper the third of his speeches, and I do not see why this matter should not come on again. I do not see why it should not be resumed, and I hope that when it is resumed it will be resumed in the fashion that I have spoken of, in the manner of preparing the requisite documents diplomatically and with the aid of the Committee of Imperial Defence. Then you will get the whole of the technical assistance from the Admiralty, as at present, but you will also get other assistance, and the whole thing will be looked at from a wider point of view. You will have a chance of sending something in advance to the United States and of seeing how far it is possible to negotiate an agreement between yourselves and the United States on broad lines. Only do not take it to Geneva until you have done that.'

But the Labour Party wanted to go much further than its leader in the House of Lords, and on November 24 Mac-Donald moved a vote of censure on the Government for its lukewarmness in the cause of peace and disarmament. In his speech MacDonald returned to his advocacy of the Geneva Protocol and charged the Government with insincerity in the professed desire to promote peace and assist disarmament, in that it had not signed the Optional Clause of the Covenant committing us to arbitration.

In reply to this last point Austen Chamberlain said:

'The case on this point was stated so lucidly, so clearly, and so temperately by the late Lord Chancellor, Lord Haldane, in a paper which he left on record when he went out of office, that I asked his permission to quote this paper to-day, if I found it necessary or useful in this debate, and I have his permission to quote it and to lay the paper if it be demanded, in accordance with the usual practice. This is a paper which expresses, of course, the personal view of Lord Haldane. It does in fact coincide with the view taken by His Majesty's present advisers, and it sets out in terms so clear, and as I said, so moderate, that I think it is better than any words I myself could employ.

'He says: "At first sight it appears natural to give the Court compulsory authority in as many cases as possible, for it looks as though by doing so the dispute which might lead to war will most effectually be avoided. In the instances of small states with unitary Constitutions this seems true, for the jurisdiction could strengthen their position against more powerful nations, but in the instance of the British Empire it is not so clear that this is true. In substance the Constitution of our Empire is not unitary, and it is perilous for the Imperial Government to proceed as if it were. We have to secure the assent of the Dominions and of India at every step. An analogous difficulty has confronted the United States. The Executive does not dare to give undertakings unless the President is sure, which he rarely is, that the Legislature will adopt his actions. That is the real reason why the President, however disposed to arbitration treaties, will rarely join them. In the case of Great Britain and the United States alike, it is thus for reasons which, although not the same, are analogous, undesirable to give an unqualified undertaking which it may afterwards prove to be impracticable to fulfil. The condition of things in the event of failure is apt to show itself more provocative of insoluble dispute than if no unqualified undertaking had been given."

'Later in the same paper he says: "Speaking for myself, I think it safer, in the present state of the Constitution of our Empire, to avoid trying to go further than the Covenant of the League of Nations. This Article binds us to arbitrate on any matter that is suitable, and which diplomacy cannot satisfactorily settle, including the interpretation of treaties, questions of international law, the existence of facts constituting a breach of international obligations, and the extent of the reparation to be made. The language used in this Article is less stringent than in Article 36 of the Protocol of 1920, and gives rise to less embarrassment. I agree with Lord Balfour in his suggestion of 1920 that resort to the Permanent Court is likely by degrees to become more and more general, and in the end it will probably become compulsory, but this requires time to enable a firm conception of Empire fully to become familiar to our own people. At present I am adverse to the explicit acceptance of a principle which will probably give rise, if so accepted, to keen controversy."

'Those are broadly the reasons which have commended themselves to His Majesty's present Government when they also had to give their attention to this matter. Perhaps I ought to add that it is, I believe, common ground to all parties in this country that even if we did sign the optional clause we should sign it only with reservations. I do not want to delay the House with a long list, but I would beg hon. members to consider for themselves what some of those reservations must be. At present there is no great body of law on the subject of naval belligerent rights. We should not know what law would be administered, and I believe it to be common ground to all parties that we should have to reserve that subject. We should have to reserve everything which concerned the relations of the Empire *inter se*. We should have to make it perfectly clear that we did not arbitrate on internal matters within the sovereign jurisdiction of the State itself; and perhaps there would be other reservations.'

The memorandum which Austen Chamberlain quoted had been prepared by Haldane as Lord Chancellor for the information of the Foreign Office. It expressed the view which Haldane held consistently that we are far too prone to look on our problems from the point of view of Great Britain and not from that of the British Empire. As we have seen, his opposition to a Ministry of Defence was based, not on the grounds that such a ministry would be unsuited to Great Britain but that it was unsuited to the British Empire. But, not unnaturally, the Labour Party was seriously annoyed to find that its leader in the House of Lords had supplied the Foreign Minister with some particularly effective ammunition. MacDonald thereupon wrote to Haldane:

'I wonder if you could throw some light upon an incident which happened in the debate here on Thursday as it has given rise to much concern in the Party and several members have spoken to me about it. Without giving me any warning Sir Austen Chamberlain produced a secret memorandum written by you on arbitration for the Cabinet, which he said you had allowed him to read if he found it useful in replying to us. Am I not right that permission to disclose such memoranda must be got from the Prime Minister in office at the time, and that certainly if it is to be used against him some warning should be given to him? We had other memoranda both to an opposite effect and also showing how your points could be dealt with. Nor did my fix end by its sudden production in debate. In the ordinary way I should ask for its publication but that would do no good without the publication of those stating another view. I think you will agree with me that if this is to be used as a precedent the door to serious abuse will be opened, and it will be dangerous in a high degree for any Government to ask for differing views so as to guide it to sound conclusions. I am sure you will also agree that no colleague should arm an opposition with material to discredit or embarrass other colleagues knowing, as Sir Austen Chamberlain said, that he was doing so. Our men feel that I was badly let down, and I cannot help feeling that some mistake was made.'

To this Haldane replied that the memorandum which Austen Chamberlain had quoted was a legal opinion of his which was in the files of the Foreign Office and that he had told the Foreign Minister that he could use it 'in accordance with the usual practice', as he would use any other legal opinion. MacDonald was not satisfied with this and wrote again on December 2:

'It was impossible for Sir Austen Chamberlain to quote your document on Thursday without using it as a stick with which to beat us. It was no use except for that purpose. It was meant by him to be part of his reply to the Labour Party's resolution. He could quite easily have expressed your views in his own words without quoting you or dragging you in. He used your memorandum only to confound us with specially disconcerting force, and had you been present and heard the laughing jeers of the House and seen the other evidence of glee on the part of the Tory Party, you could have had no mistake whatever about how you were being used.

'I still hold that, under such circumstances, (a) I ought to have been warned that the document was to be used and (b) it ought not to have been disclosed without my knowledge and consent.

'Your quotation "in accordance with the usual practice" is taken from its context. Sir Austen did not say that he was quoting it in that way, but he said, after having quoted it, that he would publish the document if I cared "in accordance with the usual practice". That is quite different. We knew perfectly well that your document was one of several in the Foreign

Office files expressing different points of view and presenting facts in different relations, and in inviting me to request him to publish it he was also aware that that would only play into his hands and hide up the completeness of the survey which the question underwent under my hands. To publish yours alone, as he suggested that I should ask him to do, would have been a still graver injustice to colleagues and to myself.

'However, it is now too late to do anything. I have heard from Sir Austen, and, though he admits no fault, he is apparently not too comfortable and suggests that I see the Prime Minister on the whole question of the disclosure of such documents. He is apparently aware of the mess that would be made if his successor were to follow his example. The Party is very angry about the incident and I must do my best to pacify the members.'

This ruffled Haldane, who wrote on December 4:

'MY DEAR MacDONALD

'Thank you for your letter of the 2nd. I cannot modify my view that the point is one, not of policy, but of law pure and simple. It was as a Law Officer that I advised the Foreign Office and I am not aware that they have in their records any opinions to a different effect. My views were well known and I think that the Foreign Office was within its rights in relying on these and citing them from its own records.

'But that is not the most serious thing. I gather from what you write that there are members of the Party who think that when opinions on such legal and constitutional subjects are expressed by any of my colleagues in the House of Lords, I should remain silent and seem to acquiesce in them. Now this I cannot consent to do. It was not on this footing that I undertook to lead the Labour Party in the House of Lords. I have tried hard to avoid friction in every way I could, I am willing to continue to try to do so, but only on the footing that I am not to be compelled to leave myself in a false position. Such a line of contact could only destroy any influence I have in that Chamber. I think, therefore, it would be well if you would release me from my position as leader there. I hate resignations and I am quite as deeply attached to the ideals of the Labour movement as when I joined the Government, but I feel that I can be more influential as a supporter of these ideals if I support them independently, no longer sitting on the front bench and exposed to misconstruction. Considerations of health as well as those I have indicated, induce me to take the step suggested. I am only restrained by my dislike of appearing to run away. I have no desire to do anything of the kind, but you may well think that as I cannot give a more definite undertaking I had better not be there so it remains with you to decide.'

MacDonald answered the next day:

'I have your letter of yesterday and am grateful to you for it. The two little bits of friction that have arisen are however quite distinct. Of the one in which I am concerned I have said my last word. It is past.

'As regards the other I have refused to let it come before us, holding that it ought to be dealt with by yourselves,[1] which I am told has been done. The question of consultation has worried me a good deal and I have well understood your difficulties. But there we are, both busy and occupied all day long with rarely a chance of meeting. Was Party ever so run? Can one make a living and head a Party as well? I doubt it. I have nothing but thoughts of gratitude and admiration for your forbearance with me.

'So, as these things have been got over, hadn't you just better go on and see how events go? The air is probably cleared for some time, and both Parmoor and Arnold assure me that they are content with matters as they now stand.

[1] The Labour Press.

Neither you nor I are what we were in health and we may soon have to recognize it in a mournful way. But, my dear Haldane, not to-day—not yet. I shall be glad and obliged if you would fall in with this view.'

So peace was restored and Haldane agreed to go on, but it is clear from this correspondence that his natural disregard of, and even contempt for, the exigences of party warfare made him at times a difficult colleague, and that he was far from comfortable in his position in the Lords.

Though this difference with MacDonald had its origin in his disagreement with the terms of the Protocol which the great majority of his colleagues in the Labour Government supported, this did not mean that he had wavered in his faith in the League of Nations. In his address to the American Bar Association in Montreal in 1913 he had said: 'Recent events in Europe and the way in which the Great Powers have worked together to preserve the peace of Europe, as if forming one community, point to the ethical possibility of the group system as deserving close study by both statesmen and students. The *Sittlichkeit* which can develop itself between the peoples of even a loosely connected group seems to promise a sanction for international obligations which has not hitherto, as far as I know, attracted attention in connection with international Law.'[1] In the last paper he wrote in April 1915 as a Cabinet Minister in Asquith's Government he had insisted that when the war ended the treaties of peace should include provision for an association of nations which should provide a permanent organization for the common study of international problems. In 1920 he had concluded his *Before the War* in these words:

'The spirit is at least as important as the letter in the doctrine of a League of Nations. Such a League has for its main purpose the supersession of the old principle of balancing the Powers. In the absence of a League of Nations, or—what is

[1]*Haldane*, vol. I, p. 336.

the same thing in a less organized form—of an entente or concert of Powers so general that none are left shut out from it, the principle of balancing may have to be relied on. I believe this to have been unavoidable when the entente between France, Russia and Great Britain was found to be required for safety if the tendency to dominate of the Triple Alliance was to be held in check. But in that case, and probably in every other case, reliance on the principle could only be admissible for self-protection and never for the mere exhibition of the power of the sword. If the principle is resorted to with the latter object the group that is suspected of aggressive intentions will by degrees find itself confronted with another group of nations that have huddled together for self-protection and may become very strong just because they have a moral justification for their action. It was this that happened before the war broke out in 1914, and it was the state of tension which ensued which led up to that war. Had there been no counter-grouping to that of the Central Powers there would probably have been war all the same, but with this difference, that defeat and not victory would have been the lot of the Entente Powers.

'Now the German-speaking peoples in the world amount to an enormous number, at least to a hundred millions, if those outside Germany and Austria, and in the New World as well as the Old are taken into account. It may be difficult for them to organize themselves for war, but it will be less difficult for them to develop a common spirit which may penetrate all over the world. It is just this development that statesmen ought to watch carefully, for, given an interval long enough, it is impossible to predict what influence these hundred millions of people may not acquire and come to exercise. We do not want to have a prolonged period of growing anxiety and unrest, such as obtained in our relations with the French, notwithstanding the peace established by the Treaty of Vienna. Of the anxiety and unrest which were ours for

more than one generation, the history of the Channel fortifi-
cations, of the Volunteer force and of several other great and
often costly institutions, bears witness. Let us therefore take
thought while there is time to do so. We do not wish to see
repeated anything analogous to our former experience. The
one thing that can avert it is the spirit in which the League of
Nations has been brought to birth. That spirit alone can pre-
clude the gradual nascence of desire to call into existence a
new balance of power. It is not enough to tell Germany and
Austria that if they behave well they will be admitted to the
League of Nations. What really matters is the feeling and
manner in which the invitation is given, and an obvious sincerity in the desire that they should work with us as equals in
a common endeavour to make the best of a world that contains us both. One is quite conscious of the difficulties that
must attend the attempt to approach the question in the frame
of mind that is requisite. We may have to discipline ourselves
considerably. But the people of this country are capable of
reflection, and so are the people of the American Continent.
The problem to be solved is one that presses on our great
Allies in the United States, where the German-speaking population is very large, quite as much as it does on us. France and
Belgium have more to forgive, and France has a hard past
from which to avert her eyes. But she is a country of great
intelligence, and it is for the sake of everybody, and not
merely in the interest of our recent enemies, that enlargement
of the spirit is requisite.

'How the present situation is to be softened, how the
people of the Central Powers are to be brought to feel that
they are not to remain divided from us by an impassable gulf,
this is not the occasion to suggest. It is enough to repeat that
the question is not one simply of the letter of a treaty but is
one of the spirit in which it is made. Conditions change in this
world with a rapidity that is often startling. The fashion of
the day passes before we know that what is novel and was un-

expected has come upon us. The foundations of a peace that is to be enduring must therefore be sought in what is highest and most abiding in human nature.'[1]

At the end of the session of 1927 both the country and Parliament were stirred and excited by the Prayerbook Measure, which was sent up to Parliament by the Church Assembly. The Measure was approved by a large majority in the Lords but defeated by a small majority in the Commons. Of the debates in both Houses Haldane wrote to his sister on December 16, the day after the Bill had been defeated in the Commons:

'We are said as a people to be becoming less and less religious, but both Parliament and the country were as much moved by the proposal to revise the Prayer Book of the Church of England as it was by the General Strike. I have not seen the Lords so full since I became a peer. As a Scot I took no part in the debate. Randall Davidson presented his case with his usual skill. There is I think no doubt that many of the rubrics of the prayer book are out of date and cannot to-day be rigidly enforced, nor is there any doubt, in my mind, that much of the language of the prayer book, beautiful as it is, is not understanded of the people, and there are not a few definite mistranslations. But the real interest of the debates was the revelation of the extent to which fundamentalism still prevails and the hold which the cry of No-Popery has on the people. When I listened to Carson thundering from his place in the Lords I felt that I was back in the sixteenth century. The black Protestantism of Northern England is to-day a stronger political force than is that of the Neri of Italy. The measure was defeated in the Commons by non-conformist distrust of the bishops, though I think that if Davidson had been able to put his case to them he might have won through. The root of the matter in my judgement is that the organization of the Church of England is out of date. The parson's

[1]*Before the War*, pp. 196 *sqq.*

freehold makes it difficult, even impossible, for the Bishops to control their clergy, when they wish to resist, and the Bishops are charged with approving practices which they cannot prevent. The arrangements for the Bishops' salaries are an anachronism. When the working man sees that the Archbishop of Canterbury's salary is £15,000 he is naturally inclined to blaspheme. But out of that salary the Archbishop has to provide for the headquarters staff for his diocese and for his province. My salary as Secretary of State for War might with equal logic have been quoted as £3,000,000 or whatever the War Office vote is. I am full of sympathy with Davidson, who has given twenty years of his life to get this measure as far as Parliament. I always remember with gratitude the help which he and Lang gave us over the Scottish Church Bill.'

The year 1927 brought a sad loss to Haldane. The big black Labrador, Bruce, died. Barrie, who was his devoted friend, wrote: 'Alas poor Bruce! He was a fellow of infinite jest. Such a gentleman and so companionable that he could represent the house, do the honours if they were absent, show us where to put our coats and hats, and conduct us to our rooms. He made that sort of impression on me. I'll not know anyone again with whom I'll care to sit on the floor—the truest companionship. I know how it saddens you.'

Having made peace with his party Haldane returned to his place on the front Opposition bench in the Lords for the opening of the session of 1928, but he was a tired man and his heart was beginning to cause his doctor anxiety. His first duty after the usual reply to the mover and seconder of the address was to pay a tribute to two of his closest friends. Haig died on January 30 and Lord Oxford a fortnight later. As soon as the address had been disposed of Lord Salisbury on February 5 rose to speak on behalf of the Government in the Lords of Haig's services to his country. Haldane followed him and said:

'My Lords, I wish to be permitted to add something to the eloquent words that have fallen from the lips of the noble Marquess, the Leader of the House. I, too, knew Lord Haig, and in one way I knew him more intimately probably than any of your Lordships. I do not refer to events in France. I visited him there, of course, more than once at his headquarters, but that is not relevant to what I am going to say. Lord Haig was distinguished by something upon which public attention is hardly yet adequately focussed. He was a military thinker of a very high order. When he went into battle it was with a plan, not merely improvised but strategically conceived and based on far-reaching objectives. That was the tone and temper of his mind. The year 1906[1] was a perilous one for the British nation. Armaments had been and were being piled up on the Continent, to such a height that it looked as though they must come down with a disastrous crash. We here as a people were doing all that we could to keep the peace with Germany and I do not think that the leaders of German public opinion wanted war. But there was a powerful military element in Germany which thought the hour had struck for Germany to assert her greatness and one cannot altogether wonder. They had an Army which for magnitude and perfection of organization was the greatest in the world; they were laying the foundations of a Fleet which, so far as its size allowed, was of the highest training and efficiency, and we could not tell, desirous as we were to avert every pretext for them to strike, whether a conflagration might not break out. In those circumstances the problem of 1906 was how to deal with it if it arose.

'We had no doubt that Germany could not, in face of our magnificent and superior Fleet, invade this country directly: we knew them too well to think that they were likely to try. But they had other means. If they could get possession of the northern ports of France, Calais, Dunkirk, and Boulogne,

[1]The year of the opening of the military conversations with France.

then, with long range guns and submarines and with Air Fleets, they might make the position of this country a very precarious one in point of safety. That problem had to be thought out, and, after surveying the whole Army, I took it upon myself to ask Lord Haig, who was then in India, to come over to this country and to think for us. From all I could discover even then, he seemed to be the most highly equipped thinker in the British Army. He came and for three years it was my privilege to work with him and to take instruction from him. He had a singularly lucid mind, the most modest of demeanours, and none the less when he had formed a conclusion he was both resolute in it and, as the noble Marquess has said, courageous. We worked out the details of the Expeditionary Force. Then Lord Haig took the Territorial Force. At first he wished to organize it in 28 divisions instead of the 14 divisions that ultimately formed its strength. That proved impossible because we could not raise the numbers or distribute them when raised in the right parts of the United Kingdom. But the 14 divisions he fashioned into a shape which was perfect as far as it went, and he took in hand the staff work and the other things that were necessary.

'But more than that: he had come back to a high position on the new General Staff which had been called into being just before he arrived, and he conceived the idea that the principle of that General Staff might be extended far beyond Great Britain so as to be acceptable to the Dominions and to India. The plan was worked out largely by himself for that purpose, and through the Colonial Office and at the Conferences which took place with the Dominions Premiers, it was communicated and adopted, and the result was that the General Staff became the Imperial General Staff, no longer a local organization but part of the military equipment of the Empire. Then we thought that the best thing that could be done was that he should return to India in a high position on the General Staff of the Indian Army, to carry out his own reforms amongst the soldiers there whom he knew so well. He did that. He accomplished his task, and he returned. We had now got to a stage when what was necessary was to train the troops up to the high standard which Lord Haig had laid down.

'For that purpose he took command at Aldershot and had under him two divisions of the Expeditionary Force. From the first it had been proposed that he should have high command in the Expeditionary Force, and he and Lord French—another very gallant soldier with modern views—worked together and discussed their plans. In the end Haig brought the two divisions at Aldershot to so high a pitch of efficiency and quality that they became an example to the other four divisions of the Expeditionary Force. More than that he spread something of the same spirit among the Territorial troops, so that it is not too much to say that it was to Haig probably more than to any other that the efficiency of the British Army was due when it had to take the field, as it had to do in 1914.

'My Lords, he has passed from us, and those who knew him, who knew the modesty of his character, who knew the clearness of his mind, who realized the inflexible resolution that lay at the back of his judgement, are mourning—mourning because such personalities are not easily produced again. And yet I feel that he has left behind him a tradition which the British Army will not readily lay down, and I think that the manifestation of feeling all over the country in the last few days has been an illustration of how the British democracy, perhaps not understanding very much, but yet with a fine instinct for the truth, recognized in Haig one of its greatest soldiers. In conception of the objects of a battle, in clear ideas of how to use his troops, I doubt whether there has been anybody since the great Marlborough who was his equal. He may not have been one of those magnetic personalities who inspire troops, as two or three great Generals of our own have done in our own time, but I end by saying what I said at the beginning, he was a great military thinker—so great that only those who had to live through years, as I had, in the closest contact with him, can realize how great he was.'

Haldane has been charged with conceit and with taking undue credit to himself for work which Haig and others had done for him. It is a charge which seems ridiculous to those who knew him at all intimately. It arose, I think, in part from his intense eagerness to give out what was in his mind on matters which interested him, and this made him an autocrat of his dinner table, but as I have shown he annoyed his closest friends by his resolute refusal to defend himself, at least until the crises of the Great War were past. The charge has been repeated by some of the critics of my first volume, and for that I feel that I may be in some measure responsible. Haldane's daily letters to his mother have been an invaluable diary for his biographer, giving his day to day impressions of men and events, and I have used them freely. But they were letters of a son to a mother, and as I have said, when attacks were made upon him, the thing that troubled Haldane most was the grief that they would cause his mother. Quite naturally, then, he made the most in these letters of any little compliments and successes which came his way. But I have been unable to find either in his book *Before the War*, which is more concerned with Germany than with his reconstruction of the British Army, or in his autobiography, that he ever took to himself half the credit which is his due for his work in the War Office. To-day Haldane is remembered by his countrymen as the creator of the Territorial Army, a fine achievement, but in reality a by-product of his reorganization. The reason why Haig called Haldane the greatest Secretary of State for War England has ever had was that he knew that Haldane had for the first time in the history of the military forces of the Crown given not only the British Army but the Army of the Empire a uniform organization for war, prepared to the last detail in time of peace, so that it could be studied and learned before the need to apply it arose. In his obituary tribute Haldane gave Haig all the credit for this. But it was Haldane who brought Haig back from India to the War Office and gave him his task, and, as Haig said, without Haldane's understanding of the problem and his constant support it would have been impossible to overcome the opposition which these proposals met in the War Office and to carry them to a triumphant conclusion through an Imperial Conference.

Lieutenant-General Sir Gerald Ellison, who was Haldane's 'devil' on his work for army reform, and knows more of the facts than any one now alive, wrote to Haldane in January 1923 in reply to a letter congratulating him on his promotion to lieutenant-general:

'Whatever help I or anyone else may have been to you, we all of us realize very fully, and no one more than Lord Haig, how useless our knowledge would have been unless you had been there to take advantage of it. Other S. of S.'s could have had, and did have, the same information at their disposal, but they would not face the music as you did.

'Perhaps it is only right to add that none of your predecessors, except Broderick and Arnold-Foster, had the extraordinarily valuable experience of the South African War to guide them. At the moment the question is whether anyone is going to be found bold enough to gather up all the lessons of this last tremendous upheaval.'

The latter part of Haldane's tribute to Lord Oxford ran:

'When Sir Henry Campbell-Bannerman passed away in 1908, it was inevitable, it was the sense of the Liberal Party, that the Sovereign would be wise to choose Asquith as the successor in the Prime Ministership. That was done and then he had a stormy eight years as Prime Minister. I will not go into the events of that time. He fought great controversies on which many of your Lordships may disagree with the course which he took, but none, I think, will refuse him a tribute to the power of mind and of character which he showed throughout; because he was essentially a man of character. Having taken a decision, he did not ask whether it was popular, or whether he would get glory by it; he simply went on upon the lines of the conclusion to which he had come. And that was his character right through the course of his public life.

'The noble Marquess has alluded to the decision which Lord Asquith took to enter the War. I remember that decision well. My noble friend Lord Grey and I were with him on the night of Sunday, August 2, 1914. We saw him, and immediately, without hesitation, his mind was made up. He did not wish to consult anybody. He did not wish to look beyond his own surroundings. He simply decided that a situation had arisen in which, much as we hated war, war was inevitable if we were to be saved from war in a further form which might entail disaster to this nation. Then he pursued his course with dignity to the end, and he preserved unbroken the devoted personal attachment of his friends. He has gone from us and the nation is the poorer. His was a great figure, a figure that could, as others had before him, but few others, wield the House of Commons. But there is something still more. Your Lordships knew him by those qualities to which the noble Marquess has alluded; but among his intimate friends, who, like Lord Grey and myself, had been, as he always used to say, his oldest political friends, there was something that brought us still more closely to him. We had worked and lived closely together through all those years and now that he has passed away, speaking for myself, I feel that much of my interest has gone out of public life.'

This was literally true. Within a brief period he made his last speech in the Lords, and set himself to prepare with a calm mind for his own end. In May his dear friend Edmund Gosse passed away. Grey was now the only one of his intimates left. In the winter recess of 1927-8 he had prepared a

booklet entitled *Mind and Reality* for the series entitled 'Affirmations' edited by Dr. Percy Dearmer. It was a summary of
his philosophy expressed in language as little technical as possible. With his own end in sight he wrote of his conception of
God and of a future life:

'There is no kind of knowledge which is wholly shut off
from the other kinds. The conceptions that are distinctive
necessitate other conceptions for the interpretation of the entirety. Mind finds itself in a limitless variety of forms. These
have to be classified in their logical distinction, and to neglect
this and to confuse them is to court intellectual disaster. The
clergy fall into this sort of error as freely as do men of science.
It must never be forgotten that the actual is what our experience presents, and that the implications of that experience are
manifold. It is the result of reflection not from one but from
many standpoints. Consequently its categories are limitless.
The unifying entirety must contain them all. We are pointed
towards this entirety, and at least in abstract terms we can
interpret its nature. But to present it as a concrete object is
impossible for a mind whose capacity for apprehension is
conditioned by the limiting condition of dependence on a
brain and nervous system. These do not merely live. They
think in so far as mind is expressed in them. But not less are
they the creatures of nature, and as such they are finite. Still
the character of thought, the essence of the self, is such that it
knows no bounds.

'So long as it confines itself to reflective methods that proceed by way of conception and do not seek to envisage, there
is no apparent limit to the capacity of even human reflection.
Nor does our actual experience disclose any limit to the
higher standpoints which it seems to imply. It is in this fashion
that we are impelled towards the conception, as the foundation of the Universe, of absolute mind. What the character of
such mind is it is only in symbols that we can picture. All that
is highest in quality points towards it, and all that is highest

in quality must accordingly find its analogies for reflection there. Itself the foundation of the self and of human personality, the distinctive qualities of personality would seem to characterize it; perfect freedom, creativeness in thinking, complete self determination. But infinite mind can be no individual confronted by a notself. Its object can only be itself. It is therefore more than personal in the sense in which we use the word. To the highest implications of personality it adds those of super-personality, of qualities which pertain to what alone is all-inclusive. It may be that we can get no nearer than this in our attempts to present God as an object for reflection. Other attempts that have been made have always tended to represent Him as of a possible object in some kind of world. But we get near to his nature best in the symbolism of religion and art. These lift us beyond ourselves and show us how true it is that we are more than we take ourselves to be. . . .

'It is to mind that we are driven as the only basis on which all this can be made explicable. Outside mind there is nothing, and apart from it nothing has any meaning. In our conditioned intelligences it is expressed, but never perfectly. Yet we are pointed to an ideal beyond our finiteness, that of mind expressing itself partially in our individual selves and, so far as it does so, not in forms that merely resemble each other, but in ways in which it is identical. Such is the mind which embraces the entire reality of which it is the foundation, and gives it the implications of which it is the unification.

'The various creeds tend towards an infinity thus conceived. Their expressions may be inadequate and they are never more than symbolic. Even the strictest metaphysic does not take us out of expressions which are no more than metaphors. But our own experience drives us by what we find in it towards the recognition of what lies above and beyond; above because it is all-embracing. That is how we fashion the conception of God, and we come to that conception as reality when we look into our own souls, as we do when we turn to the world that seems to exist outside and apart from the mind, but does not truly so exist. And so we come with the moralists, with the poets, with the artists, with the votaries of the highest among the religious creeds, to the idea which begins to press itself on us when we start to explore experience. The more things are interpreted as spiritual, the more they are found to be real.'

When his health grew worse he retired to Cloan to rest and to complete his autobiography, on which he had been at work in the winter of 1926. He was not able to do this as he would have wished. He had to hurry to a conclusion with death round the corner, and the whole period covered by this volume is dismissed in two brief chapters. The book was still in manuscript when he died, and Miss Haldane saw it through the press.

The two last public acts of his life were devoted to his first love, education. Just before he retired to Cloan to rest he kept what had become an annual engagement to address the Swindon branch of the Workers' Educational Association. He advised his audience to read two books, the Gospel of St. John and Plato's *Trial and Death of Socrates*. From these he said they would get the spirit of love and tolerance that would help to guide them through life.

Sir John Simon's Statutory Commission on Indian Reforms had left for India in January and Haldane was deeply interested in all he heard of its reception and work. In one of the last notes he wrote he said: 'Willingdon seems to me to have clearer ideas of the way in which the Government of India should take shape than any man I know.'

His last public speech was an address on June 9 to the Association of Headmistresses, in which he linked a plan for a better understanding of Indian thought and feeling to his favourite subject, the relativity of knowledge. After a summary of his theory of the latter he went on:

'That brings me to the yet wider meaning of relativity, on which I wish to say a word to you. If we have got relativity in physical science in this fashion so we may have it in a number of other things. We are all more or less affected by relativity. We look at things according to our tastes. I do not think it would attract me if you said, "Now is your opportunity to join in a dance which will last till three in the morning and be very pleasant." But there are other people to whom it would be very attractive. They like it and they look at things from a very different point of view from what I at the age of seventy-two do.

'There is no such thing as only one single standard, but there is a multiple of standards which makes experience seem very different, and yet underlying it there is a basis of common knowledge such as we saw in the Tensor system, which produces such identities as there is in the experiences of individual human beings. That is so not only with individuals but it is so with great systems of knowledge.

'Neglect of the truth leads us into narrow notions. Nowhere are we narrower than in our interpretation of the outlook of the East on the great problems of life. No doubt there are a great abundance of very ignorant people in India, probably more than here; but, on the other hand, there are an abundance of very ignorant people here who do not take in what have been the great discoveries of Indian thought.

'You need not take descriptions of images or of ceremonies from India as though they represented the whole truth. These are merely the symbols in which a great wide outlook produces itself. If you turn to the highest forms of Hindu thought, if you take the words found in the Vedantas, which followed the Vedas, or if you take words found in the teaching of Buddhism by Gautama, or in the teaching of Krishna, or any other, you find an insight into the foundations of reality which compares well with the insight we have here. We have done closer logical work here. We have gone more into de-

CLOAN

tail. We have had the enormous advantage of an abundance of exact sciences, but for penetration, for freedom from convention, there are many things in the teaching of Buddha which I think stand on the very highest level. That was why Schopenhauer, who had a constructive mind, said that Buddhism was the greatest religion the world had ever seen, and, for himself, he preferred it to any other. That was not because of certain things that had been said in the name of Buddhism. It was because Schopenhauer saw that Buddha had had the most acute insight into the nature and the problem of reality, and had come very close to his own conclusions about the importance of will in the world.

'I only give you that to show you how cautious we ought to be before we reject the solutions that have come to us from India as though they were of no importance. Indian thought, taken at its highest—and, of course, it is very variegated and a great deal in it is mere metaphor—but taken at its highest comes very near in penetration to the profoundest thought of the West.

'You find things in the East that remind you of what was said by Plato, by Aristotle, and by Plotinus, and make you wonder whether these things, that were said long prior to Greek philosophy, had not penetrated across Asia and reached the Greeks so that they were influenced by them.

'You find things which remind you very much of the great idealists of last century, which have come from India and which are there to-day, and indeed the study of East in its relation to West is one of the most instructive studies you can enter on because all those great systems bring us to much the same conclusion. Our ways of looking on the Universe are really unaffected, to use the phrase I used before, by relativity. We form images of God, the Ultimate Reality, which are wholly inadequate to His Nature, and we have to correct them.

'We fail to see that the crude notion of a body surviving

after death is no adequate solution of the problem of eternal life, and that immortality that begins on this side of the grave is not a mere empirical continuance, because empirically you could get no real equivalent of it. You will find all these things in Indian thought. You find them in Western thought too. We do well to realize that philosophy is not any one creed, that nobody is bound to work out his own special philosophy any more than he can be looked to to have a special poetry. Art has infinite forms, but underneath it lies the nature of the highest in art everywhere.

'So with philosophy; anybody who has gone through a long enough training in it has gained an immense freedom, a freedom from conventionalism which he can probably get in no other way, and the teaching of the East is highly instructive in opening up the wider outlook. It is so with religion too. There is much in the old religious teaching of the East that suggests what is highest in Christianity. There are points of difference, but there is much of resemblance; so much that I feel, if we are to get the sympathy of people in the East, we ought to begin by saying that we understand them on their deepest side, that we understand their religion and their minds, and that we recognize that it is only relativity and conventionalism which has prevented us saying "You are as we are".

'That is what I want to say about the deeper meaning of relativity. That is what I want to say to you about a subject which I have only been able to touch in its barest outline. But I am sure of this, that if there is any one study which more than any other repays, it is the study of ultimate reality and the attempt to get the grasp which the history of thought gives you of the meaning of these deeper things. There may be no ultimate system of philosophy or metaphysics. I do not think there is, any more than there is anything ultimate possibly even in religion; but at least you can get a grasp of what the whole thing means, which will lead you out of a sea of mental troubles and open up to you an enriched view of the universe.'

At the time when he gave this his last public address he was concluding his autobiography, in the last pages of which he gave a statement of his philosophy which completes what he said to the headmistresses:

'The belief that the more experience is spiritual the more it is real has influenced me through the course of life, during more than fifty years. I have said enough to make it plain that I do not mean that the particular creeds have satisfied me. They have appeared as at best symbolic of what is higher, but not more, and I will add that I think the sense of this has held me back from being looked on as in the ordinary sense a "religious man". That description imports as a rule a creed. If not, it means that one has lived the life of a saint. Now, of failure to have lived such a life no man is more conscious than I am. But for me the ultimate test of failure or success has lain in how life appears from the standpoint now stated, a standpoint which has not only influenced conduct, public and private, but has made the events of life happy and easy to live through. One can abstract oneself, with greater or less success, not only from illness and pain and depression, but even from the fear of death. There is little that matters when the principle is grasped and held to, and hesitation and unhappiness become replaced by a life that is tranquil because freed from dependence on casual ups and downs.

'As I have said, I do not think that most people would have called a life so moulded a religious one, for, at all events in my earlier days, it was largely concerned with the surrender of self to the ideals of daily life as much as with the infinite basis which life implies. Moreover, it was solitary in the sense that it took me away from the definite creeds of the Churches, and from the religious opinions which were current among those with whom I mixed. These creeds and opinions I have always treated with deep respect, but they have not embodied for me any lasting foundation for faith. They are for me symbolic, but not more, and like all symbols they appear inadequate and often untrue when put forward as expressions of belief. The fuller view of which I have spoken has satisfied me, inasmuch as it has given me a sufficient solution of the problems of existence, and has taught me that it is not on how to die but on how to live that one ought to concentrate. Death is in this view but an event which comes as the necessary outcome of the course of organic life. It belongs to what falls outside the inmost nature of spirit. We do not pass out of an independently subsisting world with it; that world on the contrary passes from us, and we can contemplate it as so passing, and thereby we are lifted above the event. This does not mean personal or individual continuance, but it does signify that as mind we are more than we take ourselves to be, when immersed in the changing events of life. The finite turns out to be inseparable from the infinite, however little it is possible to form a picture of their oneness in the fashion in which we depict to ourselves external nature. Something like this John Henry Newman seems to have had in his thoughts when, in the earlier though not in the later part of the *Dream of Gerontius*, he drew his picture of the dying saint.

'Such a view is not that current with the majority. They usually seek to express what lies beyond in language that can be no more than symbolic. But the symbolic form is not for many of us tenable, while the idealistic principle which leads up to it is apparently unassailable. At least, speaking for myself, I have found it so far not only sustaining but sufficient to rest upon....

'It would be out of place here to follow out further the kind of idealism that has throughout had hold of me. It is enough to say that its essence led me to the belief in the possibility of finding rational principles underlying all forms of experience, and to a strong sense of the endeavour to find such principles as a first duty in every department of public life. That is the faith that prevailed with me when at the Bar, when later on I undertook the reform of the Army, when I was Lord Chancellor, and when I sat on the Committee of Imperial Defence. It prevails with me to-day not less than in earlier days, and it helps in the endeavour to bring together the apparently divergent views of those with whom one has to deal. That has seemed to me throughout to be as true of the Army and of the administrative services as it has seemed in the case of judicial duties.

'I am now, when writing this, in my seventy-second year. Life will close before long, but I do not think that my outlook will alter before the world passes from me. That world has in the case of each of us been made what it is largely by the reflection which has been directed to it, and the question is whether the basis of that reflection has been true.

'No one who has set himself seriously the task of discovering the truth about the meaning of life dare feel confident that he has been wholly right in his result. Where Plato and Aristotle and Kant were not sure of their knowledge how dare we be? But then we are not living in the world to discover final truth. There is no such truth. What we find is always developing itself and assuming fuller forms. But we can discriminate quality in what we find before us. Our criticism of life, if not our constructive doctrine, becomes more firm as we gain in knowledge and in the interpretation of experience which knowledge brings. Of knowledge we can at best master only a fragment. But if that fragment has been reached by endeavour that is sufficiently passionate, the struggle towards it yields a sense of quality, of quality in the very effort made, which stands for us as being what we care for beyond everything else, as being for us truth, whatever else may not be certainly truth. And so life is not lived in vain though in the ends attained it may seem to have failed.

'I have no sense of success on any very large scale in things achieved. But I have the sense of having worked and of having found happiness in doing so. Better that than more honours and more wealth, and more esteem from men. For the happiness gained has a character in it of which nothing beyond can take the place. So far as external circumstances are concerned, I would not if I could take the chance of living life over again. A distinguished living statesman and man of the world once asked me whether, even with the aid of such knowledge experience had brought, I would like to try to begin life anew. My answer was in the negative. "For", I added, "we are apt greatly to underrate the part which accident and good luck has really played in the shaping of our careers and in giving us such successes as we have had." His rejoinder was to the same effect as my answer to his question. "I would not", he said, "myself try again, for I do not feel sure that good fortune, irrational as it has been, would attend me in the same way." The contingent plays a large part in the best ordered lives, and we do well to ask of philosophy to teach us how to make ourselves detached from the circumstances it brings, whether happy or otherwise. The best that ordinary mortals can hope for is the result which will probably come from sustained work directed by as full reflection as is possible. This result may be affected adversely by circumstances, by illness, by misfortune, or by death. But if we have striven to think and to work based on thought, then we have at least the sense of having striven with such faculties as we have possessed devoted to the striving. And that is in itself a source of happiness, going beyond the possession of any definite gain. It was this that Faust discovered at the end of a life spent mistakenly, nearly up to its close, in the pursuit of his individual pleasure. He found at last that it was in work done, not for himself, but for others, that the satisfying quality of which he had been in search lay. Then, for the first time, and in a different sense from that which was intended by the words when used in his covenant with Mephistopheles, he found that he could only say to the moment, "Stay, thou art fair." His soul was saved from the clutches of the fiend who, despite the warning given to him by the Deity at the beginning, had misunderstood man in his higher development, and had underrated what was required to give him happiness.

'So it may turn out in some degree with each of us, whatever our circumstances and our capacities. This creed is one which fits into what is highest in the various forms of religion. It is open to all of us—provided we keep ourselves humble in mind and avoid self-seeking and vanity.'[1]

At the end of June he was delighted to receive a telegram announcing that he had been unanimously elected Chancellor of the University of St. Andrews in succession to Haig. His last weeks were spent quietly amidst the Perthshire hills and on Sunday, August 19, his heart suddenly failed. The story of his laying to rest is simply and beautifully told by his sister:

'We laid him in the burial ground at Gleneagles, which had been the old family home for many centuries, the little chapel of which had recently been restored in memory of those of the family who had died in the War. Amongst the numerous mourners there was, as was fitting, a large contingent of soldiers, Regulars and Territorials, at the grave. Pipers of the Black Watch led the procession through Auchterarder and up the glen. And in the midst of the mountains he loved so well we sang the Scottish version of the 121st Psalm.

I to the hills will lift mine eyes
From whence doth come mine aid.'

The inscription on the tombstone erected in the beautiful little close of the chapel of Gleneagles runs:

[1]*Autobiography,* pp. 348 *sqq.*

RICHARD BURDON
VISCOUNT HALDANE
OF CLOAN
K.T., O.M.
Born July 30th 1856
Died August 19th 1928.
Secretary of State for War
1905–1912.
Lord High Chancellor
1912–1915 and 1924.
A great servant of the
State
who devoted his life
to the advancement and
application of knowledge.
Through his work in
fashioning her army
he rendered invaluable aid
to his country in her time of
direst need.

Chapter X

AN APPRECIATION OF HALDANE'S
PUBLIC SERVICES

I have now told the story of Lord Haldane's life, as far as is possible in his own words, and have confined myself strictly to such comment as seemed to me necessary to connect his letters and papers. I served under him for four years in the War Office as a junior, when he was engaged on his work of army reform, I met him on several occasions during the war, and after it was over he often asked me to come and talk with him in that pleasant smoking-room at Queen Annes Gate, while for some years I have now been living with his papers. So I am moved to conclude my book with an appreciation of the man's work. Haldane's public life covered so wide a field of activity that the attempt to do so is perhaps as rash as I feel the attempt to write his biography to have been. Not long after his death the Institute of Public Administration, of which he was the founder, wished to publish in its *Journal* a tribute to him, and it chose four men of great distinction who had been closely associated with him, each in a different way, to make each his distinctive contribution. His most intimate political friend, Lord Grey, wrote of him as a statesman, Sir Charles Harris of his work in the War Office, Sir Frank Heath of his achievements as an educational and administrative reformer, and Sir Claud Schuster of his work as Lord Chancellor. The Institute of Public Administration, naturally enough, did not concern itself with philosophy nor with Haldane's private life. It will be understood then that I delayed long before I returned an answer to Miss Haldane, when she asked me to write her brother's life. I agreed eventually because, on reflection, I came to the conclusion that Haldane's chief title to place in the temple of fame was his work as an army reformer.

It is the gracious custom of our educational institutions to commemorate their benefactors, and Haldane's name will always be remembered with gratitude in the University of London, not only at its headquarters, where the acerbities of internal politics, with which he battled during a great part of his life, have happily died down, but as one of the founders of the Imperial College of Science and Technology and of the London School of Economics, while he guided Birkbeck College into the university. His name is kept alive in the universities of Liverpool, Bristol, and Wales, while every university in the Kingdom should remember him gratefully as the prime mover in the institution of the University Grants Committee which now distributes more than £2,000,000 annually to the universities of Great Britain, and every research student as the instigator of the system of grants now distributed annually by the Department of Scientific and Industrial Research.

Haldane's name will also live in the records of adult education. When he first came to it adult education comprised less than 3,000 students and was supported entirely by a small band of voluntary workers. When he died adult education, largely owing to his inspiring leadership and guidance, had become a recognized department of education, with some half-million students.

One foresees that the student of public administration will trace back to Haldane's proposals many of the administrative reforms which will benefit the next generation, for he had the habit of seeing further ahead than most of his contemporaries, and his name will appear in a good many theses compiled by future students of the London School of Economics.

As Lord Chancellor his two periods of office were too brief to enable him to give complete effect to the reforms in the administration of the Law which he held necessary, but he set in train many improvements, some of which were adopted in his lifetime; others are still in process of development.

I have, I hope, made it clear that Haldane was a convinced Imperialist. Not that he was of those who wished to see the Union Jack planted anywhere in the world where a vacant space may be found for it, or an occupied space acquired, but because he had faith in the influence for good of the younger nations of the Empire on the old country. He believed that they must have the freest and most unfettered opportunities for development on their own lines, but he sought to make the connection with the motherland not merely one of sentiment, but of real material value and therefore more enduring. He looked to the legal system common to Great Britain and to the Dominions as one of the most vital of those connections. In 1923 he wrote:

'A great Privy Council Judge, such as was Lord Cairns, Lord Selborne, or Lord Watson, is always esteemed throughout the Empire. The very political experience of such men has added to their value. It is a paradox, but a very real truth, that their training as politicians had made them better judges of such a Court. Only under an unwritten Constitution, the influence of which pervades the Empire and holds it in unison, could such a curious result have emerged. We are far away from the Continental conception of a Judge as a mere interpreter of rigid codes.

'The Judicial Committee of the Privy Council is thus a real link between the Dominions and Colonies and the mother country. If it is little known to the man in the streets of the various cities which rule themselves under the aegis of the Sovereign, it has a long arm, and is a very real influence in smoothing the paths of Governments as well as of governed. It is impalpable. But few people, even of those who dwell in

London, turn into Downing Street to see it sitting. And yet it is one of the King's Courts, and is open to every citizen of the Empire and to anyone else who chooses to walk in. There the visitor may see advocates of every shade of complexion, and with the most varied accents, pleading or waiting to plead. A native King of a negro tribe is in evidence; or a holy man from the Far East, come to superintend the suit brought by an idol to recover his temple, through his next friend, who is responsible for the costs if the suit goes against the idol; a farmer; a gold miner from British Columbia; a French advocate from Quebec; all of these may be there, confronting five elderly gentlemen, without wigs or robes, but seated round the horseshoe oaken table of the Judge, and with the marks of years of immersion in legal contemplation written on their brows. It is indeed an unusual spectacle. . . . For the spirit is everything with a tribunal of a nature so anomalous from a modern point of view as is the Judicial Committee of the Privy Council. It is hopeless to search for the secret of such success as it has had merely in printed documents. For it is not in the written letter that the description of the real nature of the Court is to be found. The true description can only be given by those who, living here, or coming from afar have been in daily contact with the working of this extraordinary organization, and have experienced the extent to which it is continuously seeking to adapt its life to the needs which it has to fulfil as a link between the parts of this Empire.'[1]

With this conviction Haldane laboured to make the Judicial Committee as effective as possible. He increased the number of its members, improved its facilities for the dispatch of business, and, until his health broke down, he rarely missed presiding over any appeal in which a Dominion raised a constitutional issue. His aim was to make a unified Supreme Court of Appeal, and he believed that there should be a President of this Supreme Imperial Court distinct from the Lord

[1]Haldane, *Selected Addresses and Essays*, p. 226.

Chancellor, whose function should be the administration of the Law. I have already said enough of the improvements which he affected in that administration and of his desire for the creation of a Ministry of Justice, with its political chief sitting in the House of Commons and responsible for all the patronage now exercised by the Lord Chancellor. Haldane's portrait hangs in the somewhat dingy room in Downing Street in which the Supreme Court of the Empire sits and there his name will be remembered, as it is remembered in the educational institutions which he founded or benefited.

On every phase of public life in which he took an active part Haldane has left behind him a pregnant influence and an enduring mark, but it will not, I think, be disputed that his national reputation depends upon his eight years' work at the War Office. Most people who remember his name to-day think of him as the creator of the Territorial Army, not as lawyer, educationist, or philosopher.

A smaller but still a large number remember him as the creator of the Expeditionary Force which went to France in August 1914. Now during the years in which that Expeditionary Force was being prepared there were differences of opinion as to how it could be employed most effectively. To-day many people are of opinion that it would be a fatal mistake for us to use our little Regular Army again to extend the line of a Continental ally at the outset of a war and very possibly commit ourselves once more to raising military forces on the Continental scale. This in turn has had the effect of causing some critics to accuse Haldane of having committed us to false strategy. I have so far confined myself to stating in the first volume of Haldane's life his part in the creation of the Expeditionary Force, but to answer this criticism which opens up the vitally important question of the function of the statesman and of the soldier in deciding on the strategy of our armed forces in war, it is necessary to go further back into the story of how our plan of campaign of August 1914 was given its final shape.

The Entente Cordiale was negotiated between Lord Lansdowne and M. Delcassé, the Foreign ministers of England and France, and became operative in April 1904. One of the major factors which had influenced France in proposing the Entente had been the defeat of Russia in the Russo-Japanese War, and the consequent diminution in the military value to her of Russia as an ally, while right up to the time of the outbreak of that war the first major military problem of the British Empire had been held to be an invasion of Afghanistan by Russia. Russia's advance towards India had provoked a number of international crises, the extension of Russian railways towards the frontiers of Afghanistan was watched with suspicious eyes, and the problem of how to meet and defeat a Russian invasion of India was the subject of somewhat heated controversy between military experts at home and in India. A second major military problem was the possibility of war with France. Invasion of England by France was regarded as a military problem for which adequate provision must be made, and in 1897 Lord Wolseley, then the Commander-in-Chief, had stated that the first requirement of the Army was that it should be able to defend the country against the largest invading force that France could in favourable circumstances put across the Channel. The probability of invasion by France had been the prime cause of a succession of agitations for the strengthening of our Fleet, and Lord Roberts had replied to Lord Wolseley that the first business must be to have such a fleet as would make invasion impossible, and that the first requirement of the Army was to be able to defend India against Russia. Actually, in 1898 the Fashoda incident brought us very near to war with France. The conclusion of the Entente with France, then, brought about a complete reorientation of our military problems. France had become a close friend, if not an actual ally; she was allied to Russia, which as the result of the Russo-Japanese War was not likely to be able to contemplate an invasion of India for a long time to come. Japan was our ally. On the other hand, the relations between France and Germany were always in a state of greater or less tension, while the maintenance of the neutrality of Belgium was a traditional British military interest. Therefore quite properly the department of the Director of Military Operations, then under the charge of General Grierson, began, as soon as the Entente with France was concluded, to investigate the problem of co-operation with France and Belgium in a war with Germany. Such investigations are, of course, entirely secret, and in their preliminary stages are not even communicated to other departments of the War Office.

It was not long before the desirability of such investigation became apparent. One of the main agreements which we had reached with France was that we should give her a free hand in North Africa, while she undertook in return not to interfere with us in Egypt. France had long desired to get control of Morocco, and in February 1905 had sent an expedition to Fez. This gave the German Chancellor, von Bülow, the opportunity for a counter demonstration to the Entente for which he was seeking, and on March 31 of that year Kaiser Wilhelm II made a flamboyant entry into Tangier. In a speech at the German Legation he told the German colony that he was determined to uphold the interests of the Fatherland in a free country. 'The Empire has great and growing interests in Morocco. Commerce can only progress if all the Powers are considered to have equal rights under the sovereignty of the Sultan and respect the independence of the country. My visit is the recognition of this independence.' This was an open challenge to the agreement reached by Great Britain and France concerning French policy and rights in North Africa, and the Sultan of Morocco saw in it an opportunity for countering the French plans, which were clearly aimed at the domination, if not the complete control, of his country. He accordingly issued invitations to the Powers to a round-table conference which should consider the future of Morocco. This the French Government refused, on the advice of M. Delcassé, as a trespass on their specific field of influence. Von Bülow's retort to this was to cause his Ambassador in Paris to inform the French Government that Germany supported the Sultan of Morocco. The French Government was frightened and gave way. Preparations for an international conference at Algeciras were begun and M. Delcassé, sacrificed to appease von Bülow, resigned on June 6.

In order to clear his mind as to the possible repercussions of the new foreign policy of the Government Grierson had arranged for a war-game to be played on the supposition that Germany had declared war on France. The commander of the German Army in this exercise was Colonel, afterwards Field-Marshal, Sir William Robertson. The result of this war-game was to make it clear to those who took part in it that France would almost certainly be defeated unless she was supported very promptly by a considerable British army. At this time Mr. Balfour's administration was tottering to its fall, and, being fully occupied with its own affairs, it does not appear to have paid any marked attention to foreign policy, nor to have taken Germany's attitude as seriously as did the French. However that may be, the Directorate of Military Operations had made up its mind that if Germany attacked France she would march through Belgium to turn the French left, and this view trickled through the Committee of Imperial Defence to the Prime Minister, who in August 1905 asked his General Staff to report formally on the probability of a German invasion of Belgium and to state how long it would take to land two British Army Corps in that country. It seems certain from the wording of Grey's letter to Haldane of January 8, 1906,[1] 'Fisher says he is ready', that the First Sea Lord must have begun his plans about the same time as the Prime Minister

[1]*Haldane*, vol. I, p. 172.

addressed his inquiry to the General Staff, and that on these plans the French Naval Attaché in London and very probably the French Minister of Marine were consulted. As to the military side Robertson is quite clear that there were some general contacts with the French Military Attaché,[1] while Grey says in his *Twenty-Five Years* that plans for naval and military co-operation had begun to be made under Lord Lansdowne in 1905.[2] This was the first blunder made in the preparation of our plans of campaign and in shaping our strategy. Before the end of 1905 the Admiralty had ready complete plans for naval action in the event of our being engaged in alliance with France in a war against Germany, and some consideration had been given to military action in support of France on the Continent, yet Robertson, who was present, describes what happened at the meeting of the Committee of Imperial Defence, in which these grave questions were considered as 'a rather rambling conversation in which everybody joined'. 'The truth was', he goes on, 'that the probability of our being drawn into a Franco-German war was not yet a question to which Ministers were disposed to concede more than an academic hearing, and they maintained that even if we had to intervene our role would necessarily be almost entirely naval, and scarcely at all military in character!'[3] The first business of the Committee of Imperial Defence after the conclusion of the Entente with France should have been to have the naval and military implications of that agreement scientifically examined and co-ordinated.

Meanwhile the attitude of Germany, delighted with her victory over Delcassé, was becoming more and more aggressive. The French Government had information that von Bülow proposed to demand at the forthcoming Algeciras Conference a port in Morocco with a suitable hinterland,

[1]Robertson, *Soldiers and Statesmen*, vol. I, p. 48.
[2]Grey, *Twenty-five Years*, vol. I, p. 78.
[3]Robertson, *Soldiers and Statesmen*, vol. I, p. 25.

and was preparing, if this was refused, to go to war. In these circumstances France watched the fall of Mr. Balfour's administration with considerable apprehension, for it had no information as to what the attitude of the new Liberal Government would be. Accordingly the French Military Attaché in London, Major, later General, Huguet was instructed to take soundings, and on December 28 he got into touch with Colonel Repington, the military correspondent of *The Times*, who was a friend of his, and expressed the anxieties of France to him. Repington sent on the purport of this conversation at once to Grey, who was electioneering in Northumberland. He next day met Lord Esher and Sir John Fisher. The First Sea Lord told him that he was forming a new Western Fleet with headquarters at Berehaven by taking two battleships from the Atlantic, Mediterranean, and Channel Fleets, with the addition of six armoured cruisers and of destroyers recalled from China and the Mediterranean. He said that he believed that the Germans would beat the French, and from further conversations that Repington had with Sir George Clarke it appeared that Fisher was keeping his plans entirely to himself, that he had not concerted any plans with the French, beyond asking for some submarines at Dunkirk, that he would not guarantee the passage of a British Army across the Channel, and wanted the Army to be used in conjunction with the Navy to carry out landings on the coast of Schleswig-Holstein.[1] All the new Ministers were occupied with the General Election, and in these confused and confusing conditions Esher suggested to Repington that he should make some unofficial inquiries on the French War Office as to the kind of help they wanted from us. Repington accordingly drew up a questionnaire for Huguet to take to Paris. The most important question was:

'Have the *Conseil Supérieur de la Guerre* considered British co-operation in case of war with Germany? In what manner

[1]Repington, *The First World War*, vol. I, pp. 3 *sqq*.

do they consider this co-operation can best be carried out, (*a*) by sea, (*b*) by land?'

To this Huguet brought back on January 11 the following answer:

'La question de la coopération de l'armée britannique sur terre a été étudiée—on estime que, pour être le plus efficace, son action devra:

'(*a*) être liée à celle de l'armée française, c'est-à-dire être placée sous la même direction, soit que les deux armées agissant sur le méme théâtre d'opérations, ou sur des théâtres différents;

'(*b*) se faire sentir dès le début des hostilités; en raison de l'effet moral considérable qui en résultèra, il serait à désirer qu'un certain nombre de corps anglais, quel que soient leur nombre et leur effectif (1 ou 2 divisions, si possible), puissent être débarqués vers les 5me ou 6me jour, de manière à être transportés sur le lieu de leurs opérations, en même temps que le seront les corps français. Ils pourraient partir à leur effectives de paix en doublant les unités, les réservistes rejoindront ensuite pour porter les unités à leur effectif normal de guerre. Le reste de l'armée exécutait sa mobilisation régulièrement et partait quand elle serait achevée.

'Sur mer, la situation particulière de l'Angleterre, la grande supériorité de sa flotte, la possibilité qu'elle a de prendre à l'avance toutes les mesures préparatives qu'elle juge utiles, la met a même d'établir un plan mieux que la France, qui ne jouit pas de la même liberté d'action parce que

'(i) elle ignore quelle serait l'attitude d'Italie;

'(ii) elle ne peut pour cette raison et aussi pour éviter des récriminations, prendre à l'avance les mêmes mesures que l'Angleterre.'

From this it appears that the French were quite willing to leave the naval plans in Fisher's hands, but that they wanted the earliest possible military help from us. Their request that units should be sent over by the 5th of 6th day of mobilization to be in effect amalgamated in the French army was neither practical nor advisable. In fact the request showed that the French General Staff was not acquainted with the organization and conditions of the British Army. Our military units at home were at peace strength little more than feeders for those abroad, and in the winter particularly, when drafts had been sent out to the units in India and elsewhere, were very weak and composed largely of recruits unfit for active service. Our process of mobilization was necessarily much slower than that of the French. The French Army was organized in regiments, which remained permanently in the same garrisons. The regiments drew their recruits from the districts in which they were quartered, and when these had completed their period of service and become reservists they went back to their homes, from which in emergency they could be very quickly called up to the regimental centre. The units of the British Army were not localized. They changed their stations at regular intervals and took their turn of foreign service; their reservists had, therefore, on mobilization, to go to the regimental depots to be clothed and equipped, and were sent thence to wherever the unit happened to be, while, of course, the units, when mobilized, had to be embarked and disembarked before they could move to a place of concentration on the Continent. If the French wanted rapid help a great deal of thought and of organization would be required before it could be forthcoming.

On January 8 Grey had told Haldane that his information led him to believe that the Germans were preparing to attack the French in the spring, that Fisher had said that the naval plans were ready, and he asked Haldane if the War Office had taken any steps to assist France in such an eventuality.[1] On January 10 M. Cambon, the French Ambassador in London, saw Grey and suggested to him that the French and British staffs should be put officially into communication. To this

[1] Cf. *Haldane,* vol. I, p. 172.

Grey replied that a decision on this point must wait until the elections were over and the position of the new Government was secure.[1] On January 12 Grey went to Berwick for an election meeting and there met Haldane to discuss the problem of the part the British Army should play in the event of a war with Germany. It seems certain that they discussed Cambon's proposal that the military staffs of the two countries should co-operate in working out plans, for Haldane says that after his talk with Grey he returned at once to London and saw the new Prime Minister, Sir Henry Campbell-Bannerman, who agreed to conversations being recognized officially, provided that any study undertaken by the two staffs was carefully safeguarded so far as any possible commitment was concerned. On January 15 direct contact between the British and French military staffs began, and at Grierson's suggestion was extended to include the Belgian staff.

Haldane, back from his election campaign, met Huguet and the General Staff at the War Office and soon discovered that both were convinced that without prompt help from Great Britain France would be in grave danger of defeat. His Military Operations Department had made up its mind that the German plan would include a turning movement through Belgium, which, unless it was defeated, would place the coasts of that country and the Channel ports under German control. 'I became aware at once', he says, 'that there was a new army problem.'[2] Mr. Balfour's Government appears to have thought that the resignation of Delcassé had, for the present at least, satisfied Germany, and had not thought it necessary to keep the leaders of the Opposition in touch with developments in foreign affairs, so the existence of the new problem came as a surprise to Haldane. The situation which he found was peculiar and complex. Under the previous government no military operations on any considerable scale

[1]*British Documents or the Origins of the War*, vol. III, Nos. 210 and 219.
[2]Haldane, *Before the War*, p. 36.

on the continent of Europe had been contemplated and no preparations for such operations had been made. The First Sea Lord had a plan of his own, the details of which he refused to divulge, and he refused also to guarantee the transport of British troops to France. As to what the Army could do, on January 15 Grierson wrote to Colonel Barnadiston, our Military Attaché at Brussels, instructing him to inquire of the Belgian Chief of the Staff how, in case of need, British assistance could be most effectively afforded to Belgium for the defence of her neutrality, adding that he could say that we were prepared to send across the Channel four cavalry brigades, two army corps, and a division of mounted infantry, a force of about 105,000 men.[1] This force was evidently a paper scheme worked out secretly in the Department of Military Operations, without consultation with those other departments which had to provide men, horses, equipment, and munitions, for when these were brought into consultation the force available dwindled to 80,000 men, and the time required to mobilize even that small force and send it to its place of concentration proved to be two months.

Robertson, who, under Grierson, was working out the details of the organization of an expeditionary force, thus describes the state of the Army at the time when Haldane entered the War Office: 'The situation was the more disquieting to those behind the scenes because not enough was being done to make the best of such forces as we had, which, for the most part, were allowed to remain a heterogeneous jumble of small units incapable of effective use. With the exception of the Aldershot army corps, so called, the regular army had no formation higher than the brigade which could have been mobilized without changing its composition. Cavalry were short of horses, infantry of men, artillery of ammunition, and everybody of other requirements of war. The second line, the militia, continued to be bled for the regulars, and only a por-

[1]*British Documents*, vol. III, No. 217.

tion of it was liable for service abroad. The yeomanry and volunteers, the third line, were in most cases without any organization higher than the regiment and battalion. For thirty years and more the various categories had constantly been pulled to pieces and put together again in a different way by the twelve war ministers who had followed Mr. Cardwell, and innumerable changes had been made in areas of command, periods of training, terms of enlistment, rates of pay, and other similar details. This never-ending stream of tinkering reforms, few of which were of real benefit from the standpoint of the higher organization, had created a feeling of despair in the minds of senior officers, and the whole army longed to be spared the infliction of further nostrums as a cure for its supposed ailments. Speaking in the House of Lords in July 1905 Lord Roberts said: "I have no hesitation in stating that our armed forces, as a body, are as unfitted and unprepared for war as they were in 1899–1900." Such was the position three years after our experiences in South Africa, and nine years before the Great War.'[1]

After hearing from Haldane of the result of the preliminary investigations in the War Office, Grey on January 15 wrote to Sir F. Bertie, our Ambassador in Paris: 'As to taking precautions beforehand in case war should come, it appears that Fisher has long ago taken the French Naval Attaché in hand, and no doubt has all naval plans prepared. I have now got Haldane's consent to General Grierson being in direct communication with the French Military Attaché, but I am told 80,000 men with good guns is all that we can put into the field in Europe to meet first-class troops; that won't save France unless she can save herself. We can protect ourselves of course for we are now more superior at sea than we have ever been.'[2]

The position, then, when Haldane entered the War Office,

[1]Robertson, *Soldiers and Statesmen,* vol. I, p. 27.
[2]*British Documents,* vol. III, No. 216.

was that the Prime Minister had approved of the preparation of plans for the dispatch of an Expeditionary Force to the Continent in co-operation with the military staffs of France and Belgium, without any commitment to action by any of the governments concerned. Haldane's military advisers told him that they were convinced that Germany, if she went to war with France, would violate the neutrality of Belgium, and that unless we could support France promptly and in adequate strength France would be defeated and Germany would occupy the Channel ports.

A review of our available military resources showed that we could not support France either quickly or in adequate strength.

This was the first military problem that Haldane set himself to tackle. He devoted himself entirely to the military reforms required to make the creation of an efficient Expeditionary Force possible, and left it to his General Staff to prepare plans for the landing of such a force and its movements to a selected place of concentration, with the proviso that the security of the Channel ports must be the prime object of our military strategy. The proposals of the General Staff were from time to time considered by the Committee of Imperial Defence, but no attempt appears to have been made at any time to review the problem of war with Germany as a whole. There we made a serious mistake. No British plan for co-operation with an ally on the continent of Europe should have been worked out and presented to the consideration of that ally in separate naval and military sections. The function of the Committee of Imperial Defence is, as its name implies, to work out co-ordinated plans for imperial defence and such plans should in their final form be presented for the approval of the Government by the Committee, and not by the War Office, nor by the Admiralty, while to-day of course the Air Ministry comes very much into the picture. Unfortunately no Liberal Minister had had in 1906 any experience of the

Committee of Imperial Defence and none realized what the real functions of that Committee were, with the result that when schemes for the dispatch of an Expeditionary Force were discussed in the Committee Fisher preserved a stony silence and nursed a plan of his own, which conflicted directly with the military plan. So the military conversations took a wrong turn from the start, and they resulted eventually in our being tied to a French military plan of which we had little knowledge and on which we could exercise no influence.

This only dawned on Haldane a good deal later. As we have seen he devoted the later years of his life to an endeavour to make provision that this should not happen again. The defence of France in a war with Germany is an essentially military problem, and the French are not called upon to study the possibilities of amphibious power. Their one object was to get the maximum military help from us, and they rarely, if ever, gave a thought to our naval power. As our military contribution to the alliance was, at first, very small in comparison with their own, they held that we should fall in with their plans and obey orders. There is an illuminating entry in Sir Henry Wilson's diary describing a meeting of his on February 14, 1913, with the French Military chiefs:

'My talk with Castelnau and Joffre was about Repington's recent articles in *The Times*, where he claims that our navy is worth 500,000 bayonets to the French at the decisive point. I had written to Fred Oliver that our navy was not worth 500 bayonets. Castelnau and Joffre did not value it at one bayonet! except from the moral point of view. It was realized by these men what a serious statement this was, coming at this particular moment, and it was agreed that it should be thoroughly exposed in the French press. We went into the whole question. I can't help thinking that time is on the side of the Entente.

'After lunch Huguet and I came down here [Bourges],

where Huguet has a charming house, and we dined with Foch, who has just come here to command the VIIIe Corps. Foch is of the same opinion as regards Repington's egregious articles as are Castelnau and Joffre, and we talked till midnight.'[1]

From which it appears that there were British soldiers too who needed education in the value of amphibious power. The result of dealing with naval and military plans separately was that the French military leaders, whose influence on French statesmen in matters of defence was supreme, never had any real appreciation of the value of our contribution to the war until our armies numbered millions, and our influence on them was in the first years of the war small. If our plans had been presented from the first as combined naval and military plans this might have been avoided. It was never necessary to tie ourselves down to a precise place of concentration beforehand. All that was needed was that we should have in our possession precise information as to the French ports which would be available for us, and the railway facilities which could be provided at those ports. There would then have been ample time, between the issue of the order for mobilization and the embarkation of our first units, to settle, in conjunction with the French, the most suitable area of concentration. The fact that we had this decision up our sleeve would almost certainly have opened the eyes of the French soldiers to the liberty of action which sea power confers, and made them more susceptible to influence from us.

The Algeciras crisis passed off. When we firmly supported France Germany retreated from the position she had taken up. With the exception of Haldane those ministers who attended the meetings of the Committee of Imperial Defence, after the crisis had passed, seemed to regard plans for the dispatch of an Expeditionary Force to the Continent as an academic exer-

[1]Callwell, *Field-Marshal Sir Henry Wilson—His Life and Diaries*, vol. I, p. 122.

cise. Haldane became completely absorbed in this problem of organizing the force, to the neglect, as he confessed, of his general duties as a member of the Cabinet, and in January 1907 he was able to announce his scheme of reorganization of the Regular Army at home into six divisions and a cavalry division, which on mobilization would provide an Expeditionary Force of 160,000. The 'heretogeneous jumble of small units incapable of effective use' of which Robertson had spoken in 1905 had disappeared, and for seven years the Expeditionary Force was to be trained in the formations in which it would fight by the men who would lead it in war. Much remained to be done to speed up mobilization and to provide means of expansion of the regular Army, but the main problem had been solved.

Meanwhile Grierson was at work on his plans. Through his opposite number at the Admiralty, Admiral Ballard, Fisher was induced to withdraw his statement that the Navy could not protect the transport of an expedition to the Continent, and the Admiralty decided that it could assure the communications across the Channel west of the line Dunkirk–North Foreland. Accordingly it was agreed with the French that Calais, Boulogne, and Cherbourg should be the ports of disembarkation, and that they should provide railway transport thence towards Belgium, the underlying idea in Grierson's mind being that our Expeditionary Force should support the Belgian Army and so cover both the coast of Belgium and the Channel ports. In October 1906 Grierson left the War Office to take command of a division at Aldershot, and he was succeeded by General Ewart, who continued to work on the same lines as his predecessor. Both were careful not to commit us to any precise area of concentration, a number of alternatives being kept in view to meet possible variations in the German plan of campaign. Haldane never interfered with the working out of these plans. The Government had agreed in principle to the creation of an Expeditionary

Force and to its dispatch to the Continent in certain eventualities. It was for the experts to arrange for the transportation of the force and its place of concentration. Throughout his long tenure of the office of Secretary of State for War he adhered to the principles which he had formulated to the Staff College in the address which he delivered there in 1924: 'To me the first of these principles is that we should realize the great doctrine that it is for the Government to define the objectives, just as it is the duty of the Government to answer the preliminary question between peace and war. When this is done the carrying out of what is aimed at is for the leaders of the naval and military and air Forces.'

Such then was the position when in the autumn of 1908 the outlook in international affairs again became threatening. Towards the end of September of that year a party of deserters from the French Foreign Legion were assisted to escape at Casablanca by the German Consul. The French used force to recapture the deserters and Germany demanded an apology on the ground of violation of diplomatic rights. This the French refused, but offered to refer the matter to arbitration. The Germans demanded an apology first, but, eventually when we and most other nations in Europe supported France, Germany gave way. While negotiations were proceeding with increasing heat public feeling in the country against Germany was further exacerbated by the publication in the *Daily Telegraph* on October 28 of an interview with the German Emperor, in which, amongst other statements, he claimed to have planned Lord Roberts' campaign in South Africa. The situation was regarded as sufficiently serious by the Prime Minister, Mr. Asquith, for him to call a special meeting of the Committee of Imperial Defence, to consider our action in the event of war with Germany. At that meeting Lord Nicholson, then the Chief of the Imperial General Staff, expounded the military plan for the movement of the Expeditionary Force to France. An account of this meeting is given in Admiral Sir

R. Bacon's *Life of Lord Fisher*.[1] It was given by Lord Fisher to a friend, and is the friend's version of the story:

'During the Morocco crisis the French Government was within an inch of war with Germany, and insisted on 120,000 British troops being sent to the French frontier. The Cabinet agreed. At a meeting of the Imperial Defence Committee, when the military plans were set forth by General Nicholson, Fisher remained silent, seated opposite to Mr. Asquith at the end of a long table. The only question put to Fisher was, "Whether the Navy could guarantee transport", to which he answered "Yes". Mr. Asquith then asked him if he had anything to say; and he replied that he had nothing to say that anyone present would care to hear. Mr. Asquith pressed him and a scene took place. Fisher told the Committee that if 120,000 Englishmen were sent to France the Germans would put everything else aside and make any sacrifice to surround and destroy the British, and that they would succeed. Continental armies being what they are, Fisher expressed the view that the British Army should be absolutely restricted to operations consisting of sudden descents on the coast, the recovery of Heligoland and the garrisoning of Antwerp.

'He pointed out that there was a stretch of ten miles of hard sand on the Pomeranian coast which is only ninety miles from Berlin. Were the British Army to seize and entrench that strip a million Germans would find occupation; but to dispatch British troops to the front in a Continental war would be an act of suicidal idiocy arising from the distorted views of war produced by Mr. Haldane's speeches, and the childish arrangements for training Terriers after war broke out. Fisher followed this up with an impassioned diatribe against the War Office and all its ways, including conceit, waste of money, and ignorance of war. He claimed that the British Army should be administered as an annexe to the

[1] Bacon, *Life of Lord Fisher*, vol. II, pp. 182 *sqq*. The year of this incident is wrongly given as 1909.

Navy and that the present follies should be abandoned. At this period Mr. Asquith said, "I think we had better adjourn." This was done, but for some months onward the Defence Committee never considered, nor did the soldiers propose, any plan for helping France by means of an Expeditionary Force to take part in the main inland fighting.'

Mr. Asquith's reason for adjourning the meeting are understandable. Lord Fisher was just about to retire and the Prime Minister naturally did not want an unnecessary altercation with the great sailor. He evidently hoped that Fisher's successor, Sir A. Wilson, would prove more amenable, but no attempt was made to find out whether that was likely to be the case. Fisher's outburst had emphasized what was already generally known, that there was fundamental disagreement between naval and military strategy, and still no attempt was made by the Prime Minister as chairman of the Committee of Imperial Defence to bring the two into line. The basis of the military strategy was that unless the French Army was quickly supported by us in the greatest possible strength, it would be defeated by Germany and the Belgian coast and the Channel ports would fall into the hands of the enemy. Fisher's strategy was a reversion to our strategy of the eighteenth century; he wanted the Expeditionary Force kept back for 'sudden descents on the coast' in conjunction with the Navy. The soldiers had no difficulty in convincing the Committee of Imperial Defence that military conditions had changed materially since the eighteenth century, and that descents on the coast could not be expected to have the same effect in the twentieth century, and would be infinitely more risky. Admiral Bacon in his comment on Fisher's outburst says: 'It would be tempting to speculate on what the result might have been had our Expeditionary Force been landed in Belgium in the early days of the war, on the flank of the German advance, as Lord Fisher had argued that it should have been.' But Fisher, in fact, never argued anything of the kind; he wanted the army kept in hand for raids, and one of the chief reasons why the Expeditionary Force could not be deployed in Belgium at the outset was that the Admiralty could not guarantee the use of ports east of Calais. To get the Expeditionary Force into position, with its left on the southern ports of Antwerp, in time it would have been necessary to use the ports Ostende, Zeebrugge, and Dunkirk, as well as Calais and Boulogne. All this depended on agreed naval and military plans, which it was the function of the Committee of Imperial Defence to bring about, and it did not do so.

The Casablanca crisis passed off and Haldane continued to go on quietly with his work of organization. The Territorial Army was brought into being, the Militia became the Special Reserve, the Army was provided for the first time in its history with a complete and carefully thought-out system of organization and administration in war, the Imperial General Staff was created, and by agreement with the Dominions all their forces were trained and organized on the same system as the Regular Army. In August 1910 General Wilson succeeded General Ewart as Director of Military Operations, and within less than a year there was yet another international crisis over Morocco. France had proceeded methodically with her plan for getting control of that country, which was rapidly falling into decay. Outlying tribes were in a constant state of revolt against the Sultan and the French were employing considerable military forces to restore order. Germany claimed that matters had gone far beyond what was contemplated by the Algeciras agreement and demanded territorial compensation for herself in Africa, if France was to have control of Morocco. She put forward a claim to the greater part of the French Congo, and early in July 1911 sent a small gun-boat, the *Panther,* to Agadir, a Moroccan port on the Atlantic. The pretext for this clumsy demonstration was that Germany had commercial interests at the port, but it was easy to prove that the total business of the port was small and the German share in that business insignificant.

It is very doubtful whether Germany had any intention of proceeding to extremes. Actually, at the very time when the *Panther* arrived at Agadir, Prince Henry of Prussia with a large party of Germans was visiting England on a mission of goodwill. But M. Caillaux was the Prime Minister of France, and he was known to favour a Franco-German understanding which would very probably have broken the Entente and left us isolated. So our Government decided to take a strong line, and Mr. Lloyd George on July 21 addressed a serious warning to Germany in a speech in the City. General Wilson, with his natural shrewdness, took advantage of the situation to get our military preparations thoroughly overhauled. We tested our arrangements for mobilization and these disclosed certain defects, and the attitude which the Government had taken up made it easy for Haldane to get the money needed to make these good. One result of the appearance of the *Panther* at Agadir was that our military mobilization was speeded up by several days. Another was a drastic change at the Admiralty. As I have said, at the meeting of the Committee of Imperial Defence of August 23, 1911, it became clear that the First Sea Lord, Sir A. Wilson, adhered to the Fisher plan of confining our efforts to the sea and keeping the Expeditionary Force back for descents on the coasts of Schleswig-Holstein. There was complete disagreement between the naval and military authorities as to our strategy.

Haldane made up his mind that this state of affairs must not continue and told Asquith that he would resign unless it was stopped. He wanted to go to the Admiralty himself to create a naval general staff which would work out with the military General Staff a naval and military plan of campaign in the event of war with Germany. Mr. Asquith decided to send Mr. Winston Churchill to the Admiralty instead, and he saw to it that the Admiralty provided what the War Office needed to ensure the rapid and safe transportation of the Expeditionary Force to France. But with this exception we came no nearer to presenting to France a considered scheme for the employment of the forces of the Empire to support her against Germany. The Admiralty still maintained its ban on disembarkation east of Calais. General Wilson, very much under the influence of Foch, went ahead with his plans for the close co-operation of our Expeditionary Force with a French plan of which our information was scanty. Just at this time another development played into his hands. With Grierson and Ewart as Directors of Military Operations the idea of co-operation with the Belgian Army in defence of the Belgian coast had always been kept in view, though in Ewart's time the interest of the Belgian staff had clearly begun to wane. Now Belgium had become alarmed by the succession of crises, and by the increasing strength of the German Army. She feared, not without reason, that Germany would regard any agreement between Belgium and ourselves, or between Belgium and France, for joint action in the event of war with Germany, as a breach of neutrality and would use this as an excuse for invading Belgium. In fact when the Germans occupied Brussels in 1914 they discovered in the archives in the Belgian War Office the correspondence of 1906 between General Grierson and Colonel Barnadiston and General Degoutte, the Belgian Chief of the General Staff, and they published this as justifying their invasion of Belgium. The result of this change of feeling in Belgium was that when at the time of the Agadir crisis renewed approaches were made at Brussels, we were informed that if we landed troops on the Belgian coast or crossed the Belgian frontier, except at the express invitation of the Belgian Government, Belgium would regard this as a hostile act and would oppose us in arms. So direct military co-operation with Belgium dropped out of the picture, and when the crisis of 1914 burst upon us Wilson's plans were ready to the last detail for the concentration of our

Expeditionary Force on the French left behind the fortress of Maubeuge.

Haldane left the War Office in the spring of 1912, but before he left plans had been completed for the mobilization of an Expeditionary Force of 160,000 which could begin embarkation on the eighth day of mobilization.

On August 5, the day after we were at war with Germany, Mr. Asquith called a War Council of which somewhat different accounts have appeared from several of those who were present. Wilson, for example, says that Haig wanted to keep the Expeditionary Force back till we saw how the German plan developed.[1] Haig himself says that he was definitely in favour of immediate co-operation with the French in the greatest possible strength, but wanted us to keep back a considerable number of regular officers and non-commissioned officers to train our reserve forces, as 'we must organize our reserves for a war of several years'.[2] There is, however, general agreement that both Lord Roberts and Lord French spoke of going to Antwerp and operating with the Belgian Army with that fortress as our base. Now we could not go direct to Antwerp without violating Dutch territorial waters, which was politically impossible when the prime reason of our going to war was Germany's violation of Belgium neutrality. Landing at Ostende and Zeebrugge was ruled out because at the Council Churchill, First Lord of the Admiralty, announced that the Dover defile was sealed and that the Admiralty could not guarantee protection for transports east of it. The only opinion that Haldane expressed at the Conference was that we must support the agreed plans of the French and British General Staffs and should send the whole of our Expeditionary Force to France as soon as possible.

Those who argue that our plan of campaign of 1914 was a disastrous departure from our traditional strategy appear to

[1]Callwell, *Wilson*, vol. I, p. 158.
[2]Duff Cooper, *Haig*, vol. I, p. 130.

be of opinion that it would have been possible for us, in the conditions which prevailed in August 1914, to have landed on the Belgian coast and acted on the flank of the German advance, and they are disposed to criticize Haldane for not having insisted on this. I hope I have made it clear that this was not so. Landings at Ostende and Zeebrugge might have been possible if the Admiralty had been pressed to make plans for covering them, but they were not, though they made no bones about escorting the 2nd Cavalry Division and the 7th Division to land at those ports early in October 1914. If we had landed at Ostende, Zeebrugge, Dunkirk, Calais, and Boulogne, we could have got five divisions and a cavalry division behind the Scheldt with their left on Termonde in touch with the Belgian Army in Antwerp in time to meet the German advance through Belgium, and it is quite possible that this threat to his flank would have contained enough of von Kluck's army to enable the French to readjust their dispositions when they discovered the real nature of the German invasion. The King of the Belgians appealed for help on August 3, and arrangements for disembarkation on the Belgian coast could, from a military point of view, have been made between then and August 12, when our first units were ready to embark, provided always that the plans of the Admiralty for covering such a movement were complete. They were not, for the Admiralty was never asked whether, if Belgium called on us for help, they could revise their veto on disembarkation east of Calais. Without a great deal more information as to the naval situation at the outbreak of war than is given us in the *Naval History of the War* it is not possible to form a considered opinion whether landings at Belgian ports would have been possible from a naval point of view. Even if they were it would have been taking a military risk, at which even Sir John French, with his well-known courage, might have balked, to have gone on with a military concentration in Belgium when he learned, before any part of the

Expeditionary Force had embarked, that the Germans had entered Liége. It is, however, a just criticism of our preparations that our naval and military plans were in the main kept in separate compartments, and that the eventuality of an appeal for help coming from Belgium was not considered.

Whether our concentration was in Belgium or behind Maubeuge, or, as Kitchener and others preferred, about Amiens, the essential was that our Expeditionary Force should arrive in time to attract to it the greater part of von Kluck's 5th German Army. The French had gravely underestimated the strength of the German army on the Western Front and had not considered it to be possible that it would make a wide turning movement through Belgium west of the Meuse in great strength. Neither we nor the French had thought it possible that von Kluck's 5th Army of 200,000 men could be passed quickly through the narrow defile of Aix-la-Chapelle, a very remarkable feat of march discipline and organization, so it was not until late on August 22 that the real situation in Belgium dawned on those at French headquarters.

The sketch map opposite shows what would have been the position of Lanzerac's 5th Army had we not been able either to cover its left flank or to attract to ourselves the attention of von Kluck's 5th German Army in some other way. It is then certain that if our Expeditionary Force had not been ready for action by at latest the sixteenth day of mobilization (August 20) the left of the French line of battle would have been completely enveloped, and the German plan for the defeat of the French Armies by the fortieth day of mobilization successful, with the inevitable concomitant that the Germans would have been in possession of the Channel ports. No demonstrations or landings on the coasts of Belgium or Schleswig-Holstein could have averted that.

It was Haldane's speeding up of the mobilization of the Expeditionary Force, one of his objectives from the time when he entered the War Office, which made it possible for the Force to arrive in time to save the French. It did in fact arrive so much sooner than the Germans expected that its presence at Mons came as a complete surprise both to von Kluck and to German General Headquarters. It was Haldane's organization of the Expeditionary Force, as far back as 1907,

Position evening Aug 22nd assuming absence of B.E.F.

which gave it its quality. The seven years of training it received in the formations in which it fought in the war, under the men who led it in war, gave it a cohesion and character such as no other British Military Expedition had ever had when it left our shores. Therefore the claim made for him by his family on his tombstone that 'in fashioning her army he rendered invaluable aid to his country in her hour of direst need' is a just claim.

After he had been dismissed from office Haldane naturally enough gave much thought to the way in which our plans in war had been prepared, and he came definitely to the conclusion that the Committee of Imperial Defence had not exercised the functions it should have exercised, nor exerted its authority sufficiently over the Admiralty and the War Office. On more than one occasion when we were discussing the events which led up to the war he told me that he always blamed himself for not having brought the differences between the Admiralty and the War Office to a head earlier. It certainly would not have been easy for him to have done so. Many, certainly a majority, of his colleagues in the Cabinet were averse to any kind of commitment which might involve us in a European war, and a row with the Admiralty might well have frightened them and the Liberal Party in the country into vetoing the preparations which he had in train. He was only able to get his military reforms through Parliament by using the greatest tact and by bringing about economies in military expenditure. That, however, was all of the past; looking to the future he was constantly thinking of how best to improve the organization and increase the authority of the Committee of Imperial Defence. As I have said, he welcomed very warmly the recommendations of the Salisbury Report and in particular the creation of the sub-committee of the three chiefs of staff, of Navy, Army, and Air. He had always held that one of the defects of the Committee of Imperial Defence was that it brought soldiers and sailors around a table in which Cabinet Ministers were in a large majority, and that the sailors and soldiers were shy of opening their mouths in such company, and in particular were averse to appearing to disagree with the political heads of their departments. He believed that for this reason the Committee often failed to get the true opinion of the Services. He was convinced that a sub-committee of the three chiefs with the Prime Minister's deputy in the chair would not only elicit the views of each Service, but would be an effective means of removing differences between the Services and bringing plans into agreement.

Haldane was so seized of the importance of this that when soon after the publication of the Salisbury Report Mr. Baldwin's Government was defeated, he decided to take office under Mr. Ramsay MacDonald in order that he might devote his abilities and experience to improving the organization of the Committee of Imperial Defence, and he devised the peculiar arrangement by which Lord Cave took over the legal work of the Lord Chancellor in order that he might spend his afternoons in the offices of the Committee of Imperial Defence in Whitehall Gardens, after dealing in the morning with the administrative business of the Lord Chancellor's office. He put this as in importance even before educational reform. During the comparatively short time that he was in office he succeeded in making the sub-committee of the three chiefs of staff a reality, and in so doing rendered a great and final service to his country. For he made it as reasonably certain as anything in human affairs can be certain that if we went to war again we should do so with naval, military, and air plans scientifically co-ordinated, and that if there were alternative plans these should be presented in such a way that the Government could make its choice with full knowledge of the technical issues involved.

LORD HALDANE'S DEGREES AND HONOURS

M.A., Edinburgh
M.A., Göttingen
Hon. LL.D., Cambridge
     Edinburgh
     Bristol
     Liverpool
     Manchester
     Sheffield
     McGill
Hon. D.C.L., Oxford
     Durham
Hon. Ph.D., Göttingen

Privy Councillor, 1902
Fellow of the Royal Society, 1906
Viscount, 1912
Knight of the Thistle, 1913
Order of Merit, 1915

LORD HALDANE'S PUBLISHED WORKS

Essays in Philosophical Criticism (in conjunction with Professor Seth) (Longmans), 1883.

Translation of Schopenhauer's *World as Will and Idea* (in conjunction with Mr. J. Kemp), 3 vols. (Trübner & Co.), 1883.

Revised edition of Dart's *Vendors and Purchasers* (in conjunction with Mr. Sheldon), 1886.

Life of Adam Smith (Walter Scott), 1887.

Education and Empire (John Murray), 1903.

The Pathway to Reality, 2 vols. (John Murray), 1903.

The Conduct of Life (John Murray), 1904.

Army Reform and other Addresses (John Murray), 1907.

Universities and National Life (John Murray), 1912.

Higher Nationality (John Murray), 1913.

The Ebbing Tide (Mills & Boon), 1916.

Before the War (Cassell & Co.), 1920.

The Reign of Relativity (John Murray), 1921.

The Philosophy of Humanism (John Murray,) 1922.

Human Experience (John Murray), 1926

Mind and Reality (Affirmations) (Ernest Benn), 1928.

Selected Essays and Addresses (John Murray), 1928.

Autobiography (Hodder & Stoughton), 1931.

INDEX

INDEX